THE GENTLE DYNAMITER

Tom Mooney, socialist agitator and labor activist.

The *Gentle* DYNAMITER

A Biography of Tom Mooney

Estolv Ethan Ward

Ramparts Press
Palo Alto, California 94303

Library of Congress Cataloging in Publication Data

Ward, Estolv Ethan, 1900-
    The gentle dynamiter.

    Includes bibliographical references and index.
    1. Mooney, Thomas J., 1882-1942.   Trials (murder)
—California—San Francisco.   I. Title.
KF224.M6W37   1983   345'02523   82-80645
ISBN 0-87867-089-0   347.3052523
ISBN 0-87867-090-4 (pbk.)

Photographs reproduced through the courtesy of the Bancroft
Library, University of California, Berkeley, and from the private
collection of Herbert Resner, San Francisco.

Published by Ramparts Press, Palo Alto, California 94303.

First Edition

Library of Congress Catalog Card Number 82-80645
ISBN 0-87867-089-0 (cloth)
ISBN 0-87867-090-4 (paper)

Manufactured in the United States of America

Contents

ACKNOWLEDGEMENTS

Tom Dan Dycke was not the first person to tell me I should write the story of Tom Mooney, but because he was a literary agent he was the first man whose word was gospel. That was eighteen years ago, and I've been on the job to which he assigned me ever since.

I found doing a book on the vastly complex history of Tom Mooney's life and times much more difficult than telling yarns about him to friends; thus Van Dycke's attempts to find a publisher for my first efforts were of no avail. But I have always given thanks for that first push he provided, and am happy to acknowledge the encouragement and advice he gave during the earlier years of my task.

Eventually I came to realize that my script was too long and full of detail, and therefore I turned to an editor and writer in whose opinion I had great confidence, Al Richmond. After reading my script he suggested drastic literary surgery. The main feature of his clinical approach was that I should toss away my cloak of modesty and make full use of my personal knowledge of Mooney and his case.

The result is the book you are now reading. If you find it readable you will be helping me, by osmosis, in giving Al Richmond adequate thanks.

During the years of research I received invaluable assistance from past and present members of the staff of the Bancroft Library, University of California at Berkeley — Robert Becker, John Barr Tompkins, Mrs. Helen Radnor, Cecil Chase, and Vivian Fisher, among others; also Carol Schwartz, librarian for the International Longshoremen's and Warehousemen's Union.

All through the many years and several versions of *The Gentle Dynamiter*, I had the devoted and enthusiastic support of my wife, Angela, plus her indispensable help in doing the research and the typing and re-typing of the manuscript. Thanks, my dear.

E.E.W.

Prologue

Tom Mooney! The name rang a bell wherever men and women could read the printed word, for in 1935 he was the most famous convicted murderer in the world.

And when one day he entered the courtroom of the California Supreme Court and took his seat at defense counsel's table, no one other than those in the know could have told by dress or demeanor that he was any kind of a criminal at all.

But among those who did know the tragedy of Tom Mooney's life was a young member of the court's staff who put his job and his reputation on the line by crossing the courtroom and offering his hand. I was that man.

At that time I was the court reporter and bailiff, and I served at the pleasure of the justices. And when I put out my hand I knew full well that my act would certainly irritate and probably infuriate most or all of those seven men. But the sight of Tom Mooney overcame all other considerations in my mind. After nineteen years of hearing about him, talking about him, here was Mooney in the flesh.

I felt a sudden, urgent need to offer my loyalty to him and his cause, although I could only look him in the eye and clasp his hand, my lips locked to all but the most banal of utterances:

"I've always wanted to meet you, sir."

9

Still, I was careful to refrain from uttering any word that Mooney could rush to his printer for publication in a pamphlet.

The man I faced was slightly under medium height, with a stocky body that seemed to be composed of a series of circles: round face, round head, round eyes, round belly. The eyes were dark, set under massive black eyebrows; his glance was bright, expressing unusual courage and determination. His hair, once as black as his eyebrows, was now grey and receding. He was neatly dressed in a suit of dark grey with a faint pinstripe, and at a casual glance the rare person who had not already seen that face a thousand times in print might have taken him for some sort of successful professional man.

Mooney was as Irish as his name, but he was not a professional — unless being under lock and key for nineteen years made him a professional prisoner. Also he was one of the world's most famous men, infintely better known than any of the seven solemn men who had the power to keep him in San Quentin Prison for the rest of his life. He had been convicted of murder, yet most American citizens, high and low, knew that Mooney had killed no one; everyone, practically, except the California Establishment — including six of the seven justices of the California Supreme Court.

Even those six probably did not believe that Mooney had actually taken a human life. They merely believed, in essence, that if he hadn't it had been an oversight on his part.

These thoughts whirled in my head as I returned to my station in front of the long, high bench where, in a moment or two, the seven black-robed figures would seat themselves. They entered, and I brought the audience to its feet with the three traditional knocks of my knuckles on an oak table and the historic cry: "Hear ye, hear ye, hear ye!"

Then, my duties finished, I gave thought to what I had just done. The job I had just laid on the line was a sinecure, a lazy man's pipedream that paid $300 per month — a handsome little living in 1935. Why had I taken such a chance?

I could blame it on my father. He was an anomaly, combining a quiet belief in Socialism with a keen understanding of the legal and practical aspects of the shipping industry that had made him quite successful in San Francisco, then queen of Pacific Coast waterborne commerce. On our dining room table there always lay the latest copy of Eugene V. Debs' *Appeal to Reason* from which I learned early in life that there were better things to hope for than the capitalist system and its cycle of boom, depression, war, boom, depression, and war, over and over. I learned about women's suffrage and pacifism and the union struggles of those times, and was proud that my father paid union wages on the ships he controlled and refused to participate in strikebreaking — then the customary response of most shipping men when seamen sought more money, better conditions.

Most of my reminiscing, however, focused on the events of 1916, when I was 17 years old.

My reverie ended as the morning court session came to an end; the justices left the bench; Mooney, his lawyer, and the deputy sheriff assigned to guard the prisoner disappeared. Of course, my outlook on many things, including the mysteries of injustice, had changed over those nineteen years. At 17, I had not seen any direct connection between myself and men like Mooney. I was sympathetic, but only as an onlooker. During World War I I had been all too eager to go and fight the Hun, and thought changing the name of the innocent hamburger to "Liberty Steak" was eminently right and proper.

Now I was seeing and feeling things that made me want to make my own commitment to peace and to the cause of labor. I saw Mooney as a sign-post pointing out the right road — and it was not long before I took that road.

I was soon to leave my easy job with the court, but before I did, I heard the Chief Justice order his law clerk to refuse Mooney's plea. Indeed, that was one of the things that catapulted me into the hurly-burly of the great CIO organizing drive of the Nineteen-Thirties. Soon I was visiting Tom Mooney regularly at San Quentin Prison, sometimes alone, more often as a member or leader of some delegation.

I was in the room when a Governor-elect, despite great political risk, agreed to set the famous prisoner free after twenty-two and a half years in San Quentin.

I was one of the crowd that jammed the Assembly Room in the State Capitol at Sacramento on that great day when Tom Mooney finally received just treatment, despite the courts of law.

And I was in a hospital room, not long after, to visit Tom as he lay dying a slow and miserable death.

War and peace . . . the years flew by; at last I decided to attempt what friends had been pressing me to do for a long time, to put down on paper what I knew about Tom Mooney. To make sure of myself and my memory, I spent nearly four years doing research at the University of California's Bancroft Library and in old newspaper files, checking out the vast maze of facts and lies the Mooney case had left behind.

Although I use the first person when describing matters personally known to me, the bulk of this book is taken from my research, with reference notes available to every reader.

Estolv Ethan Ward

1

Setting the Stage

The Mooney case began, literally, with a bang in 1916; a bang so loud and murderous and politically significant that for decades it made headlines wherever men printed newspapers.

The United States was seething with great controversies — labor struggles, the question of involvement in World War I in Europe, our "little war" against Pancho Villa in northern Mexico, pacifists versus jingoes, and a heated Presidential campaign.

In the labor struggles, led mostly by members of the Industrial Workers of the World (known better as "Wobblies"), the boss had on his side the press, the law, the courts, and the cops. The working man had only the ability to withhold his labor; no laws giving workers the right to organize and bargain collectively, no National Labor Relations Board, no friends on high. The employer used policemen and vigilantes (often the same men in civilian garb) and judges and jails; workers frequently retaliated with guns and dynamite.

San Francisco, in 1916, bore the reputation of "The best damned union town in America," and the employers, sensing the nation's warlike mood, saw an opportunity to reverse this situation and make the city by the Golden Gate the best damned open shop region on the West Coast. As a result there were several strikes all sizzling at once during the summer months. The longest, bloodiest, and most crucial of these was that of the longshoremen. There was a nasty racist tinge to this imbroglio, because in those days most unions, including longshore, were "lily-white." Thus the employers, seeking strikebreakers, traditionally went straight to the Black ghettos to hire desperate, hungry men. (In 1916 there was no public welfare, no such thing as a social relief agency for Blacks, no hint of unemployment insurance.)

These men, knowing full well the danger attached to every dollar they might earn, came to work armed and ready to fight.*

In 1916, shootings, knifings, beatings, killings, and riots broke out on the waterfronts of San Francisco and in Seattle and Tacoma, with lesser violence in the smaller ports. In San Francisco, leaders charged, without rebuttal, that the first murder and, in fact, the first violence, had been committed by the strikebreakers.

The strikers, determined to keep their closed shop contract, declared this issue was not negotiable. Otherwise, their demands seemed mild. Longshoremen had been getting along with two classes of labor, the lower at 50 cents an hour for straight time of eight hours and 75 cents for overtime; the higher at 55 cents an hour and $1.00 for overtime. Now the men were demanding the establishment of a single work classification at this higher rate.

The conflict came to a head when the San Francisco Chamber of Commerce called an employers' meeting, set up a vigilante "Law and Order Committee," and raised a million dollars (no mean sum in those days) to smash the workers, restore the open shop, and protect those sweet low wages. Crowds of businessmen swarmed into the courtrooms of judges who might be tempted to mete out even-handed justice. A group led by Captain Robert Dollar, a a ferocious old shipping and lumber magnate, called upon the District Attorney and threatened to hang him from the nearest telephone pole if he dallied in using his power in their behalf — this meant looking the other way when the scabs were violent but cracking

---

*Pitting Black against white in labor struggles went on unabated until 1934, when Harry Bridges and men like him moved to promise Blacks union membership and equal opportunity with whites if they refused to scab in that year's famous longshore strike — a promise kept after a victory that ended the open shop in the West Coast shipping industry.

down with a vengeance when any striker was caught in a slug-fest.

On the docks, the strike was brought to a quick and miserable end, with the union broken, their contract reduced to waste paper, and the open shop reigning supreme. The scabs slunk back to their ghettos; it was to be eighteen long years before genuine unionism returned to the Pacific Coast waterfronts.

Meanwhile, U.S. General John Pershing and a few thousand of his troops were 300 miles into Northern Mexico, trying to catch and eliminate Pancho Villa — known to Americans as a bandit and to most Mexicans as a liberator — while our government officially declared itself unable to decide which side to take in an enigmatic civil war our neighbors were trying to keep among themselves. Jingoes, notably Theodore Roosevelt and men of his ilk, were demanding that we do to Mexico what we had done to Cuba and the Philippines in 1898, namely, move in and take over.

There were many Mexicans in California, and most of them, reacting to the invasion of their homeland, considered it their patriotic duty to give Americans as much trouble as Americans were giving their countrymen. The result: scares about "mysterious Mexicans" in various places, mostly the agricultural valleys; a bombing in an Oakland railroad station that injured ten persons, supposedly set by three Mexicans; fights wherever Mexicans and Anglos confronted each other.

Even more disturbing were the Germans, from diplomats to saboteurs. The United States was shipping great quantities of munitions and other war necessities to the Allies, and the Germans were doing their utmost to cut off this valuable assistance — using professionals to touch off fires and explosions in warehouses and on terminals and barges in various American ports. Franz Bopp, German consul-general in San Francisco, and some of his men were under Federal indictment and awaiting trial, accused of masterminding the Western portion of this activity. Yet sabotage attributed to the Germans still plagued munitions merchants, with tremendous destruction of property and occasional loss of life.

San Francisco authorities also worried about the Anarchists. Two of their foremost spokesmen, Emma Goldman and Alexander Berkman, were "living in sin" near Mission Dolores Park. Miss Goldman was speaking nightly in a small hall on Fillmore Street on such inflammatory topics as "Birth Control" and "Revolutionary

Art," and that sinister character, Berkman, was always there, handing out pamphlets on all sorts of unspeakable subjects. He had done time in prison for shooting a Pennsylvania steel magnate, and many felt he should never have been let free.

Also to be watched were more than a few loud-mouthed street corner speakers, mostly strikers, shouting words taken directly from the publications of the Wobblies.

Clashes between pacifists and jingoes grew heated as the United States edged closer to deciding what it could or should do about that draggly war in Europe, already two years old and going nowhere. The pacifists, though scorned in some quarters as "Mr. Milquetoasts," were by no means all meek, humble and powerless. They were strong enough that President Wilson, campaigning for re-election, found it expedient to offer the slogan "He Kept Us Out of War" as the main reason why he should be returned to office.

Yet Wilson had also marched in a New York spectacle billed as a "Preparedness Day Parade." Such parades, serving dual belligerencies, first against union labor and second against all nations we disliked, such as the Mexicans and maybe the Germans, had been held in several of the larger Eastern cities.

The last of these "parades" was set for San Francisco for July 22nd, 1916. The pacifists saw this as a provocative act and held a big protest rally at Idora Park in Oakland, with speaker after speaker crying out against the munitions makers as war makers, out to make dollars by the murder of millions. And then, two days before the parade, an even larger protest rally was held at Dreamland Rink in San Francisco, with five thousand persons jamming a hall that normally held only three thousand, and hundreds more standing outside.

"Preparedness" supporters found these pacifist speeches incendiary, particularly as they came from the mouths of men many notches higher in the social order than the common soapbox rabble rouser. For instance, Rudolph Spreckels, chairman of the Dreamland affair, was widely and favorably known to almost everyone in San Francisco: a multi-millionaire, scion of the great Spreckels sugar clan and president of one of San Francisco's largest banks; he was a man with something dangerously akin to a social conscience.

Spreckels stood up against Hearstian and Rooseveltian clamor for war with Mexico. At the rally, William McDevitt, a local election commissioner speaking for the Socialist Party, paraphrased George Bernard Shaw: "If I were in a heroic mood I would advise somebody to shoot in . . . . the back every representative of a corrupt munitions maker or corporation in the parade . . . All nations should use one flag, the flag that is the color of the heart's blood." Paul Scharrenberg, California's top labor leader, spoke of Preparedness parades as "Indian war dances."

Meanwhile, sinister postcards and letters kept coming through the mail to the editors of the city's five daily newspapers. All these missives claimed sympathy with "the masses," and threatened dire things to the paraders. Two hundred postcards, all in identical handwriting, attacked the more or less prominent citizens who were to lead various contingents of the huge demonstration as members of the "brutal, greedy, parasitic, thieving and warmaking class," and promised them "immediate exterminating." The letters, among other threats, said " . . . we want to give . . . THE HYPO-CRITICAL PATRIOTS WHO SHOUT FOR WAR BUT NEVER GO a real taste of war."

If such happenings were not enough to give the authorities pause, there was also Tom Mooney, who was causing almost as much trouble in San Francisco, single-handed, as the striking longshoremen. A militant, a Socialist, and a suspected dynamiter, Mooney had stood trial more than once for alleged attempts to illegally transport explosives with the purpose of destroying electric transmission lines of the Pacific Gas and Electric Company. So far, he had escaped conviction, but one of his associates, a battle-hardened youngster named Warren Billings, had been less lucky and had served a prison sentence. Mooney, his wife, Rena, and Billings, were involved in a desperate struggle to unionize the employees of the Market Street Railway, a division of the United Railroads (URR) a private corporation, so they might enjoy the same wages and conditions that obtained on the competing city-owned railway system. Only a few days before Preparedness Day, Rena and several carmen had been arrested for attempting to start a strike by stopping a Market Street Railway car at a crucial downtown intersection in the evening rush hour. And, barely a month before, after an unsuccessful organizing meeting for streetcar men, three transmission towers supplying the privately-owned carline had been dynamited in the dead of night. Mooney and Billings were the suspects.

It was no accident that it was Tom Mooney who raised the hue and cry in labor circles that the Preparedness Day parade might well prove dangerous to the union cause. He had been quietly tipped off about the threatening letters and postcards by Frederick Ely, labor editor of the *Bulletin*, whose editor-in chief, Fremont Older, was a famous crusading liberal whose paper reflected Older's personality and policies. The tip went to Mooney because he was the man most likely to get things done, and he behaved in keeping with his reputation. First he got a resolution through his own union, the Molders, and then took it to the San Francisco Central Labor Countil and the Building Trades Council; the gist of it was a warning that provocateurs might attempt to blacken labor by blowing up the Preparedness parade. The resolution was adopted, and this may very well have moved Paul Scharrenberg, no flaming radical, to denounce the parade. It was certainly the reason why no union member worthy of the name could be seen in that fateful parade, unless his union was so weak that the boss could lay it on the line: "March, or else!"

Preparedness Day came clear of the fog that normally enshrouds San Francisco in summer; a day to encourage any outdoor pleasure, including a parade. Plenty of precautions had been taken for this great patriotic event. At least one policeman stood at every intersection along the parade route; roving automobiles full of armed police sought Anarchists and troublemakers and plainclothesmen filtered through the onlookers lining the curbs to see the fun.

Suddenly there was a boom heard throughout downtown. Most people thought this was some sort of parade signal, but it proved to be the signal of death, for the explosion sent lead bullets and shards of other metals flying in all directions. The immediate toll: six dead, four dying, forty injured. In the words of one eyewitness, "It looked like a battlefield!"

The populace went into shock. As the first awful hours went by, this turned to outrage. The air rang with hysterical promises that vengeful justice would be done. And done without delay!

Before midnight of that day, an opinion had begun to form in high places. The suspects . . . . forget about the Germans, the Mexicans; Labor, maybe; Anarchists, probably. But which laborite, which Anarchist? Or Socialist? Or pacifist?

Up came a man who wished to be helpful: Martin Swanson, a

Blast site: District Attorney Fickert (far right) and Frederick H. Colburn, banker and Chamber of Commerce official, used a sledge-hammer to make the damage appear greater.

super-sleuth for hire to any employer who wished to keep trade unionism from infecting his workers. He had a man in mind, a man he had trailed for years on behalf of the United Railroads and the Pacific Gas and Electric Company, a man he had kept under close surveillance for the past couple of weeks. This man fitted several possibilities — Labor, Socialist, Anarchist, pacifist. Swanson whispered the name to all the important men he could, including the district attorney.

The name caught fire in the brains of those to whom Swanson whispered. Yes! Yes! Of course! Even Older of the *Bulletin*, the most fearless and liberal man in his field, thought so too. Thomas J. Mooney. . . .

Young Rena and Tom Mooney

2

Despair

1917 — — —

It was Friday night, February 9, in the Hall of Justice, and the ugly, square building on Kearney Street blazed with lights. There was excitement in the air, for the word was that the Mooney jury was ready to come in. Attorneys, court attaches, newspapermen, friends of those who had been killed or maimed in the Preparedness Day tragedy; Mooney and his aged, trembling mother, his brother and sister; and here and there a mere sensation-seeker, waited impatiently to see what the twelve "good men and true" had to say. The hysteria of the past few months was muted for the moment, but it was there, holding its breath.

The Judge, the Honorable Franklin Griffin, entered and took the bench. The bailiff rapped for order. A side door opened and the jury filed in. "Billie" McNevin, the man who, as he had predicted, had been elected foreman, looked over the crowd until he caught the eye of Eddie Cunha, the Deputy District Attorney who had prosecuted Mooney. Quick as a wink, McNevin drew his finger across his throat. Cunha nodded. He understood the signal. This silent and highly improper communication went unnoticed by all except a few, including one man who knew Cunha and McNevin very well — a lawyer named Ed McKenzie who had stopped by the courtroom door out of curiosity. At the time the incident was none of his business, but it was to haunt him for years to come.

"Guilty of murder in the first degree," was the verdict. Actually the word might well have been "murders" since the Preparedness bomb had killed ten persons. However, District Attorney Charles M. Fickert had decided upon separate cases, each to be tried by itself, just to make sure — and to prolong the excitement, feed the public hunger for revenge, and boost the name of the avenger toward high political heaven.

Guards clamped handcuffs on the prisoner and led him off to the city prison. His dear ones, shaken and silent, went their mournful way. The chief defense counsel, Bourke Cockran, a former Congressman and a gilt-tongued Irish orator, was crestfallen, for he had promised himself and his client an acquittal; now he was moved to catch the first train out of California, to places where he might hope to find some semblance of sanity and decency.

Edward A. Cunha, however, was ecstatic. It was his first break as a deputy district attorney, and he had made good, but big! A slender, fiery brunet, Eddie Cunha stood at the courtroom door, shouting to all who would listen that on the strength of the Mooney conviction District Attorney Fickert would be wafted into the Governor's mansion in Sacramento; Eddie, himself, of course, would get Fickert's current job.

The jailhouse that night held at least five very sad, despondent inmates: Tom; his youthful helper, Warren Billings; Tom's wife, Rena; and two friends, a taxi driver named Israel Weinberg and an official of the Machinists' Union, Ed Nolan. All had been arrested in a police dragnet and charged with the bombing. Billings, the first to be tried, had already been convicted of murder and sentenced to life in prison. To the prosecution, however, Billings was merely the stepping stone to Mooney. He was the man they were determined to hang.

Almost as thick as the gloom in those prison cells was the atmosphere in the office of Maxwell McNutt, the brilliant local attorney who had assisted Bourke Cochran in Mooney's defense. He had defended Mooney in previous cases involving accusations of dynamiting, and although McNutt was himself a most law-abiding citizen, he had come to like Mooney and trust him.

Therefore, when Tom told McNutt, eye to eye, that he and

The accused: Israel Weinberg, an officer of the Jitney Union, Warren K. Billings, Rena Mooney, Tom Mooney and Edward D. Nolan, official in the Machinists Union.

Prosecutor Eddie Cunha and District Attorney Charles M. Fickert, men who selected and coached the perjurers used to convict Mooney.

Rena had not set that bomb-laden suitcase at Steuart and Market Streets, the lawyer believed him. It was not a case where the clever lawyer takes his client's story with a grain of salt but does his best to get the man off scot free. Mooney was honest; McNutt would swear to it.

McNutt may have thought the prosecution witnesses were the weirdest collection of God-damned liars he had ever seen — but he couldn't prove it. There was one possible exception in that parade, a big, burly fellow named Frank C. Oxman, dubbed "the honest cattleman" by the press. He was amiable, forthright, impressive. McNutt was sure the jurymen had taken a liking to this witness. And yet, he was either lying in his teeth or the victim of hallucinations, for Mooney simply had not placed that suitcase full of dynamite. Nor had Billings. McNutt would have staked his life on that.

The other prosecution witnesses were easy to dismiss — grifters, derelicts, little people on the make. Oxman, though, was wealthy, a respected citizen of a farming locality up in the state of Oregon. While wealth was no guarantee of honesty, it was difficult to imagine what the prosecution could offer such a man to testify falsely. Oxman had sworn under oath that he had seen Mooney and Billings place a battered imitation leather suitcase alongside a saloon at the site of the explosion and had heard Mooney say to his young friend, "Let's go; the bulls will be after us." On the witness stand, the old cattleman had declared, with country-bumpkin innocence, "I remember, because I thought a bull was a male cow!" The courtroom had rocked with approving laughter. What chance did a man stand against a witness like that?

The defense problems seemed insuperable. For one thing, there was virtually no public support. With one or two brave exceptions, the labor movement chose to deplore the tragedy and ignore Mooney. Even his political home, the Socialist Party, had tried to expel him, and would have succeeded except that his own unit, the San Francisco Hungarian branch, stood steadfast. (Under the Socialist Party's constitution, a member's own unit could veto an expulsion move.)

Also, the defense treasury was a morass of debt. While Bourke Cockran had charged no fee, the defense had felt obligated to meet his expenses, and you could not expect a man of his caliber to sleep on a cot in some friend's back bedroom. Cockran's bill at the St. Francis Hotel, one of the town's best, went unpaid for what seemed like eons.

The immediate problem facing the defense was the fact that the guilty verdict was, in effect, the starter's pistol in a race against time. Under California law, newly discovered evidence was admissible only until sentence was passed. Once Judge Griffin pronounced those lethal words, ". . . to be hanged by the neck until dead," only a reversal by the State Supreme Court or a gubernatorial pardon could rescue Mooney from the gallows. And neither event was in the cards.

Knowing as well as anyone the unstable nature of most of the prosecution witnesses, Fickert and Cunha wanted no delay in the sentencing. Judge Griffin was accommodating and named a date fifteen days after the verdict.

Only two weeks! Somewhere, somehow, there had to be evidence. But where? The exhausted, impoverished defense had not the faintest clue as to its whereabouts.

Public hysteria continued for months after the Preparedness Day bombing. Some flavor of the times is provided by the story of Eugene Randolph, a young technician for the Pacific Telephone and Telegraph Company, and an innocent bystander if ever there was one.

On September 8th, the day before Admission Day (a big holiday for Northern Californians) Randolph was sent from San Francisco to the rural town of Santa Rosa to perform some emergency repairs in the local telephone exchange. The job kept him overnight, and he finished his task about noon on the holiday. Planning to hurry back to San Francisco, he picked up his overnight bag, a black leather Gladstone, and left the cool of the telephone company building for the blinding September heat of Fourth Street, the town's main thoroughfare. He found himself at the tag-end of the Admission Day parade, in which the Native Sons of the Golden West (and also the Native Daughters) had marched with flags and banners and bands under the leadership of Mayor "Sunny Jim" Rolph of San Francisco, resplendent in silk hat, cowboy boots, and ineradicable smile. The street was full.

The heat made young Randolph slightly dizzy, and looking around for a cool spot he saw the Sonoma County court house, surrounded by a green lawn dotted with trees. As he settled onto the grass his black bag caught the attention of a noisy group that seemed a little drunk. "Look!" exclaimed one of them. Black was known as the Anarchist color. In a moment a score of men were staring at Randolph and his bag; in two moments, two score.

"A bomber!" muttered one. "Anarchist!" shouted another. "Let's get him!" cried a third. "Lynch him!" "String him up!"

A ring formed around the telephone technician. Drunken faces were leaning in. Randolph was not exactly surprised; he only found it incomprehensible that this should be happening to him. He had marched in the Preparedness Day parade at his employer's behest. He had heard that bomb go off a block and a half behind him, and like thousands of others had thought it must be some kind of a signal. Later, like all of his fellow workers, he had speculated that somebody — probably some Anarchist — would be made the goat, with questions of guilt or innocence lost in the uproar. But to find *himself* the goat! It was impossible! But, it was happening.

Randolph rolled from a sitting position onto his back, knees drawn up, feet ready to kick. This pose held off the rush for half a second, just enough time for two uniformed policemen to burst through the ring. They told Randolph something he already knew:

"You're in trouble!"

They hustled Randolph through the unruly throng and into the courthouse. The crowd sought to follow. Hastily the officers locked the door, then ran to secure all the other entrances to the building.

Now safe from the mob, the policemen turned on Randolph. "What's in that bag?" they demanded. He showed them: nightshirt, slippers, shaving kit, toothbrush and powder, hair brush and a change of underwear. He displayed credentials proving his occupation and his reason for being in Santa Rosa.

This satisfied the cops, but much of the mob was still around the courthouse, hopefully eyeing its doors. For two hours, until the last of the would-be lynchers wandered off in search of other diversions, Randolph was kept in protective custody.

Then, timing it precisely, the police sneaked Randolph out of the courthouse and put him aboard a train just ready to pull out for Sausalito. Even then, the officers did not relax. Fearing for his safety, they took Randolph to the mail section of the baggage car and placed him in the care of an armed clerk. In this fashion, thankful to be alive, Randolph made his way back to San Francisco.

Among the millions of Americans who read of Mooney's conviction, some were stirred into activity — for a variety of motives: cupidity, indignation, revenge, malice, and even a desire to rescue justice. One of these was a deeply religious woman living in the San Joaquin Valley, south of San Francisco. Another, a man of very different tendencies, resided in the small town of Grayville in southern Illinois, near the Indiana border.

Grayville contained about two thousand inhabitants and, as in most communities of that size, everybody knew everybody else's business. The deeply religious woman had grown up there, and she and her family had come to regard a man named Frank Oxman — "Cliff," as he was known — with something less than respect or admiration. He had been mixed up in some shady land deals, though he had bought his way out of this trouble. Infinitely more scandalous was an act which to this woman fell into the lowest possible category of human behavior. He had deserted his fine wife and lovely children, leaving them destitute, and run off with another woman; to the state of Oregon, so it was said. If this should be the same F.C. Oxman who had been the key witness against Mooney, she thought Mooney's lawyers ought to be informed of Oxman's past.

On the other hand, what she had read about Mooney made him seem abhorrent to her, and she dithered about what to do. Finally she hit upon a plan: she wrote a friend in San Francisco, another devout woman, asking her to send an anonymous letter to Maxwell McNutt. The friend obliged, but by the time that letter reached the defense, a month had passed. The crucial moment had come and gone.

The man in Grayville moved much more quickly. He was F.E. "Ed" Rigall, owner of the local pool hall and billiard parlor, and just about the sportiest of small-town sports. Smooth-faced, with widely set big blue eyes and a Cupid's-bow mouth, he wore his wavy platinum grey hair parted in the center and was fond of snazzy clothes — something of a lady killer, by his own account, though a little on the short and stocky side, with too much meat on the nose and not enough on the chin. After reading a squib in the Grayville paper about Mooney's conviction, Rigall instructed his assistant to mind the hall, and then trudged across town to an office with gold lettering on the window: "C.O. Ellis, Attorney-at-Law."

Attorney Ellis was a man of high standing in Grayville. He had twice been mayor, and he carried himself with a dignity which contrasted strongly with the aura of the pool hall owner. Only one flash of human frailty marred Ellis's impeccable professional appearance — the narrow, pin-striped bow tie worn like an X fallen sideways, and beneath it a blazing diamond stickpin. Claude Ellis knew and was known to every resident of southern Illinois; it was no secret to him that Ed Rigall had recently returned from a trip to San Francisco.

Ed sat down and began to talk, and what he said brought Ellis to full attention. In mid-December, 1916, Rigall had received a letter written on the stationery of the Terminal Hotel, San Francisco, and signed by F.C. Oxman, suggesting that the recipient come West and testify in some litigation. As all Grayville knew, there were two F.C. Oxmans, the father known as Cliff and the son called Frank. The latter had been Rigall's chum and drinking companion, having remained in town long after his father's departure. By now, however, the younger Oxman had disappeared; probably gone West like his father before him.

Although in the dark as to what might be expected of him, and even about which Oxman had written, Rigall was taken with the prospect of an expense-free trip to a part of the country he had not yet seen, so he had shot off a wire saying he'd come; please send money for railroad fare and expenses. Oxman had replied promptly, still vague as to the nature of the litigation, but promising to send money forthwith if Rigall would testify to seeing Oxman in San Francisco on July 22, and asking him to say nothing of the matter. Soon Rigall was "riding the cushions" westbound, a round-trip ticket plus $27 in spending money in his pocket.

As Ellis was to discover, there were several versions of what happened after Rigall arrived in San Francisco, but the one he heard that day in Grayville was most favorable to its author. Rigall said he had soon learned that the father, not the son, had sent for him, and that he was being asked to testify in a sensational murder case about which he knew not a damn thing. If he took the witness stand for Oxman, he would have to commit perjury. Rigall said he made up his mind not to testify, but also decided to keep that to

Ed Rigall, Indiana poolhall owner brought to San Francisco to bolster Oxman's perjury. Rigall declined to lie for the prosecution.

himself until the right moment. He was being wined and dined and otherwise entertained by police and prosecution bigwigs, and the atmosphere of plot and counterplot intrigued him. He would play along for awhile.

The Mooney trial was on and the prosecution was nearing the climax of its case. The District Attorney, who had a flair for sensational publicity, made daily headlines by promising to produce an Oregon cattleman of great wealth and probity whose testimony would certainly send Mooney to the gallows. There were also hints that at least one other witness would appear to corroborate Oxman's story. The newspapers had spelled the name differently — Regal, Reigal, Riggal — and were fuzzy about this person's first name and origins; some reported he was an Oregon cattleman, others placed him as from Chicago.

Rigall told Claude Ellis that on the night before Oxman was expected to take the witness stand, Rigall had been called into conference with Deputy D.A. Eddie Cunha at the Hall of Justice, to rehearse the testimony he was expected to deliver. This, Rigall now said, seemed to be the moment he had been awaiting, so he confessed for the first time that he had not been in San Francisco on July 22, 1916. As a matter of fact, Rigall knew damned well where he had been that day — at Niagara Falls, New York.

According to Rigall, Cunha had taken this turn of events philosophically, agreeing that the whole matter should be forgotten. He did have, however, one small request. Would Rigall kindly stick around until after Oxman testified? Should Rigall suddenly disappear, the star witness might get cold feet. The pool hall owner could see the logic of this and agreed to stay on — for a price.

So Oxman had testified without corroboration that he had seen Tom and Rena Mooney, and Billings, arrive at Steuart and Market Streets in a jitney driven by Weinberg, a few minutes before the explosion occurred, and had watched Mooney direct Billings to place a suitcase at the point of blast. To clinch his story, Oxman produced a pencilled notation he claimed to have made of the jitney's license number. Later, evidence was introduced showing that Oxman's notation tallied exactly with that of Weinberg's jitney.

Within hours, the Grayville pool hall man was on his way homeward with $150 more of the District Attorney's expense money in his pockets. End of story.

Ellis finally spoke: "It's a hell of a thing to see a man go to the gallows on that kind of testimony."

"I know that," replied Rigall.

"Didn't this man Cunha ask, when you came clean with him, how or by what means Oxman got in touch with you?"

"Oh, yes. I told him I'd had a couple of letters from Oxman. Mr. Cunha asked where they were; he wanted to see them. But I kidded him along. I had them right in my pocket while I was talking to him, but I said I'd left them on the dining room table at home in Grayville, and I could get them for him, provided my wife hadn't come along and burned them up, or something. He asked me to send them if I could find them. When I got home I found that Oxman had written a third letter, to my mother, suggesting that she come along too; he might need her for an extra witness."

"So what did you do?" asked Ellis.

"I wrote Mr. Cunha telling him about Oxman's letter to my mother, and said I'd found the other two and would he rather I sent the letter to him personally or to Mr. Fickert. I never got an answer."

"Then you have those letters now, I suppose?"

"Right here in my pocket." He brought them out, envelopes and all; Ellis unfolded them and went into a silent study for possibly ten minutes. Then he refolded them, returned them to their envelopes, and put them into his own inside coat pocket.

"Better let me keep these," said Ellis. "You can never tell — something might happen to you."

The consultation went on for hours, Ellis demanding detail after detail, Rigall answering questions as fast as they came. Finally the lawyer gave his advice:

"All right, Ed. I think you ought to send this Mr. Cunha a telegram to stir him up a bit. Won't do a bit of harm."

Together the men drafted the message:

CONGRATULATIONS ON YOUR CONVICTION. THINK MY EVIDENCE WILL GET PARTY A NEW TRIAL. F.E. RIGALL.

The pool hall man went to the telegraph office and sent his message night letter. This took place late Saturday afternoon, less than 24 hours after Mooney had been found guilty.

Eddie Cunha may have spent the weekend in glorious exultation. But when he arrived at his desk in the Hall of Justice on Monday morning, the sweet afterglow of his victory was probably dimmed by the waiting wire from Grayville, Illinois. The young prosecutor's reaction is recorded in the telegram he fired back that same day:

CANNOT UNDERSTAND YOUR TELEGRAM. YOU TOLD ME YOUR FRIEND WAS THOROUGHLY TRUTHFUL AND RE-LIABLE. WE HAVE PLENTY OF OTHER WITNESSES AND CONCLUSIVE EVIDENCE SUPPORTING HIS TESTIMONY. AM ASTOUNDED AT YOUR SUGGESTION THAT YOU HAVE TESTIMONY TO HELP DEFENDANT. IT IS YOUR DUTY TO REVEAL TO ME AT ONCE ANY AND ALL FACTS WHICH YOU HAVE BECAUSE I CERTAINLY WANT THIS DEFEN-DANT TO HAVE A NEW TRIAL IF HE IS ENTITLED TO IT.

WIRE ME QUICK ALL DETAILS AT ONCE. EXPLAIN IN
DETAIL YOUR TELEGRAM AND YOUR ATTITUDE. BE
CAREFUL AND FAIR BECAUSE ANY WITNESS WHO HAS
TESTIFIED FALSELY IN THIS MURDER CASE MUST HIM-
SELF BE PROSECUTED FOR MURDER. YOU SHOULD HAVE
TOLD ME ANYTHING YOU KNEW BEFORE THE WITNESS
TESTIFIED. AFTER WIRING WRITE ME EVERY SLIGHT
NOTION EVEN WHICH YOU HAVE ON THIS CASE AND
SEND ALL DATA. I AM SURE YOU KNOW NOTHING TO
GET DEFENDANT NEW TRIAL BUT I FEEL PERSONALLY
RESPONSIBLE AND WOULD LATER ON HAVE GOVERNOR
CHANGE PENALTY OR PARDON IF I DEVELOPED ANY
KIND OF DOUBT. AT PRESENT I AM THOROUGHLY SATIS-
FIED EVEN WITHOUT YOUR FRIEND'S TESTIMONY JUST
AS JURY WAS IN FIRST CASE BUT I WANT EVERYTHING
CLEARED UP IN MY MIND. WIRE IMMEDIATELY TO ME
AT OLYMPIC CLUB, SAN FRANCISCO, CALIFORNIA. ED-
WARD A. CUNHA.

Cunha received no reply. Rigall, at his attorney's behest, simply
sat, waiting.

The continued silence from Grayville could only have fed Eddie
Cunha's worst fears; Rigall had definitely come down on the defense
side! Despite his pious protestations of fairness, Cunha leapt into
action to protect his victory. He went to his boss, Charles Fickert,
and demanded that police guards be set at all railroad stations and
ferries with orders to arrest Rigall if he should dare to return to
San Francisco. Then, in case Rigall should manage to slip through,
Cunha took a train for Portland, Oregon, for a conference with
Oxman. The upshot of that meeting was that the cattleman came
back to San Francisco with the nervous prosecutor, ready to shout
Rigall out of countenance, should that be necessary.

During Cunha's brief absence from San Francisco, his plans
suffered a setback. His request for police guards to stop Rigall was
vetoed by Police Captain Duncan Matheson, who had been in charge
of certain phases of the investigation into the bombing. This blunt
and upright police officer, known widely as "the honest cop," had
met Rigall and stiffened visibly when Fickert passed on Cunha's
request. In the first place, Matheson was beginning to dislike and
distrust Fickert. In the second place, Matheson found Rigall utterly
without credibility. Matheson had dealt with crooks all his official

life, and Rigall was one of the most obvious con men he had ever laid eyes upon.

"I will not order a single policeman to spend as much as one minute trying to intercept Rigall," Matheson thundered.

As the fifteen-day time limit ran its course, stirrings of life were seen in defense circles. Tips and guesses and tantalizing bits of information came in, first a trickle and soon a flood, from earnest, well-meaning people — plus as many more who only seemed earnest and well-meaning. It took time for McNutt to dismiss the phonies, particularly since he was hamstrung for funds to hire investigators.

On the dot, on February 24, 1917, fifteen days after the verdict, final argument took place before Judge Griffin. Cunha came in, gambling that he still had the edge. If Rigall did not appear, it might be dangerous to produce Oxman. Better to keep him in the wings, ready to be called. Otherwise, Oxman's presence might touch off questions and speculations most detrimental to the prosecution.

Cunha was doubtless expecting to see the broad, pale face of Ed Rigall at any moment. Defense Attorney McNutt, the ring of hope in his voice, presented affidavits challenging the prosecution on various points, including a random stab at Oxman's veracity. Cunha's fears could only have diminished with every phrase he heard his opponent utter.

With the threat of Rigall's appearance gone, Cunha, when his turn came, flung himself into impassioned argument for a hanging. With a great show of scorn he picked apart McNutt's affidavits; lofty with pride, he described Oxman as eminently successful, a man of unimpeachable character. It was the finest argument of his young career, and it impressed Judge Griffin. A large, reputedly kindly person with a high forehead and dignified stride, the Judge had found Oxman likable and believable, and Cunha's argument made it easier to carry out his duty. He was not the traditional "hanging Judge," but Cunha's polemics must have soothed any inner doubts, and he was able to pronounce upon the prisoner at the dock the fateful, lethal words. Mooney's execution was set for May 17, 1917.

At the moment those words were inscribed in the clerk's minutes, the barrier went up. No new evidence could be brought, no matter how terrible the injustice might be.

Still, the defense could not rest — although the court could no longer consider new evidence, the public could. If public opinion could be swayed from anti-Mooney to pro-Mooney, then a gubernatorial pardon would be an enticing possibility.

Another two doleful weeks went by before attorney McNutt received the anonymous letter from the religious lady in San Francisco. Unsigned communications were no novelty in the Mooney case, but this letter rang a strong, clear bell. In relaying the message, the writer had been purposely vague as to her friend's location, but the lady who had known Cliff Oxman apparently lived in the agricultural region somewhere between Fresno and Porterville. It was an enormous area, and a doubtful errand, but the defense, grasping at any straw, sent a man to Fresno to advertise in the Valley newspapers, begging the informant to come forward. No one responded.

The anonymous letter did not, however, prove a dead end. It did reveal Oxman's origins and hinted they might be worth investigating. McNutt thought enough of the prospects to write a good friend of the defense in Chicago, but not enough to tell Tom Mooney of this act.

The mid-western friend was "Big Ed" Nockels, secretary of the Chicago Federation of Labor. On his way home, Bourke Cockran had spent an hour with the labor leader and Nockels had agreed to organize a series of mass meetings to drum up funds and furor to save Tom Mooney. Now Nockels asked John Walker, president of the Illinois Federation of Labor, in Springfield, to send someone to Grayville to follow up on the suggestions in McNutt's letter.

In mid-March, a couple of strangers arrived in Grayville. They put up at the hotel, which was operated by Ed Rigall's mother, and talked to the hotel porter, who directed them to the pool hall. Rigall immediately assumed the strangers were from San Francisco, fobbed off a few hints to whet their curiosity, and then sent them to Claude Ellis.

Though Ellis had advised his client to make no response to Cunha's frantic telegram, reaction had been much slower than the lawyer had anticipated. Now, however, it was at hand. First, he had to determine which side these strangers were on. Discovering they were from the defense, Ellis put the Oxman letters on display and stepped back. The visitors were visibly surprised and elated. Ellis mentioned, casually, that the letters might have a money value, whereupon the men from Springfield grew cautious. They had come to inquire, not to deal. While the letters seemed important, they did not feel qualified to judge their value, or even their authenticity.

They thanked Ellis and withdrew; soon Nockels in Chicago had their exciting report. The situation needed a man familiar with the case and more skilled in dealing with skulduggery than Ed Nockels. He chose Frank Mulholland of Toledo, Ohio, a lawyer of excellent repute who was general counsel for the International Association of Machinists. Ed Nolan, indicted along with Mooney and Billings and now in jail awaiting trial, was the San Francisco member of the executive board of this International, and Mulholland had been sent to sit in on the bombing trials to determine whether this was a genuine labor case; and if it was, to obtain sufficient information to prepare a proper defense of Nolan.

Mulholland was soon feeling out Claude Ellis and reading the Oxman letters. They brought from him the astonished declaration: "I never expected to find anything like this in Grayville! I expected to come down here and find out something about Oxman's character."

Ellis suggested the letters ought to be worth at least ten thousand dollars. Mulholland did not quarrel, he simply refused to bargain. He proposed that one of the San Francisco defense lawyers, armed with exemplars of Oxman's known handwriting, should come and inspect the letters before any arrangements might be made. Lawyer Ellis could not help but agree with such circumspection.

Shortly thereafter Ellis returned to Grayville from an overnight trip up-state to find that his office had been broken into and searched. Every drawer had been emptied, the files had been tossed about, every law book had been riffled. Ellis could find nothing missing, and as he put his belongings back in order, he may have allowed himself a smile. He was not likely to be caught leaving anything as precious as the Oxman letters in his office.

Could the defense have hoped to find a way of saving ten thousand dollars? Was the prosecution trying to prevent consummation of a deal? Ellis knew — the defense people had warned him — that all telegrams sent to Mooney headquarters in San Francisco were copied and made available to Fickert's men. Everyone had been most careful, but a leak could have occurred.

Ellis could not have suspected the defense of trying the burglary for very long: he had just returned from a second meeting with Mulholland, who knew he was carrying the letters. No, it could not have been the defense.

An unexpected turn of fate suddenly brought Ed McKenzie, the criminal lawyer who had seen the Mooney jury foreman flash the death signal, plop into the middle of the case. McKenzie, a short man with a wedge-shaped face, the most prominent feature of which was the protruding forehead, shiny and prematurely bald, had nothing slick or oily about him: on the contrary, his bluntness was so pronounced that it sometimes worked against him.

At first, McKenzie had felt closer to the prosecution than to the defense, partially because prosecutors were merely opponents, whereas defense lawyers were his competitors. In fact, he had a special bond with the prosecution for his younger brother, Harry, was on the District Attorney's staff. Harry McKenzie and Eddie Cunha, both unmarried, even shared a room at the Olympic Club. Eddie had confided many of the secrets of the Mooney case to his roommate, and Harry had passed them on to big brother Ed.

One of those secrets had confirmed McKenzie's impressions on the night the Mooney jury brought in its verdict — the jury foreman and the prosecutor were in cahoots. Furthermore, Eddie Cunha had confided to Harry that Mooney's conviction had been in the bag from the beginning: the jury had been rigged.

But Ed McKenzie lived night and day around the Hall of Justice. He hobnobbed with police officials, judges, bailbond brokers, newspaper reporters and bartenders, and there were firm codes of loyalty. Idle tattling was frowned upon, and since the bombing trials were none of his business, these secrets went no further.

With Mooney presumably enroute to the gallows, and Billings already incarcerated at Folsom Prison, Fickert next proposed to try Israel Weinberg. Weinberg was a Jewish carpenter and contractor who had come to San Francisco with his wife and son from Cleveland some ten years before. Weinberg drove a "jitney" — a poor man's taxicab — to make a living, and was an officer of the jitney drivers' union. He had been friendly with Tom and Rena Mooney, and had driven them around town on various occasions — his sole connection with the case until he had been implicated in the bombing by the damning testimony of Oxman.

Fickert, publicly embroidering every move and hope of the prosecution into acts of great courage to protect the public from red-eyed Anarchy, was still making daily headlines in the local press, and when he announced that his next target would be Weinberg, a group of rabbis bestirred themselves. It did not take great perspicacity to detect anti-Semitic undertones in the accusations against Weinberg, and the rabbis decided to help him. For legal assistance they went to Tom O'Connor, a handsome Irish criminal lawyer of the old-school, a flamboyant type, wearing a gates-ajar wing collar and a necktie almost as unruly as his long black hair. EdMcKenzie was O'Connor's junior partner.

These lawyers suggested to Weinberg's supporters that they call on Fickert and plead with him to postpone the trial; the new defenders needed time to familiarize themselves with the case. The rabbis called on the District Attorney, who was most gracious about the postponement. He was agreeable, but he was also seductive, for he called his visitors' attention to the bombing exhibits on display in his office: photographs of the horrible carnage at the bombing scene; sticks of dynamite and a timing device, allegedly owned by Mooney and Billings; guns and ammunition and copper wire seized on a boat which Mooney had rented in 1913.

These sights so alarmed the rabbis that they went back to O'Connor and McKenzie, paid them for their two days work and washed their hands of Weinberg.

At this juncture, Weinberg's wife came in panic to O'Connor and McKenzie. An extremely timid person, she was hysterical in fear her husband would go on trial for his life with no one to defend him. Moved, the lawyers enlisted another prominent criminal lawyer, Nate Coghlan, and the three promised the distraught woman they would do their best to defend Weinberg, fee or no fee. They followed up this promise by making a deal with the International Workers Defense League. This organization, formed some years earlier to help radicals and unionists facing court battles, was practically bankrupt after the Mooney and Billings trials. So the lawyers had little more to go on than incorrigible optimism and the offer of a lot of hard, uphill work with scant promise of reward in either money or prestige.

McKenzie was just getting his feet wet in the case when news came of the find in Grayville. The ten thousand dollars asked was overwhelming: the IWDL was deeply in debt and had barely enough cash on hand to buy postage for an appeal for more donations. But, this was an opportunity that could not be passed up. McKenzie was chosen; he could best be spared to make the trip, and he had the ability to make the best of his mission. Ticket money was scraped together and he took the eastbound Overland train with the understanding that the Defense League would send on as much money as it could collect in the days before McKenzie came to grips with Rigall and Ellis.

McKenzie headed first for Toledo to talk to Mulholland, only to find that that gentleman, much in demand throughout the mid-West as a speaker, was off somewhere on tour. However, Mulholland was to meet with Samuel Gompers, head of the American Federation of Labor in Washington, D.C., two days hence. McKenzie gave chase, successfully. Realizing that the Defense League was unlikely to raise $10,000, or any appreciable part thereof, in sufficient time, the two lawyers went to William Johnston, the president of the International Association of Machinists. With the honor of his union and Ed Nolan's welfare very much in mind, Johnston agreed to lend the Defense League $10,000. Carrying this sum in cash, Mulholland and McKenzie took the train for Chicago after setting up a meeting with the Grayville men by means of a telegram bearing the pre-arranged code signature "Edward Murphy." In Chicago, McKenzie found that the Defense League had sent a telegraphic money order for $1,000. This he never cashed.

The four men met as agreed at the La Salle Hotel, but McKenzie, grimy and weary after more than a week of train travel, demanded time for rest and refreshment. He bathed, changed clothes, dined and took a short nap; it was well along in the evening before they all settled down to negotiations in Mulholland's room.

Claude Ellis spread the Oxman letters and their envelopes on the bed; McKenzie read them and compared the handwriting with the exemplars he had brought along. Although not a handwriting expert, McKenzie had read several books on the subject and had handled lawsuits centering on disputed documents. Finally he announced his opinion: the letters were genuine. The bargaining began.

Ellis played coy, talking this way and that before letting it be known that $10,000 would be acceptable. The moment the price was mentioned, McKenzie announced that he had the exact sum in cash. This, however, did not mean he was ready to hand over the money; far from it. He was resolved not to pay a penny for those letters unless he could be convinced that there was no other way of obtaining them.

He closed with Ellis: "You're a lawyer, and you damn well know that once we pay money for those letters they lose 95 percent of their value to us. The other side will accuse us in court of having bought them; we will have to admit it, and that admission will blacken the evidence so seriously that it might well result in the conviction and execution of my client."

As he was to remark years later, McKenzie was well aware that Ed Rigall was "no sweet magnolia." It was painfully obvious that the Grayville men were out for a holdup. Even so, McKenzie was of two minds: he was revolted at the thought of paying blood money, yet those letters were of paramount importance — perhaps the demand for money could be considered a side issue compared to the offense they laid bare. A too-righteous course might risk the death of Mooney, plus the possible conviction and death of the other defendants. Only four years out of law school, McKenzie searched his conscience: what legal ethic should prevail under these circumstances? The more he questioned himself, the more certain he became that it might be right to pay.

Near midnight, a knock came at the door. "Why, that must be Mr. Waterman!" ejaculated Mulholland. He seemed embarrassed; the meeting had dragged on far beyond his expectations. He opened the door quickly, and there indeed stood Mr. Waterman, a middle-aged gentleman in shirt sleeves and leather slippers. He had just returned from an hilarious banquet to find a note from Mulholland at the hotel desk; now he expressed delight at seeing his wonderful friend, Mulholland, once again. The somewhat maudlin Mr. Waterman also took an instant liking to Mulholland's wonderful friends, those three strangers sitting there looking daggers at him.

The lawyer from Toledo began to talk a mile a minute, grimacing like a movie comedian to prevent his confreres from suggesting that Mr. Waterman get the hell out. This Mr. Waterman was *the* Waterman of Waterman Fountain Pens, and he admired Mulholland for his oratorical virtuosity. On arriving at the La Salle Hotel, Mulholland had noticed the millionaire's name on the register, and had left a note suggesting he drop by.

There seemed nothing for it but to sit up with Mr. Waterman, and so they did, hour after hour. His garrulity had no end; and he knew more jokes than could be told in a single night. It was nearly dawn when Mr. Waterman yawned, hiccupped, and fell silent. Then Mulholland took him by the arm and led him, unprotesting, to his room.

Negotiations resumed in an atmosphere saturated with irritation and fatigue. McKenzie, however, had suffered the least, and now felt stronger than the Grayville men. As he pressed his argument, he intercepted a glance between Ellis and Rigall that could be interpreted to mean, "He's right!" Seizing this imagined opportunity, the San Franciscan took up the matter of an affidavit Ellis had prepared for Rigall's signature setting forth the conditions under which the Oxman letters had been received and acted upon. The affidavit was essential, but its effect would be enormously enhanced if the signer presented himself in court, ready to testify.

Rigall demurred. He was not going into court in San Francisco without a trusted lawyer at his side. All right, McKenzie urged, let Mr. Ellis come too. It would be perfectly proper for the defense to cover his expenses and pay for his lost time.

The pool hall operator began to see some new possibilities. His wife, he suggested, would enjoy a trip to California, and might be useful as a corroborating witness. McKenzie shook his head: if Rigall wished his wife's company, let him bring her at his own expense. Even Oxman hadn't offered to pay for the wife. Well, then, how about Rigall's mother? She had been the recipient of Oxman's third letter. McKenzie yielded.

Now pleased, Rigall said: "All right, you pay three expenses and take care of Mr. Ellis, and show us as good a time as the District Attorney and the cops showed me . . . . Well, we'll do it!"

Plans were made to insure that Rigall and party arrived safely in San Francisco, and then the meeting broke up. It was eight o'clock in the morning. McKenzie pocketed the letters and Rigall's signed affidavit and returned the $10,000 to Mulholland. Then he excused himself and hunted up a reliable photographer who made copies of the letters, page by page. Once they had been safely reproduced on film, McKenzie returned to his hotel room and fell into bed, spent.

Within hours after McKenzie's return on April 11, San Francisco was pregnant with rumors of some sort of scandal concerning the "honest cattleman." Although Editor Fremont Older of the *Bulletin*, like so many others, had been convinced that Mooney was guilty as hell, he was the first man the defense confided in. This respect for Older proved justified; one good look at the Oxman letters turned Older into a furious, dedicated believer that Mooney and his co-defendants were victims of a conspiracy to increase the Preparedness Day murders from ten to fifteen — the last five to be committed by so-called process of law. Older withheld publication for a few hours while the lawyers made legal moves, but by nightfall it became obvious that the story was too big to hide any longer.

At 8 o'clock that evening, the *Bulletin* came out with a special extra, called a "Jack-rabbit" edition, with the top half of the front page shrieking "OXMAN FRAMED MOONEY," and a hastily composed text below. Newsboys raced through the downtown streets and alleys shouting their wares, and soon a jailer brought a copy to Tom Mooney in his cell. Thus he learned for the first time of a town called Grayville and of its poolhall operator, Ed Rigall.

In the rush to publish, part of the flavor of the exposure got lost. Some iron-bottom on the *Bulletin*'s copy desk, a man who could not stomach faulty grammar and misspelled words, had cleaned up Oxman's letters. Not until the next day, when the *Bulletin* reprinted the letters in facsimile in its regular editions, did the public get the full feel of the wealthy Oregonian, the "honest cattleman."

The first letter, Oxman to Rigall, was dated December 14, 1916, a day or so after Oxman had come to San Francisco as a prospective witness for the prosecution. It read:

Dear Ed Riggall:

has been a long time since I hurd from you I have a chance for you to cum to San Frico as a Expurt Wittness in a very important case. You will only hafto ansuer 3 & 4 questions and I will post you on them. You wil get milegage and all that a witness can draw. Probly 100 in the clear so if you will come ans me quick in care of this Hotel and I wilt mange the Balance it is all O.K. but I need a witness Let me no if you can come Jan. 3 is the dait set for trile. Pleas keep this confidential. Ansur hear.

Yours Truly

F.C. Oxman.

Oxman's second letter to Rigall, had been written on December 18, after Rigall had agreed to come:

Your telegram recived I will wire you Transportation in plenty of time also expce money. . . . I thought you can make this trip and see California and save a little money. As you will be alued to collect 10c Per Mile from the state which will be about 200 I can get your expence and you will only hafto say you saw me on July 22 in San Frisco and that will be easy dun. You know that the silent Road is the one and say nothing to any Body the fewer People no it the Better when arrive Register as Evansville Ind little more mileage.

F. C. Oxman.

The third letter, Oxman to Rigall's mother, apparently had been written on Christmas Day. It read:

Dear Mrs. Rigall:

As I am sending Ed transportation tomorrow 26 it might be that I can use you also about the 10 so if I can obtain you a ticket that you can see California if you would like the Trip adress me care this hotel tell F.E. to say nothing until he see me Can Probly use a Extry witness been a long time I don't see you.

F.C. Oxman.

April, 1917, was a month when any event short of Armageddon was lucky to make Page Three of an American newspaper. A few days before the Oxman disclosure President Wilson, five months after winning re-election on a promise of peace, had asked Congress to declare war on Germany and Congress had obliged. Headlines everywhere concentrated on the bustle of a nation preparing to do battle, but as soon as Older saw the Oxman letters his newspaper permitted the war to take care of itself. His hatred for injustice and his innate pacifism led him to bury the oncoming combat on his inside pages, while he fed the public every bit of scandal his reporters and the defense attorneys could dig up against the bomb prosecutors and their witnesses. One item that Older particularly enjoyed publishing was a facsimile of another item brought back by McKenzie from Chicago: a courtesy card entitling F.E. Rigall to the amenities of the Olympic Club during his initial sojourn in San Francisco — signed by Charles M. Fickert.

As if in a balloon, the prisoners shot up from despair to highest hope. Sympathizers who had kept their feelings to themselves now came boldly forward, proclaiming belief in the innocence of all the suspects. On the streets and in the County Jail, it seemed clear that the tide of opinion was turning. To Mooney and his codefendants, freedom seemed nearly close enough to touch. The defense lawyers were jubilant; it might take a few days — perhaps even a few weeks — to smooth out the obstacles, but surely there could be no permanent barrier on the path to vindication.

District Attorney Fickert was reportedly visiting his mother on her ranch in Kern County, far south. On the night of the extra, Prosecutor Cunha was nowhere to be found. Reporters worked like hunting dogs to sniff out anyone willing to speak for the prosecution, and got only a reluctant grumble from Police Captain Duncan Matheson; he had only seen Rigall a couple of times, never liked the man's looks.

On the legal front, the revelations had one encouraging effect almost at once: on April 25, Judge Griffin wrote the state Attorney General saying the Oxman letters had convinced him that Mooney deserved a new trial. But, as Griffin also wrote, he no longer had jurisdiction over the case, and could only urge the Attorney General to join in the call for a new trial.

McKenzie now came to the court of Superior Judge Frank Dunne to ask for a warrant charging Oxman with attempted subornation of perjury. Dunne was a stern, cold man who had earned a reputation for honesty and courage in the municipal graft prosecutions some years earlier. Recently he had been much in the news; he had presided at Billings trial, and was scheduled to conduct the trial of Rena Mooney.

In the Judge's chambers McKenzie spread out the Oxman letters and waited for the reaction. Judge Dunne handled the precious letters, then tossed them back across his desk.

"Something anyone might write under the circumstances," snapped the Judge. "I see nothing actionable in these letters."

F. C Oxman, key witness to Mooney's conviction, in Jail waiting for a grand jury whitewash of his perjury.

In the morning after the extra came out, the *Bulletin* contacted Cunha, who spoke of an "honest mistake" as the reason why Rigall had not testified for the prosecution, his story differing only slightly from the yarn the pool hall man had spun to Claude Ellis. This prompted Duncan Matheson to tell *his* version of why Rigall had stayed in the background. In an interview, published prominently by the *Bulletin* but played down or ignored elsewhere, Matheson declared he had warned Fickert that everything about Rigall smacked of the bunco artist. The police captain revealed that he had shouted at Fickert: "I want no part of crooked testimony." His version of Rigall's failure to testify was the one most favored by the skeptics.

Fickert, who surfaced a bit later, laughed off the whole affair, saying the "honest cattleman" could and would explain everything. Hectic negotiations took place with Fremont Older acting as the go-between for prosecution and defense. These grew intense, with McKenzie now backing Cunha into one corner after another with knowledge gained through his brother Harry. At one point McKenzie thought he had struck a satisfactory bargain with his opponents including the District Attorney: find a gimmick that would remove any taint of wrong-doing from the prosecutors, and they would lend their good offices to any move that might secure freedom for all five defendants — maybe new trials for Mooney and Billings; maybe an appeal to the State Supreme Court; maybe a joint demand for pardons from the Governor. (McKenzie was to cherish this idea of a possible "bargain" for many years before he came to realize its fallacy.) But, just as the defense thought the deal was cinched, Fickert came out with a public blast at Mooney and his lawyers that killed any hope for justice from the Hall of Justice. The lawyers had concentrated so heavily on the legalities of the case that they had failed to consider the political situation, which could not be changed overnight merely because some jackass wrote a letter.

The public mind had been made up about these defendants. That mind could be changed, but the job would take tremendous expenditures in time, money and effort.

Meanwhile, Billings languished in Folsom Prison; Rena Mooney, Israel Weinberg, and Ed Nolan were in the County Jail awaiting trial for murder; and day by day the time grew closer when Tom Mooney was doomed to be hanged by the neck until dead.

Billings trial: In huddle on left: James Brennan, Billings' prosecutor, Edward Cunha, Mooney's prosecutor, Lt. Stephen Bunner and Charles Fickert. On other side of table: defense attorneys Edmund Lomansky and Maxwell McNutt, and Warren Billings. In the dock at far right: Israel Weinberg, Edward D. Nolan and Tom Mooney.

3

Shouts From Across the Sea

The world had other concerns in that Spring of 1917. Statesmen everywhere lay awake worrying about the working man — particularly radical working men. The war, now in its third year, seemed deadlocked, with no end in sight. News trickled out of Germany about crippling strikes, waged in defiance of the Kaiser and his Junkers. Workers were restive in Holland, England, Japan; even in beleaguered France, war weariness was setting in.

In America the militarists had triumphed; the United States had officially gone to war. The pacifists were quiet — unless they were as brave as Eugene V. Debs, now headed for a Federal Penitentiary. The nation was fresh and full of fight, yet there was grumbling among American workers. Wobblies marched across the Western states, urging men to organize and fight for their rights. There were great labor tragedies like the mass deportation of copper miners from Bisbee, Arizona, and the terrible lumber strike in the Pacific Northwest. Outside of California, the case of Mooney and Billings was barely dawning upon the public consciousness.

Russian exiles, most of them revolutionaries who had escaped the Czar after the unsuccessful revolt of 1905, were beginning an exodus from the United States. New opportunities were opening for them in their homeland, and the safest route was by sea from Pacific Coast ports to Vladivostok and thence by trans-Siberian railroad to Petrograd. Seattle and San Francisco were the exit ports, and many a Russian Red wore a Mooney defense button in his lapel when climbing the gangplank of a trans-Pacific steamer. Approximately five hundred Russians passed through San Francisco that spring, and many stopped by the County Jail to offer Tom Mooney and his fellows a word of cheer. They promised to help their segment of the human race emerge from feudalism; in so doing, they proposed to end forever the exploitation of man by man.

One cold day, 75 Russian Anarchists arrived in a body at the County Jail to visit Mooney. The handful of jailers on duty were frightened out of their wits. The visitors could not help but notice the pale faces and trembling hands of the men with the weapons and the keys; the sight made them laugh.

The jailhouse was not the only point of interest for the departing Russians. Many were Anarchists, and some of these made pilgrimage to the unpretentious flat on Dolores Street where Alexander Berkman and Emma Goldman held forth. It had been the editorial office of *The Blast*, a radical sheet for which Mooney had written an article or two — something used by his accusers in his trial. This office had also been the locale of a "secret" conference between Mooney and Billings, after Detective Martin Swanson, shortly before the bombing, made an offer to Billings if only he would rat on his fellow unionist. That conference, it turned out in the trials, was not so secret, after all. The police had watched comings and goings at the Dolores Street flat with glee.

But Berkman and Emma Goldman were touring Eastern cities raising money and other support for the Mooney's defense, and also paving their own pathways to prison by opposing the draft and otherwise speaking out against the war effort. However, there was a chatelaine on duty at the Dolores Street place, the slender, red-haired Eleanor M. Fitzgerald, "Fitzie," whose fiery attractiveness, mental as well as physical, made her especially popular with male visitors.

On one of these Russian visits, Fitzie obeyed a hunch; she took pen and paper and wrote out a message to an old Russian friend, Bill Shatoff. In that note she apparently suggested that if the Russians should raise a clamor for Mooney's freedom this might focus world attention on his plight. Shatoff was an engineer who had helped build the more modern portions of the Russian railroad system; when Fitzie had last heard of him, Shatoff was said to have been placed in charge of the defense of Petrograd by the new provisional government, headed by Alexander Kerensky. Fitzie sewed this message into the jacket lining of one of her visitors, and on its way it went.

Under the Czar the Russian war effort against Germany had never been virile; under Kerensky it was approaching complete futility. Nevertheless, the Russians tied down German divisions which the Allies would prefer not to face on the Western front. At the same time, a group of Russian radicals exiled in Switzerland found it impossible to get home, since they were surrounded on one side by the Entente, and on the other by the Allies. The members of this group called themselves Bolsheviks, and their leader was a firebrand destined to become world-famous under the political pseudonym of Vladimir Ilyich Lenin. His immediate program for Mother Russia was anathema to the Allies — peace with Germany at any price, even loss of territory.

For Lenin the only possible route home lay through Germany. With the assistance of the Swiss Social Democrats, Lenin and the Germans devised a formula. The Bolsheviks would be transported to the eastern frontiers of Germany in a well-stocked private railroad car, kept under lock and key while in transit, with impeccably neutral Swiss nationals handling outside contacts for food and drink and the like. This enabled the exiles to swear, when they stepped on to Russian soil, that they had exchanged no word, no signal, no scrap of paper with the enemy during their historic journey.

The Bolsheviks arrived safely in Petrograd on April 16, 1917, proclaiming to the handful who heeded them that they alone could solve the problems of the Russian people. Kerensky's provisional government, willing at that moment to let all men be heard, treated the new arrivals with courteous unconcern. Lenin and his cohorts were provided with a small, vacant palace and left to make all the propaganda they could. This opportunity was not wasted.

Soon the press in faraway places, including San Francisco, reported that "German propaganda" was rampant in Petrograd. Allied statesmen, getting nervous, openly announced once-secret pledges;

Russia would be given control of the Bosporus and other territorial plums if only she would stand fast with the Allies until the defeat of the Entente. Lenin retorted: "Down with imperialism! Trūe Russians want no aggrandizement from capitalist war!"

On April 18 Professor Paul Miliūkoff, Kerensky's foreign minister, publicly assured a French-British delegation that every agreement — including those made by the Czarist regime — would be kept. This statement made good reading in Allied cities; in Russia, however, the reaction was quite the opposite. Demonstrations and disturbances occurred around the clock in Petrograd as the inhabitants, in mounting anger, decried Miliukoff's promise. The Kerensky government trembled in inexperience and indecision while fundamentals such as preserving order and protecting the lives and property of the citizens were honored mostly in the breach.

Four days after Miliukoff made his *gaffe*, on Sunday, April 22, 1917, United States Ambassador David R. Francis gave a dinner party at the American Embassy. He was a tall, imposing man, scion of a prominent Kentucky family. Americans were immensely popular with the "new Russian," and Francis enjoyed official good will and public esteem.

As the Ambassador greeted his guests at the Embassy, a new political tremor was in the making in or near Lenin's headquarters. The revolution had attracted radicals of many nationalities, including a number of Italian anarchists, who were excellent agitators and popular with the Petrograd mobs, already tuned to so high a pitch that they responded to almost any radical appeal. Whether Bill Shatoff acted as a result of Fitzie's message — if he ever received it — is not clear, but someone, somehow, had heard that in California an innocent labor organizer named Mooney was being railroaded to the gallows; and this man touched off a fiery discussion about justice under capitalism.

One of the Italians, misled by a trick of phonetics or perhaps more esoteric confusions, launched into a tirade against the execution of "Muni," converting the Irish-American Socialist instanter into an Italian-American Anarchist; the call to action was for all to proceed forthwith to the American Embassy and "clean out the place." Darkness was falling as the crowd began to move and the authorities became aware of its destination and purpose.

At the Embassy, the Negro valet, Philip Jordan, approached

the Ambassador at the dinner table with a whispered message. A police official was on the telephone, warning that a mob, either led by Lenin or incited by him, had begun to move along the Nevsky Prospekt toward the Embassy, behind a vanguard displaying a big, black flag. The police officer urged the Ambassador to take steps to defend the Embassy or to flee, as the Petrograd authorities were in no position to do much more than sound the alarm.

Not easily frightened and conscious of his diplomatic rights, Francis instructed his valet to thank the official for the warning, and to order him to provide an armed guard for the Embassy. After these instructions had been carried out, however, the Ambassador had second thoughts:

"Phil! Load my revolver and bring it to me!"

This ripple between master and servant had not escaped the notice of the guests. Like their host, none had the slightest idea who Mooney might be, but they wasted little time in speculation. Acting with more haste than courtesy, they deserted the dinner table, donned their wraps and departed, advising the Ambassador as they said "Good night" that he would be wise to follow their example.

Lenin was not leading the mob. He was not likely to be found doing anything under a black banner. Lenin's color was Red. The mob was in no hurry, and its members paused here and there while the Italian orator exhorted onlookers to swell their ranks. At one point, the group passed some Red Flag people holding a street meeting.

"Where are you going?" asked the Red Flags.

"To clean out the American Embassy," replied the Black Flags.

The Reds thought poorly of attacking Americans, and there were shouts and scuffles; but the Black Flags far out-numbered the opposition and passed on.

Soon there was a hammering at the Embassy's main gate. It was the police officer who had telephoned, leading a detachment of six men. He was excited and uncertain, an unimpressive little fellow with unruly hair the color of dead straw and a face like a potato patch in winter. Francis commanded this officer to station himself and his men at the gate and to shoot anyone who tried to pass without Ambassadorial permission. Francis also ordered all the lights in the embassy grounds turned on. Then he took his post in the open doorway, prepared to handle anyone who might get past his guards.

As the sounds of the approaching mob drew closer, forty militiamen came up on the double to reinforce the guard at the gate. The Ambassador, glints sparkling from the barrel of his weapon, stood waiting in the lighted doorway.

But the mob never came. A few stragglers, most of them drunk, wandered into range and were arrested. The distant noises died away, a nearby cathedral bell tolled midnight, and tension gave way to weariness. Scouts reported that a band of Cossacks, Czarist to the core, had fallen upon the Italians and their followers and scattered them every which way among Petrograd's darker alleys.

The forty militiamen departed, the Ambassador closed his main door, ordered the lights turned down, put the revolver in a handy place, and went to bed. The seven policemen stayed on; at dawn, the valet found them still on guard, shivering and hungry.

Two days later, on April 24, Ambassador Francis sent a cable to the United States Secretary of State, Robert Lansing, asking: "Who is Muni? What crime committed?" He added a brief report of the incident, minimizing the affair and concluding: "Wouldn't cable this insignificant incident but fear sensational reports may create impression that order not enforced here where quiet prevails and life and property safe."

Word passed throughout Petrograd that a friendly nation had been insulted. Russians of conservative persuasion formed in different parts of the city and marched to the Embassy, passing in intermittent procession and calling upon Ambassador Francis to receive their informal salutes. These apologetic groups consisted mainly of school teachers and their charges, plus middle-aged women. Male participation was sparse.

On April 30, Secretary of State Lansing replied, telling the Ambassador, among other things, "Defendants and trial judge (Judge Griffin) urging Attorney General of State confess error and not await decision Supreme Court. . . ."

On May 10 Lansing sent a memorandum to President Wilson setting forth the gist of the case and reporting that Mooney was under sentence to hang on May 17 — one week away. Lansing informed the President about two demonstrations on Mooney's behalf, the one at Petrograd and another at Tampico, Mexico on

May Day. Lansing further reported that Samuel Gompers, head of the American Federation of Labor, had stated that labor organizations throughout the world had interested themselves in Mooney's fate. To cap all this, the Secretary told the President about the Oxman letters, appending copies of those famous documents, and taking pains to point out that even the trial judge had called for a new trial. He recommended:

> In view of the situation in Russia on account of the agitation of the laborites, which has spread over a large part of the disturbed countries of the world, causing at the present moment a very delicate stage not only in the affairs of Russia but in the international situation, I deem it of great importance to bring this case to your special attention for consideration as to whether some action should not be taken by you to prevail upon the Governor of California to suspend the execution of Mooney or to commute his sentence until the charges of perjury against the witnesses used by the prosecution have been thoroughly investigated.

Within 24 hours President Wilson quietly telegraphed Governor Stephens of California asking that he commute Mooney's sentence to life imprisonment. If that could not be done, the President suggested the granting of a stay of execution pending further judicial inquiry into the case.

The President doubtless realized that this action would bring an outcry from conservatives in California and throughout the nation against "that meddler in the White House." However, the President felt constrained to heed other outcries just then: those of the world's radicals, who if not appeased might slow down the workers, disconcert the soldiers, and diminish the chances of victory. He needed a crust of bread to toss to the disaffected.

That crust was hope for the life of Tom Mooney.

Early Mooney legal defense team. J. F. Finerty, Frank P. Walsh, Mooney, Ed Nockels and Leo Gallagher.

4

Turnaround

There was an error, strictly speaking, in Lansing's original memo to President Wilson. True, May 17 had been set as the execution date, but this had no meaning at all in terms of death according to schedule; it did not provide sufficient time for the California Supreme Court to act on the automatic appeal from any sentence of death. No matter how loud the howl for Mooney's blood, like any other man condemned under California law he would not die until the State's highest court reviewed his case. And this court was in no hurry.

This gave Tom Mooney a most precious thing — time. It also gave Governor Stephens a proper and easy answer to the President's request. The prisoner, now recovered from the numbing effect of the conviction, was taking the lead in the fight for justice. Leadership came naturally to him; all his life, no matter what the issue, no matter how crushing the odds might seem, he had always dared to take the lead.

His father, Bernard Mooney, had been a miner and a militant organizer for the Knights of Labor in struggles so intense that in one fight he had been wounded and left for dead by anti-unionists. The family had fled, more than once, from gunmen sent out by the mining companies. The father had died of "miner's con" (now known as silicosis) when Tom, the oldest of three surviving children, was ten. The widow , Mary, had come to America from County Mayo, Ireland, and never did learn to read or write. The bereft family moved to Holyoke, Massachusetts, where Mary Mooney found employment in the rag room of the Union Paper Mill, ten hours a day and six days a week, for a wage that her son later described as "four large silver dollars."

Tom became the man of the house, and actually managed to bring in a few dimes. In addition to attending school, he sold newspapers, carried lunches made at night by his mother to working men who paid 25 cents a week for this service, and did whatever odd jobs came to hand. He later remembered one winter toward the end of the nineteenth century when a big fire in downtown Holyoke partially consumed the local opera house, a shoe store and a dry-goods store. This was a heaven-sent opportunity, and Tom and his little brother, John, would get up at 4 o'clock in the morning and trudge through deep snow to scrounge around the ruins for shoes and winter clothing.

One of young Tom's favorite exploits was organizing a group of boys to gather boxes, barrels, and other wooden castoffs for the annual bonfire at Shelly's Field, which was touched off at one minute after midnight on the Glorious Fourth. People came from blocks around to see the blaze and set off fireworks — and little boys could stay up till dawn.

There was at least one striking preview of Tom's adult troubles and triumphs. At St. Jerome's parochial school, children of the poor were allowed to attend barefooted during the warm months; on Sundays, however, they were expected to wear shoes and stockings to morning Mass and Sunday School and to Vespers in the afternoon. Tom had no shoes, because his mother had no money. Mrs. Mooney solved this problem by having one of the educated neighbors write an excuse which Tom took to school on Monday morning. The lad presented this excuse to Father McGee, a muscular young fellow who tyrannized his pupils and distrusted any variation from his strict regimen. The Father ordered Tom to hold out his hand, palm up. Then, in front of the class, the priest administered ten hard lashes with a rawhide whip. Tom stood the blows without a whimper, but could not completely control his tears, which coursed down his cheeks in humiliation and anger, as well as pain. At the noon recess that day, Tom went home, prepared a skimpy lunch for himself, John, and little sister Anna. Then he took four lunch pails to customers at the mill. These chores accomplished, he went to the nearest public school and got himself assigned to the same grade he had just left at the Catholic school. Tom told no one, not even his mother, about this rebellious transfer until Father McGee came inquiring of Mrs. Mooney why her son was not attending school. When his mother asked, Tom replied that he was going to school faithfully, every day. The priest demanded to know what this school might be, and Tom told him. Public school! Imagine! The Father ordered Tom to return to the school of his faith, but the boy said "Never!" Apparently Mother Mooney more or less agreed, for she refused to back up the priest, and Tom never again entered the doors of St. Jerome's. From then on, Tom's respect for the clergy, of whatever denomination, sank to a virtual nil.

As he approached adolescence Tom had the usual yearnings for athletic prowess, but these faded when, at age 14, he became an apprentice foundryman at the Dean Steam Pump Company. Foundry work is desperately hard and dirty, sure to take every ounce of the energy even a young and husky Irishman could muster. In 1902 just before his twentieth birthday, Tom became a full-fledged member of the International Molders' Union; it was a membership to which he would cling for all his years.

During his apprenticeship, Tom developed a hankering to see other parts of the world. He also came to realize that he was sorely in need of more education. Always careful with money, Tom saved diligently for five years working as steadily as possible and finally, in 1907, left the foundry to see what manner of life lay on the other side of the Atlantic Ocean.

He toured England, Scotland, Ireland (of course), France, Belgium, Holland, Germany, Austria-Hungary, Switzerland, Italy, Spain and the Azores Islands. He kept his nose in a book much of the time, trying to use each waking hour to improve his acquaintance with the culture of each land, its art and architecture, its history. He worked his way through castles, cathedrals, palaces, art galleries and museums as earnestly as if preparing for an academic career.

One day, in an Amsterdam museum, Mooney fell in with another young American, a brewery worker from Cincinnati, Ohio. Within an hour they were chums, and before that day was done Tom was hearing all about the wondrous hopes for a better world if only Socialism could come to power. Just think! Equality and justice for everybody! No more rich, no more poor! Tom loved every word, every dream. In a day or two he became certain of himself, his life, his aims. He would bend every thought, make every effort to achieve Socialism.

On the way home, Tom read every book on Socialism he had been able to purchase in Europe. He familiarized himself with the theory and practice of this ideology, came to know the names of Socialism's heroes. Holyoke had become too small for him, and he drifted first to Chicago, where he tried without success to matriculate at the university — impossible in those times for a poor wight who had not traveled properly up the academic ladder.

The drift continued Westward; the panic of 1907 was it its height and work was virtually impossible to find. Finally Mooney, now 25, arrived in Stockton, California, where he found three things — work, membership in the Socialist Party, and a young music teacher named Rena. There was immediate magnetism between the two, but there was also an obstacle: Rena had a semi-invalid husband. However, Rena soon mustered up the courage to beg this husband for freedom and forgiveness, and soon the necessary legalities began so she and Tom could marry.

Tom found radical associations and activities exhilarating; Rena, completely enraptured, gladly went along with his every thought and deed. Tom had an exceptionally sturdy body and abundant energy; ebullient and optimistic, he could talk and act—and often prevail—against great odds. He had found answers to life's problems in Socialist literature, somewhat as the Bible guides those who are deeply religious. With Rena as assistant, he sold Socialist tracts wherever he went, a zealot among zealots.

That year, 1908, Eugene V. Debs undertook a nationwide campaign for the presidency that was to gain a million votes for him and and for socialism. As was the custom at that time, Debs traveled by special train, speaking from the rear platform wherever listeners could be found. This train, dubbed "the Red Special," had come to Stockton—and there was Tom, hustling through the crowds, selling pamphlets by the armload. His boldness attracted attention, and he was promptly enlisted by the campaign party; off Tom went

Rena and Tom Mooney (right) with young friends distributing radical papers.

for a few wonderful weeks of super-salesmanship throughout the West.

This adventure was soon followed by another. Tom entered a contest sponsored by *Wilshire Magazine*, which offered a free trip around the world to the person selling the most subscriptions within a certain time. This strongly socialist magazine was financed by a spectacular Los Angeles real estate operator whose name has come down to posterity, not through his journal but by means of Southern California's famous Wilshire Boulevard.

With Rena helping, Tom did his damndest, and came so close to winning that a second prize was hastily arranged: all expenses paid trip to the International Socialist Congress in Copenhagen in 1910. There, accompanied by brother John, he listened to and met some of the great personages of the left, functioning in the somewhat promising atmosphere of the Twentieth Century's early years. On his way home, Tom visited the British Trade Union Congress, then in session at Sheffield, England.

Perhaps this added visit caused Mooney to begin thinking of socialist action in stronger terms than making speeches and selling literature. His first move was to join the Wobblies. Yet, while Mooney remained friends with many a Wob all his life, his actual membership lasted only three months; he felt the idea of One Big Union was too all-embracing to be practical, and there were other points of disagreement. Better to work from within the older unions, he thought, those that had enjoyed some semblance of success.

This line of thinking drew Tom and Rena to San Francisco, which had two attractions for a young and vibrant organizer: it was "the best damn union town" in the West, and it was headquarters for the Pacific Gas & Electric Company—the dominant utility firm in Northern California, wielder of vast political power and a citadel of anti-unionism. Its thousands of employees were in need of organization; Mooney felt that need in his bones, and there were brave PG&E men who came around and whispered that maybe with a strike here and a strike there, a utility workers union might be born. Mooney listened and dreamed; the next step, as with other radical union men of that day, was to use dynamite.

There was something about electrical transmission lines that fascinated Mooney. Draped upon enormous towers that led from hydro-electric turbines in the mountains through the countryside to the cities, there to be fed to homes, offices, factories and streetcars, these lines were vulnerable. Bring down only one tower—the right one, of course—and San Francisco could be plunged into darkness, paralyzed. Do that again, and yet again; hit-and-run, and the utility magnates might realize that their purposes would best be served by dealing with the unions.

Easier said than done. Purchase of powder from Giant Powder or Hercules would be tantamount to insisting on arrest as soon as the first blast went off. But, there was Warren Billings, the tiny man who looked like a boy, to go scouting around rock quarries and other places where explosives were used; steal the stuff; find the crucial towers and wreck them. While Rena Mooney made what money they had by giving piano lessons, Tom began a harrowing existence, with plots and derring-do and failures and hairbreadth escapes from company detectives like Martin Swanson and from the law, which accused Mooney more than once but failed to make the accusation stick. Until Preparedness Day.

International Socialist Congress, Copenhagen, 1910. John and Tom Mooney on bottom step, left. Behind Tom is Klara Zetkin who helped found the German Communist Party. Lower right is Alexandra Kollotani of Russia holding hands with Luella Twining of California, between them is Morris Hillquit.

Many years later, when there was nothing to be gained or lost by frankness, Tom Mooney admitted that he had been a dymamiter, a saboteur of industrial installations. He was proud of what he had done, for to him, at that time and under those conditions, it had seemed to him the only way to fight. Although physical danger was implicit in many of his early deeds, he personally had a distaste for violence, and often boasted that he had never in his life resorted to fisticuffs. He was no terrorist; all his sabotage attempts took place in lonely, rural spots where there was no chance of causing injury or death to any human being. Tom was very keen about that distinction.*

While newspaper accounts of the Petrograd incident lifted the spirits of the defense, it was several months before Mooney and his helpers had any idea of the smashing impact of that demonstration. It was little more than pleasing to know there was international solidarity among the radicals; no one knew that President Wilson had intervened in Mooney's behalf.

In San Francisco that April, 1917, the defense was as busy as a three-ring circus, with Mooney acting as ring-master. Fremont Older and Judge Griffin weren't the only important personages to change their minds. Police Captain Duncan Matheson and Sergeant Charlie Goff, leaders of the police effort to eradicate Mooney, found the Oxman letters much more disturbing than had Judge Dunne. This led them to the office of Editor Older, who greeted them with cool courtesy. Older told his receptionist to see that there were no interruptions, closed his door, and settled back. Soon Older and his visitors got into a wrangle over conflicts between the testimony of Oxman and the other key prosecution witness, an itinerant waiter named John MacDonald.

The "honest cattleman" had testified that Billings, under instructions from Mooney, placed the lethal suitcase, then joined all the defendants other than Nolan, headed south on Steuart Street — away from Market — in Weinberg's jitney.

But MacDonald had testified that Mooney and Billings, after placing the suitcase, departed on foot, walking at different diagonals across Market Street, through the parade. MacDonald never claimed to have seen Rena, Weinberg, or the jitney.

Goff theorized that the defendants might have crossed Market

*Herbert Resner, an attorney who was in charge of the Mooney Defense Committee during the final stages of his incarceration, and William Schneiderman, former chairman of the California Communist Party, who knew Tom Mooney intimately, endorse this impression of the man. To him life was precious, the most important thing a human could have. In that sense, I always thought of Tom as being a truly gentle man.

Street, then crossed back and boarded the jitney for the ride south on Steuart Street. However, the timing of these events as given by Oxman and MacDonald under oath was so nearly identical that the editor was able to respond, "You're running out of time." This coupled with the Oxman letters and a host of additional suspicious circumstances, impressed Captain Matheson. He turned to Goff and said:

"Charlie, it won't do. There's something wrong." and Goff nodded in agreement.

Older was adept at prying admissions and opinions out of reluctant mouths, and he must have felt the thrill of accomplishment at hearing those words from The City's most respected policemen.

Encouraged, Older tried another gambit; he showed the officers an anonymous letter he had received concerning Estelle Smith, a buxom, blowzy woman who had been a prosecution witness. She was employed at a dental parlor on the second floor of a two-story building at 721 Market Street, four-fifths of a mile from the explosion. Smith had testified that Billings, carrying that fateful suitcase, had come to the dental office on Preparedness Day and asked permission to go up on the roof, as had others, "to take photographs" of the parade. She also said she had noticed a Ford jitney, similar to the one described by Oxman, at the curb in front of the building. (The prosecution theory was that Weinberg had driven Tom and Rena, *against the parade* down Market Street to 721, there picked up Billings and his suitcase, and proceeded easterly, again *in the face of the westerly marching thousands*, to the place of tragedy.)

The anonymous letter said that Smith, rattled by the Oxman revelations, had been telling people that Oxman tried to bribe her into testifying that she had seen Weinberg in that jitney in front of 721.

This did not surprise Captain Matheson, for he had already heard that story from Estelle Smith, in person. "In relating her story to me," Matheson told Older and Goff, "she said that Oxman had called several times to see her at the dental parlors where she worked, asking her to go out to dinner with him and suggesting that afterwards they might go to the theater or take in some of the beach resorts; in other words, he offered to show her a good time. She said she put him off, whereupon, finally, he suggested that she could make the sum of five figures for herself if she would only say she had seen Weinberg. She said she had never seen Weinberg, couldn't identify him. Oxman urged her to say so anyway, that there was a lot of money in it. She said she refused all his offers."

As soon as the police were gone, Older telephoned defense attorney Tom O'Connor, and within the hour Estelle Smith was pouring out her tale before the defense lawyer and a notary public. Her affidavit not only confirmed Matheson's recounting, but added that she had asked Oxman if the "five figure" offer came from Fickert; the cattleman had replied:

"Oh, no, it comes from those higher up than Fickert."

Furthermore, Estelle said she had confided her Oxman story to Fickert and Cunha, but they had chosen to ignore it — and her.

Following hard upon the Oxman letters, this made a grand headline for the *Bulletin*, but it was only one of many; they kept coming, one revelation after another, like stormy waves. Matheson, never too pleased with Fickert, now began to fight the District Attorney more openly. The day after his first frank talk with Older he called the editor to report that he had just faced Fickert with a demand for the release of Ed Nolan, the forgotten man of the case.

Nolan had been arrested, indicted, and left alone in a cell for nine long months. True, he was a friend of Mooney and Billings, as any left-wing labor leader might well be. True, he had allowed Mooney to keep his motorcycle in the Nolan basement. And true, a police raid of that basement revealed (in addition to the motorcycle) some odds and ends; things likely to be kept in a machinist's home workshop. Despite a police claim, later discredited, that some saltpeter (which can be used in the manufacture of explosives) had also been found in Nolan's basement, nothing was ever shown against the man.

Nonetheless, Nolan had been held incommunicado for nearly a week after his arrest, and kept in jail from August through April, separated from wife and family and union. Perhaps the crowning indecency was that he had been totally neglected. Nobody asked him anything. He complained to a friend: "They just wanted to indict somebody, and they did. I was throwed in the can and buried and Matheson or nobody else came to see me."

On April 25, very shortly after Matheson raised the question, Nolan's door was opened and he was told to get the hell out, as quietly as possible, please.

As usual, Fickert rushed to the newspapers, particularly the Hearst press, which controlled two of San Francisco's five dailies. His story was that Estelle had told him that Oxman had taken a shine to her and invited her out — but nothing more. This left the average reader wondering which to believe, the *Bulletin* or the *Examiner*; and a more difficult choice, whether to trust Fickert or Estelle.

District Attorney Fickert knew that in a difficult trial a friendly press was half the battle. In the fall of 1916, one of his many announcements before the Billings trial was that he would produce a couple of "society women" to testify that they had seen some of the suspects in compromising activities on Preparedness Day. Eventually the "society women" turned out to be a couple of seamstresses, Mrs. Mellie Edeau and he spinster daughter, Sadie. The mother was extremely dominating; the daughter a doormat. At the trial they, too, testified that they had seen Billings in front of 721 Market Street.

Newspaper accounts of this testimony caused raised eyebrows across San Francisco Bay in Oakland, at a tailor shop where the Edeau women had worked for a few days shortly after the bombing. Mrs. Edeau had talked about the tragedy at great length, boasting that she and Sadie had seen two men, "kind of old," place a black and silver suitcase at Steuart and Market Streets. She further embellished her tale with gory details of the actual blast — the dead and injured lying about, the arrival of the ambulances, and all the rest. She also said she and Sadie might testify; they had been to the police about it.

The tailor in charge, Thomas Stout, checked in his log book. Yes, Mellie and Sadie Edeau, the same women. Although not too familiar with San Francisco, Stout had the strong impression that the intersection of Market and Steuart streets must be very close to the Embarcadero. Would a spot numbered 721 be that close to the waterfront? He smelled stale fish, but shrugged his shoulders and decided to forget the whole thing.

But then came the Mooney trial, the conviction, the sentence to be hanged — much more serious than the life sentence Billings had received, in the tailor's opinion. He struggled with his conscience for a couple of days, then called his fellow tailors into conference and found two who clearly recalled the Edeau women and their tales, and were willing to repeat what they had heard. Stout telephoned the San Francisco *News*, which was somewhat pro-labor; this brought a reporter, and soon Stout and his friends were giving their affidavits to the defense. These affidavits were among several presented by Maxwell McNutt to Judge Griffin on the day Mooney was sentenced but on their own, the contradictions exposed by the three honest tailors failed to convince the judge. After all, the Edeaus' testimony had not convicted Mooney; Oxman's had — and no one in the courtroom that day, other than Eddie Cunha, had yet heard of the Oxman letters.

Still, someone on the defense team got the notion that further inquiry into the tailors' affidavits might yield a dividend. They had heard Mrs. Edeau say she had been to the police; perhaps there would be a report in the Oakland police records. By a happy chance, one of the underlings in the O'Connor-McKenzie law firm was a close friend of Walter J. Peterson, Oakland's chief of police. Bingo! The cub lawyer took the ferry across the bay, returning in a couple of hours in seventh Heaven.

Mrs. Edeau *had* gone to see Chief Peterson, all right, and she had asked for an escort to San Francisco to see the suspects. She had asked Peterson if she could give San Francisco police a fictitious name, saying she was hesitant about "getting mixed up in this terrible thing." Peterson said he had told her to use her maiden name if she liked, but if she did make an identification she must come out with her true name and agree to become a prosecution witness. She had told Peterson she had been at Steuart and Market Streets; 721 Market had never been mentioned. The chief detailed one of his best men, Inspector William H. Smith, to accompany the seamstress.

On the ferryboat, the policeman and the lady had quite a talk; she repeated the story she had told the tailors and the police chief. At the Bomb Bureau in San Francisco a cop had shown Mrs. Edeau a book with pictures of suspected dynamiters. One of the pictures was of a dark-haired, round-faced man with a heavy moustache, and she was told this was Tom Mooney. She didn't find the face familiar, so the cop laid a finger across the moustache, saying Tom had shaved since the picture was taken. The finger didn't help. Then Sergeant Goff took Mrs. Edeau and Inspector Smith, with another woman and six or eight men, upstairs into City Prison. There they had been shown Mooney and Billings, each by himself, in widely separated cells.

As they were leaving the prison, Mrs. Edeau had said to Inspector Smith: "I have never seen these men in my life before." Smith could not be sure Goff heard this remark. He was certain, however, that Goff knew she had made no identification; otherwise she would never have been permitted to leave without making a formal statement.

A well-trained officer, Smith had made notes of the incident in his pocket diary as soon as he and Mrs. Edeau parted company. The next morning he had used the notes as the basis for a written, official report to Chief Peterson, who required such daily reports from all Oakland police officers.

The day after their small journey Inspector Smith decided to do some further questioning. He went to the Edeau home and there encountered Sadie, who happened to be alone. She evaded his questions, declaring she had seen nothing and had no interest in the case.

"But weren't you with your mother at Steuart and Market Streets on the afternoon of July 22nd?" Smith had asked.

"I was there if she was there."

Yet, the Edeau women had been very bright and knowledgeable at the Billings trial, and later at the Mooney trial, identifying both defendants easily and, for good measure, Rena and Israel Weinberg — in front of 721 Market Street.

Inspector Smith was more familiar with the bombing cases than might be expected of an outside cop, because he had been detailed to assist the San Francisco authorities for five or six weeks. Therefore it seemed quite natural when Fickert asked to see the Oakland police inspector during the Mooney trial. Smith kept the appointment, bringing along his pocket diary. During the interview Fickert made remarks which Smith took as a hint that he was being asked to corroborate the Edeaus. Rather than let the District Attorney go on fumbling, Smith took out his diary, opened it to the right page, and wordlessly handed it over.

The District Attorney read; he crimsoned. "You'd make a damned good witness for the defense!" he snarled. "You better keep your mouth shut!"

Shortly after testifying against Tom Mooney, Mrs. Edeau apparently felt she had some explaining to do, and sought out Inspector Smith at Oakland police headquarters. She opened by saying· her testimony must have seemed strange to him. (The defense was to find out later that the seamstress, at first rejected as a prosecution witness, had worked her way back into the bombing cases by going to her clergyman with a "confession" which caused that worthy to telephone a tip to Fickert.) Now she explained to Smith that she had been too nervous and excited on their visit to San Francisco City prison to make the identification.

"That's all very well, lady," Smith replied, "but I remember very clearly your talking about being at Steuart and Market Streets. You never said a word about 721. How come?"

"Well, they showed me an enlarged picture in the office of the District Attorney and told my daughter and me that the picture of two women in front of 721 Market were our pictures; and that's how it came about."

The Edeau affair reached a climax on the afternoon of April 12, the day the *Bulletin* published the facsimiles of the Oxman letters. O'Connor, McKenzie, the cub lawyer, and Fremont Older went to Oakland and met Peterson and Smith. They were shown Smith's diary and his written reports about taking Mrs. Edeau to San Francisco, and the later conversation with Fickert.

Then, with Inspector Smith leading the way, the visitors went to the Edeaus' modest home. Confronted unexpectedly by Inspector Smith and four strange men, Mrs. Edeau, alone and obviously upset, ushered them into her parlor.

Calmly, the attorneys told Mrs. Edeau that she had been caught in perjury and that the sooner she made a clean breast of the affair the better it would be for her. Her response was instant eruption into hysteria; for a time nothing coherent could be learned from her. Thinking she might calm down with only one inquisitor on hand, all but O'Connor stepped outside. The florid Irishman, playing his impressive appearance to the utmost, told her that Oxman was either in jail, or soon would be. Fickert, he said, was undoubtedly headed for prison himself; the prosecution's case had fallen apart.

If she now told, fully and frankly, who had bought or browbeaten or wheedled her into lying under oath, she might win mercy.

This was like throwing gasoline on an open fire. Screaming unintelligibly, Mrs. Edeau dashed to the parlor table and came out with a loaded revolver. (Since testifying, she had complained of being annoyed and had given notice that she was armed and ready to defend herself.) Her thumb was on the hammer, her forefinger on the trigger. O'Connor moved fast, catching her by the arm and forcing her gun hand up and back. When the others rushed in her finger was still on the trigger, but the muzzle pointed at the ceiling. Inspector Smith plucked the weapon from her, uncocked it, and removed the cartridges.

Earlier, before going for her revolver, Mrs. Edeau had telephoned Chief Peterson and demanded he come to her home forthwith. "I need protection!" she had shouted into the transmitter. Now, as blood pressure subsided, Peterson arrived. His presence had a remarkable effect; the crazed look left Mrs. Edeau's eyes; she thanked him profusely for his prompt response. Soon the whole lot of them were sitting peacefully in the parlor, with Peterson doing the questioning.

The Chief showed his considerable experience with difficult customers, leading Mrs. Edeau backward and forward, time and again, over the discrepancies in her stories. How could she have been in two places four-fifths of a mile apart at the identical moment?

"Well, if you want to know," Mrs. Edeau finally explained, "I might have remained in the flesh at Steuart and Market Streets, but the brown eyes of my dead husband led me to 721 Market Street."

"That's not clear to me, Mrs. Edeau," said Chief Peterson. "Please explain it."

"Well, what I mean is, in the flesh I was at Steuart and Market Streets, but my astral body was at the other place. What I testified I seen at 721 Market Street I seen with my astral eyes."

Mellie Edeau and daughter, Sadie, key prosecution witnesses. Mrs. Edeau later insisted that, although she was miles away at the time, "What I seen, I seen with my astral eyes."

So now, less than two months after Mooney's sentencing, here was Oxman, the "honest cattleman," with a hole in his credibility wide enough for a herd of doubts to stampede. Here were two lesser witnesses in such disrepair that their sworn testimony caused laughter or scorn — or both. For years afterward it was the custom of local wits, whenever someone got off a blatant lie, to jest that one part of his conflicting story must have been witnessed by his real self while the opposing part must have been seen by his "astral body."

Only one major prosecution witness still escaped the sneers and jeers brought on by defense disclosures. This was the itinerant waiter, John MacDonald, who, like Oxman, had placed Mooney and Billings at the point of blast.

MacDonald was a wispy individual, so frail and battered it was difficult to guess his right age. On Preparedness Day he had just come out of San Francisco County Hospital after the latest in a series of major operations. He was unsteady on his feet, unable to work, and simple in the head. He may not have known it, but at the time he was suffering from syphilis.

Minutes after the blast, MacDonald, shuffling along from one waterfront saloon to the next, began to tell anyone who would listen that he had seen two men set the lethal suitcase. He was only one of several drifters telling such stories, and no one paid him any mind. Then the newspapers began to tell of reward money; this was something MacDonald could use. He came to the Hall of Justice, with not a penny to his name. He gave a statement to two cops, and then was taken to the City Prison to view the suspects.

When he emerged from the Hall, life had changed for the ailing waiter. He had lodging at police expense in a cheap, clean hotel. Within days he began boasting that he was slated to be a witness against the bombers; also that he was making steady money, $3 per day, and had been promised a ride "on the cushions" back to his old home in Baltimore when the trials were over.

So he testified before the Grand Jury that indicted the suspects, and at the trials of Billings, Mooney, Rena and Weinberg. There were some discrepancies in the first three of these five recitals, mostly as to timing, but the prosecution waved these away as quite common — a witness's memory is often clear on the essentials but faulty as to minor details. It was years before anyone learned that MacDonald's first descriptions of the men he thought he saw placing the suitcase — descriptions given before he was shown the suspects in the jailhouse — did not tally at all with the actual appearance of Mooney and Billings.

When MacDonald's role as a witness became publicly known, things got difficult for the tottery waiter. Most of Mooney's friends were poor and powerless, but they were eager to strike blows for their cause. The manager of the hotel where MacDonald was kept got a threatening letter. On the street someone tossed pepper in the waiter's eyes, hands reached out to rough him up, shoulders blocked and jostled him in crowds. He was given a uniformed cop for a bodyguard. Later, when this protection proved insufficient, arrangements were made through Frank Drew of the San Francisco Chamber of Commerce, one of Fickert's advisors, to send "Mac" to a ranch in central California to keep him out of harm's way between trials. After they were over, MacDonald vanished, not to be heard from again for several years.

In May of 1917, after spending nearly ten months in jail, Rena Mooney came to trial. She had spent her time quietly, playing her violin, chatting with the prostitutes and other female inmates, and crocheting doilies to be sold at auctions by one of the many Mooney Defense Committees, which had emerged in New York, Chicago, Detroit and elsewhere to raise funds for what was becoming a great labor cause. By the time her trial opened, the public pressure for vengeance had dwindled; the Oxman scandal and other revelations had changed the air.

Judge Dunne had been scheduled to preside at Rena's trial, but he had by this time become so closely identified with the prosecution that at the last moment a judge from Santa Rosa, Emmet Seawell, was called in. While the defense knew little about the new judge, there was a feeling of relief; no one could be worse than Dunne. The prosecutor this time was Louis Ferrari, a deputy district attorney of cooler temperament than James Brennan (who had prosecuted Billings), or Cunha or Fickert.

However, there was nothing cool in Ferrari's opening statement to the all-male jury (the trial opened just before woman suffrage made women eligible for jury duty). Behind the defendant's placid, homely countenance, he argued, lurked a "Lady Macbeth," a female of vile schemes and demoniac personality "who was always at the elbows of the conspirators urging them to new and further acts of violence."

The prosecution took advantage of a recent State Supreme Court ruling which, for the first time, made admissible "conspiracy evidence" not directly linked to the crime at issue but purporting to show the defendant's tendency toward that sort of crime. Such evidence had not been admissible in the trials of Billings and Mooney.

So out came a long string of policemen with tales to tell about Tom, Rena and Billings going back as far as 1913.

In 1913 there had been a long and desperate strike against PG&E. Sacramento cops told Rena's jurors how, during that strike, they had watched at their local railroad station as Billings got off a train from Oakland with a suitcase. They said that Billings, known as "The Kid," had met Mooney near the station; that Mooney had ridden away on his motorcycle, while The Kid, with plainclothesmen shadowing him, went by street car to a saloon where a trap had been laid.

Upon entering the saloon, Billings was arrested, the cops testified; in the suitcase, they found 65 sticks of dynamite; in the prisoner's pockets, percussion caps to set off the explosives, and burglar's tools. The conspiracy? Rena, said these policemen, had been seen taking notes in the courtroom during Billings' trial, and was known to have visited The Kid while he was in jail in Sacramento.

This testimony was corroborated by R.G. Cantrell, a PG&E property agent who, working with Martin Swanson, the private detective, had various contacts with Billings from the Sacramento incident on through to Preparedness Day. He said he and Swanson were lying in wait at the Sacramento railroad station when Billings arrived, and had observed The Kid talking to a man whom he later learned was Mooney; also he and Swanson had witnessed Billings' arrest. His Sacramento trip led to Billings' conviction for transporting explosives and his incarceration at Folsom for 18 months.

The prosecution also wanted the jury to hear about another incident in 1913. Near San Francisco, just above the Straits of Carquinez, California's two largest rivers join forces for their final journey to San Francisco Bay and the Pacific Ocean. Witnesses declared that in the summer of 1913 Tom and Rena Mooney had visited a resort called Glen Cove, situated on the straits close to a giant steel electrical transmission tower. Other witnesses testified that in December Tom and two other men had purchased a small fishing boat, not in the best condition, for $30, and that they had loaded this craft with some gear and shoved off on Christmas Day.

A storm had come up; the boat had sprung so many leaks that all three men had had to bail furiously to keep her from sinking. After 36 terrible hours they had limped into a landing at a small wooden fishing pier near Point Richmond. It was early morning and they were exhausted; they tied up their boat and walked into the nearby town, spending the day sleeping in a small hotel. Late in the afternoon they had awakened, and after stopping to eat, gone back to the boat.

While the trio slept, a man named Ruiz — formerly a Richmond cop, now a pipeline inspector for Standard Oil Company, which had large installations nearby — had ransacked the boat. Ruiz appeared at the Point Richmond police station with a small arsenal he claimed to have found under a tarpaulin on the boat: including a rifle with a silencer; a shotgun, its barrel painted with aluminum so it could be sighted at night; some copper wire rigged with percussion caps; and various kinds of ammunition — but no dynamite. Richmond police set a watch on the boat; when the three men returned late that afternoon arrests followed.

At Rena's trial, the Richmond police chief could not swear that he had actually seen the "arsenal" being taken from the boat, but he did testify that Mooney had given a fake name when arrested and that two of the three men had hand guns. Furthermore, the chief had noticed Rena in attendance at her husband's preliminary hearing in Richmond. Ruiz also testified saying that just before the lawmen pounced, one of the suspects had pulled back the tarp and yelled: "She's been cleaned out!"

Mooney had been tried three times on a charge of plotting to blow up the Glen Cove transmission tower; an act which would have deprived much of the bay region of electric power for quite some time. But Rena's prosecutor did not dwell too long on those three trials, because the first two had ended in hung juries and the third had brought acquittal. (It was in these trials that Mooney and Maxwell McNutt began their long connection; the defense lawyer had saved his client by clinging doggedly to one point — the absence of dynamite. If the "arsenal" had in fact been planted on the boat, those who played the trick had failed to provide the key ingredient that might have made a plausible prosecution case.) To counter claims of frame-up, Rena's prosecutor brought in testimony that after the trials, Mooney had made affidavit that the rifle, the shotguns, and the two handguns were his property, hoping to retrieve these weapons from the local sheriff. This testimony got the ears of Rena's jurymen, but when her defense attorney, Ed McKenzie, demanded the prosecution produce that affidavit, which should have been kept on permanent record in Contra Costa County, the document had inexplicably become lost.

Rena was again brought into the background picture the prosecution was trying to weave with testimony that she had been present when Tom was on trial in Sacramento for complicity with Billings in the transportation of dynamite — taking notes, visiting her husband and other prisoners. On occasions, she had been seen bestowing a kiss here and there; once, it was said, on Billings.

Then Prosecutor Ferrari did something which seemed at first to be against his interest — he called as a witness one of the most loyal adherents the defense ever had, Rena's sister, Belle Hammerberg. The prosecutor's purpose, however, was to add to his conspiracy theory a letter written in 1914 by Mooney. A copy of this letter (for Mooney made and kept copies of everything he wrote) was among papers and files Rena had left with her sister for safe-keeping several weeks before Preparedness, because of obvious surveillance by Swanson and the police.

This letter was to Mother Jones, a woman famous throughout the American Left. Her principal stamping grounds were the Rocky Mountain states, where for many years she led miners into battle against employers whenever they had sought better wages and working conditions. Tom had asked her to make a Pacific Coast speaking tour to raise funds for the International Workers' Defense League, of which he was then secretary. In this letter, Mooney had written:

> There were several hundred thousand dollars' worth of damage of property of the Pacific Gas and Electric Company destroyed by the strikers in various ways here. I was in hiding for four months myself, and was finally arrested and kept in jail for five months, going to the highest court in the State on habeas corpus and then had three trials on the first charge — having high explosives in my possession unlawfully — at Martinez, with two of the best and highest paid criminal lawyers prosecuting me for the gas company, and a fourth trial at Sacramento, all finally resulting in my release.

Without the help of the Defense League, Tom had written Mother Jones, he would surely have gone to San Quentin Prison at that time.

After the arrest of her sister and brother-in-law, Mrs. Hammerberg had remembered these documents and, worried as to their significance, sought the legal advice of a dear friend, Tom Straub, a PG&E attorney. He had looked at the letters and advised her there was nothing to fear. But he warned her not to offer these letters to anyone — unless the District Attorney happened to ask for them. This was how Tom's letter to Mother Jones got into court to be used against Rena. Ferrari managed to question Mrs. Hammerberg about the letters for some time without naming the man who had given her this advice. Finally the prosecutor asked who he was.

Belle answered: "The same man who brought me the message from the District Attorney."

Up came Ed McKenzie, interjecting: "What message?"

"That if I would testify against Mrs [Mr.] Mooney. . ."

"Objection!" cried Ferrari. "Sustained!" said the judge. And there sat Belle Hammerberg, her mouth legally shut.

Still, McKenzie was not a man easily put down, and on cross examination he had in Belle a most cooperative witness. He led her through harrowing tales of browbeating by Deputy D.A. Brennan, and by Detective Swanson, who had tried to get her to say things she couldn't say, because they were not true. Of one thing Belle Hammerberg had been and always would be certain: Tom and Rena Mooney had not been running around in a jitney bus setting a bomb on Preparedness afternoon. This she knew of her own knowledge because she had watched that parade with the Mooneys from the roof of the Eilers Building.

McKenzie then tried to get Belle to complete that sentence about the D.A.'s message. Again the answer was blocked; the witness could not speak. Whereupon McKenzie broke the legal logjam by roaring out the assertion so the jurymen could not help but hear, that the PG&E attorney had come to Belle with an offer from Fickert, "an inducement, namely, her (Rena's) liberty if she (Belle) would testify against Thomas J. Mooney."

Registering intense indignation, Belle said to Straub (according to the *Bulletin*'s account of that tumultous day in court): "If they're going to hang Tom they'll have to hang Rena too."

The prosecution now turned to the United Railroads, another corporation fighting unionization of its employees. A procession of witnesses, mostly carmen, described a strange meeting that had been held on the night of June 10, 1916, six weeks before Preparedness Day. The story unfolded thus:

In preparation for a "secret" strike, about 200 persons gathered that night at the old IWW Hall on Seventeenth Street near Valencia to discuss the miserable wages and working conditions on this corporation's traction system. Mooney was said to have made a deposit on the much larger main hall at Dreamland Rink, to hold it in readiness for a meeting to run from 11 p.m. to 2 a.m. that night. Mooney had also ordered a telephone installed at the IWW Hall, so it could be used as a strike headquarters. The plan, according to some of the witnesses, had been to determine at the small meeting whether a surprise strike was feasible. If the situation seemed propitious, the men would have marched to Dreamland, pulling crews off streetcars en route and enticing them, on the spur of the moment, to join the union and go instantly on strike.

Tom made a speech at the IWW Hall fairly early that evening but many of the witnesses said he disappeared shortly thereafter. In any event no men marched on Dreamland, (the balance of the hall rental was never paid), no crews came off streetcars, and the special telephone was used only that one night. Among the 2200 men employed by the United Railroads were so many spies, finks, and company agents that the idea of the workers being able to combine in pursuit of any secret plan seemed far-fetched.

The prosecution loudly supposed that during the hours when Tom was not in sight Rena had locked the IWW Hall door and stood guard over it. This supposition, however, was scotched by most of the witnesses. They testified she had stood near the door, warning that more than a hundred company men were lying in wait outside; saying it would be safer to remain together inside. Jurors were told of one chap, recognized as a company spy, who had to be knocked down and sat upon, lest he go running to tell what had transpired in that hall — or rather, what had *not* transpired, for it was obvious there would be no strike that night. The meeting, however, had droned on for hours.

There was testimony to the effect that Mooney was in a side room of the IWW building all that time, talking on the telephone and conferring with special groups. However, a few witnesses lent substance to the theory that Tom had slipped away on some secret mission. The prosecution conjecture was that Mooney had met Billings, and Weinberg, in his jitney, had driven the pair to a point south of San Francisco near a transmission line on San Bruno mountain which supplied power to the URR transit system.

This was talk — all sound and not an iota of substance; however, there was nothing imaginative about the fact that at 3:30 the next morning, June 11th, three towers of that transmission line were blown off their foundations. If the intent had been to halt streetcar service, the blasts were a fizzle. The flip of a switch at the power house by-passed the damage, and there was no interruption in service.

The prosecution indulged in yet another excursion far afield from the Preparedness Day bombing with testimony that on June 23, 1916 — twelve days after the San Bruno mountain bombing —

Billings had been sighted, again with a suitcase, taking a bus from nearby Daly City to a spot near the Tanforan race track about a mile south of San Bruno. A teamster named Mike McIntosh swore that by coincidence he had camped exactly where Billings allegedly left the bus, and turned his horse out to graze. And behold! That horse trampled upon that suitcase, and upon an alarm clock it contained, plus dynamite, with percussion caps wired to batteries!

While unreeling all these tales, the prosecutors loaded a courtroom table with an array of guns and wires and percussion caps. On the floor underneath the table were the sticks of dynamite and the dry-cell batteries assertedly taken from the suitcase in the ditch near Tanforan. Every now and then Ferrari would call attention to this display by going over and playing with various items, much as a curious child might have done. Finally, one of the jurymen interrupted the proceedings, pointing out that some of those dynamite sticks were wired and capped, and could blow up at any moment. Instantly that dramatic jumble of "conspiracy evidence" took on an urgent meaning to everyone in the courtroom. The judge said: "You may remove them as quickly as possible, so far as I am concerned." This was done, and people breathed more easily.

When the defense turn came, the scene shifted dramatically. The courtroom was inundated with children, mostly girls, music pupils of Rena Mooney. "Lady Macbeth" disappeared; in her place stood a kindly, much-loved teacher. Borrowing a line from the same Shakespearean play Ferrari had used to defame Rena in his opening statement, McNutt said the case against her was but "A tale told by an idiot, full of sound and fury and signifying nothing."

To refute prosecution claims about the day itself, the defense presented testimony to prove that the man who came to the dental parlor at 721 Market Street was not Billings, although there was a strong facial resemblance. Through pictures and the testimony of Belle Hammerberg, it was made clear that the Mooneys, plus a relative from Los Angeles, a Mrs. Timberlake, watched the Preparedness Day parade from the roof of the Eilers Building, at 975 Market, where Rena had her music studio and living quarters, at the crucial time when the fatal bomb was being set at Steuart and Market Streets over a mile away.

As the judge was placing Rena's fate in the hands of the jurors, the authorities prepared for trouble. Extra police and deputy sheriffs

Rena and Mother Mary Mooney and Belle Hammerberg.

stood guard at the juryroom door, and corridors approaching this room were roped off. Even so, crowds got close enough to see the shadows of gesticulation flitting across the ground-glass panel in the locked doorway. A cry was plainly heard: "You're an Anarchist!" Bailiffs stood ready to rush in and break up any fights. Soon the jurors were moved to a more sequestered place.

At noon of the second day of its deliberations, a rumor (later proved correct) came that the jury stood eight to four for acquittal. That night the foreman notified the judge that the jury was hopelessly deadlocked, but the judge ordered the weary twelve to go back and try again. Late in the afternoon of the third day, on July 25, after fifty hours of turbulent debate, the jury reached its verdict — not guilty.

The courtroom jubilation was immediately squelched by Judge Seawell, who rose and spoke directly to Rena, his face cold and stern. He would not comment on the verdict, he said, because she

still faced seven other murder indictments. Then he rapped his
gavel and strode to his chambers.

Rena paid little heed to the judge. She ran first to the jury box,
kissing the men who had acquitted her, one by one. Then she embraced Belle, then Mooney's mother, and on and on among the
relatives and friends. Weinberg's wife fainted, as she had done
when Tom Mooney had been found guilty. The other defendants
could not join in, for throughout the trial, except when testifying,
they had been kept in their cells in City Prison. Now they were
hastily gathered in the jail reception room and Rena ran to them,
unattended. She flung herself into the arms of her husband, laughing
and hugging and weeping all in the same breath. Meanwhile the
jail reverberated with the cheers of the other prisoners and the
banging of their tin cups against cell bars.

Undaunted, Fickert now prepared to try Weinberg, finally bringing
him into court to fight for his life, in October, 1917, sixteen months
after his arrest. Confident that a Russian-Jewish bomber would be
easy pickings, the District Attorney did not bother to personally
participate. Instead he spent most of that period acting as private
attorney for a lady named Dody Valencia in a spectacular inheritance
case.

Although this fourth bombing trial was mostly a replay, there
were a couple of new sensations. This time Mollie Edeau's explanation
that her physical body was at Steuart and Market Streets while her
astral body was at 721 Market Street, little more than a good newspaper yarn for months, finally got into the official record. Even so,
the prosecution used this and other testimony of doubtful value.
After all, they had to make an effort; they dared not use Oxman,
even though his trial for subornation of perjury had been a farce,
ending in acquittal the month before.

Police Captain Duncan Matheson's change of heart had already
gone far enough for him to state under oath that there could not

Israel Weinberg in the dock, with his wife and son.

possibly have been such a thing as the prosecution claimed — the journey of Weinberg and his jitney bus loaded with Rena, Mooney and Billings, plus that suitcase, down Market Street in the face of the up-coming parade, without such an event coming to the attention of the police. Even so, there were gasps of surprise when the defense put on eighteen cops who had been on traffic duty that day on Market Street. One after the other, they took the witness stand and swore — as they had in Rena's trial — they had seen no jitney bus go down that street against the parade.

The Weinberg jury took only 23 minutes to bring in their verdict of acquittal. Some of the jurors later said there had been no need for the defense to present any evidence at all; the prosecution's case had fallen flat on its face.

5

The Hangman Cometh

When Rena Mooney was acquitted, everyone expected she would be out of jail in a day or so at most. However, the stern look on Judge Seawell's face proved prophetic: once the verdicts were delivered in both Rena's and Weinberg's trials, Judge Dunne resumed command.

He had presided in Billings' trial, and soon after that had begun to display a fondness for Fickert and his claims that alarmed the defense. He had pooh-poohed the Oxman letters. He had presided over Oxman's trial for subornation of perjury — and contributed mightily to the decision for acquittal. His bias was no secret: though he did not formally disqualify himself, he had called Seawell to sit in his place for the last two trials. But now Dunne was back in the saddle, so with Fickert still calling for Rena and Weinberg to be tried on one of the other murder indictments, the defense was forced to come to Dunne to plead for release on bail.

Judge Dunne's violent reaction to such pleas made the front page of every newspaper in the bay region. He called defense attorneys and supporters of the accused "blackguards, crooks, Anarchists, and suborners of perjury." In the next breath he added: "There had been no dynamiting since these men have been locked up."

The legal teams changed goals; at first, the prosecution had been in a great rush to hustle the defendants into court: now it sought delay after delay. On the other hand, the defense now found the tide running in its favor and was pushing full steam ahead for new trials. This game had numerous complexities. Fickert tried to funnel all bombing case matters into Judge Dunne's court, while defense lawyers steered for more liberal judges. While Fickert and his crew dragged their feet on every possible pretext, several of the Superior Court judges to whom the bombing cases had originally been assigned lost patience and began to demand that the District Attorney either bring the accused to trial or dismiss the indictments. When a judge named Cabaniss put this demand in regard to several of the remaining indictments against Weinberg, Fickert chose to dismiss rather than try the jitneyman again. This, however, did not mean that Weinberg went free — the acquitted man still faced two murder indictments — both assigned to Judge Dunne.

Dunne was immovable. Finally, the defense went over his head and asked the State Supreme Court to settle the bail question. That court unanimously ordered Dunne to set Weinberg at liberty with bail set at $7500 on each of the two remaining indictments. Dunne had only one card left to play: bail is usually presented in the form of negotiable bonds, and the presiding judge has the right to determine the validity of those bonds. But the defense deprived him of this chance to obstruct Weinberg's freedom by putting up the $15,000 in cash; this he could not question. Raising that kind of money was difficult and caused personal hardships for some of the many who turned over their savings — but it got Weinberg out of jail.

The man who had entered that jail a forlorn and tormented foreigner emerged like a conquering hero. The prisoners among whom Weinberg had lived for twenty months lined up at the bars of their cells to give him a farewell salute, cheering, banging their tin cups, extending rows of hands to be shaken by the departing jitney driver. The solemn, anxious look faded from Weinberg's face; he was radiant as he embraced wife and son and turned his nose to the fresh, free air.

Among the last of the inmates to say goodbye was Tom Mooney. By the warmth of his Godspeed Tom dispelled the recurring rumor of friction between the defendants. He told Weinberg that he had talked with Rena and: "We wanted you to go first." Mother Mooney was on hand, as always whenever anything was up even remotely connected with the fate of her son. Belle Hammerberg was there, weeping tears that must have been part sorrow, part anger, and part happiness.

The defense attorneys had arranged a surprise luncheon celebration at the Palace Hotel. Weinberg was in the mood, and his young son, Edward, was thrilled at the prospect; with Blanche Weinberg, however, it was different. There had been times during the waiting and the fear when she had seemed about to lose all mental stability. Now the thought of going to such a fine place and seeing all those fancy people staring at her was too much for her. So she excused herself, saying she must hurry to prepare her house for Israel's homecoming — as though it had not already been prepared and prepared and prepared again!

Eight days later, as Maxwell McNutt prepared to make a similar appeal to the State Supreme Court on behalf of Rena, the certainty that he would be overruled again finally penetrated Judge Dunne's hide. On March 30, 1918 he let Rena go free on bail, growling that he personally disapproved of such leniency, but that in view of the position taken by higher authority he did not wish to "appear stubborn."

So they were gone from the County Jail; first Nolan, then Weinberg, and now Rena. Billings was in Folsom Prison. Only Tom remained, his time growing shorter day by day.

Those were tumultuous times. World War One was on everybody's mind, but for many Tom Mooney and his cause came a close second. The first six months of American military participation had produced no impressive gains for the Allies. Serious industrial unrest continued in the western United States, and in other Allied countries. At home and abroad, the focal point of many labor protests was the Mooney-Billings case — not only in Petrograd, but in England and Holland. There were reports of German aviators dropping leaflets over Italy telling of the terrible injustice America was perpetrating against an innocent man, an effort designed to induce Italian soldiers to lay down their arms and go home rather than fight side by side with such an indecent, inhumane nation.

By the late summer of 1917, the American Secretary of War, Newton B. Baker, was ready to declare he was "keenly awake to the perversion of justice in the Mooney frameup and is apprehensive of serious labor disturbances unless justice is done." Champ Clark, Speaker of the House of Representatives, permitted his name to be used as honorary chairman of a national Mooney defense committee.

Eastern newspapers began editorializing that the Mooney case was evidence of an anti-labor conspiracy that had greatly embarrassed American relations with Russia. San Francisco was dubbed "the city that doesn't care." National labor leaders, emerging from the blue funk that hung over all defense efforts in late 1916 and early 1917, went to the White House to beg the President for remedial action. Wilson received memoranda from his closest advisor, Colonel House, and several members of his cabinet, suggesting some form of federal intervention.

In September of 1917, Wilson gave muscle to all this hue and cry by announcing the appointment of a Federal Mediation Commission to investigate the causes of labor unrest — including the Preparedness Day bombing convictions. The Commission consisted of amply qualified men whose findings could not be ignored. Two were labor leaders, two were wealthy and highly respected industrialists, and the chairman was Secretary of Labor William B. Wilson. Felix Frankfurter, then a professor of law at Harvard, acted as secretary and legal counsel.

The Commission started West as Oxman's perjury trial neared its close. Fremont Older, who had previously commented editorially in the *Bulletin* that Judge Dunne was making prejudicial remarks in favor of Oxman and that the special prosecutor appointed to try the case had very pointedly refused to call important witnesses, now speculated in print that the Fickert crowd seemed to be in great haste to acquit the "honest cattleman" and get him out of town before the Federal commissioners arrived.

There was a highly political element in all this hubbub: earlier in the year, anti-Fickert forces had started a move to recall the District Attorney. By the fall, a heated political campaign was well under way. But in December, San Francisco voters — perhaps moved by a mysterious bomb explosion at the state Capitol in Sacramento on election eve — proved they were in no mood to oust Mooney's prosecutor: Fickert defeated the recall move quite handily.

The defense suffered other setbacks on the legal front. Acting on a request from Judge Griffin, and on his knowledge of the Oxman letters and Rena's acquittal, California's Attorney General, U.S. Webb, officially informed the State Supreme Court that he was willing to agree that there was error in Mooney's trial, and asking for a new trial. Shortly after this, the defense made a motion to the same court asking for a reversal and a new trial — with the Attorney General again consenting. Both moves were denied by the court in short order, the first in August, the second in September.

As the year 1917 went into its closing month, an incident occurred which had no apparent connection with the fate of Tom Mooney: the sudden resignation of Mr. Justice Frederick W. Henshaw from the California Supreme Court. Some few in the inner circle of power, prestige and wealth may have smiled wryly at this news, but to the man in the street it meant little or nothing. Judge Henshaw, in his letter of resignation to Governor Stephens, said he had been "advised and believed [I] can be of more service to the United States than to the State." To inquiring newsmen Henshaw hinted that his new work would be confidential, and therefore could not be described. (A year later, however, it would be described in detail by officials of the United States government in terms that must have unnerved the resigned justice.)

President Wilson's Mediation Commission had come and gone in November, and as far as San Franciscans knew had washed its hands of Mooney and Billings. A rumor that the Commission would never report on the case went the rounds and was published in those newspapers which supported Fickert and his doings.

So it was a jolt to official complacency when Fremont Older came out with shrieking headlines of January 26, 1918, publishing extra after extra on the Commission's report.

After summarizing the background, the Commission said:

Instead of an ordinary criminal case . . . there thus emerge elements of a clash of forces of wide significance. On the one hand, a community long in the grip of bitter labor struggles and outraged by peculiarly wicked murders. Accusation is made against a group whose leader has been widely associated with views which justify violence, at least in industrial conflict. The public mind was therefore easily aroused to a belief in the guilt of the accused. An attitude of passion was stimulated by all the arts of modern journalism. It is not surprising, then, that Billings and Mooney were tried in an impregnating atmosphere of guilt. . . . Just as Mooney symbolized labor for all the bitter opponents of labor, so he came to symbolize labor, irrespective of his personal merits, in the minds of workers and their sympathizers. The Mooney case soon resolved itself into a new aspect of the old industrial feud instead of a subject demanding a calm search for the truth. . .

When Oxman was discredited, the verdict against Mooney was discredited . . . (and) the terrible and sacred instruments of criminal justice were, consciously or unconsciously, made use of against labor by its enemies in the industrial conflict . . .

The just disposition of the Mooney case thus affects influences far beyond the confines of California, and California can now be depended upon to see the wide implications of this case.

After discussing various aspects of California law, the Commission concluded:

It impairs the faith that our democracy protects the lowliest and even the unworthy against false accusations. War is fought with moral as well as material resources. We are in this war to vindicate the moral claims of unstained process of law, however slow at times such process may be. These claims must be tempered by the fire of our devotion to them at home.

The report had an effect like tossing cold water into a hot and greasy frying pan. Judge Dunne snapped that it was "what I expected from Bolsheviki Frankfurter." Fickert bellowed that the Commission had interviewed everybody except the prosecutors, had rejected law enforcement officers' attempts at consultation, and had not allowed time to answer briefs filed by the defense. (This after the prosecutor had twice asked for, and been granted, time to file an answering brief and had failed to meet the final deadline.)

Always circumspect, Judge Griffin declared that while he had no personal opinion as to Mooney's guilt or innocence, the Commission's findings confirmed his belief that the prisoner deserved a new trial. Mooney, talking to reporters who flocked to his jailhouse, was full of new hope, confident now that vindication and freedom would come — and in the next breath, took care to thank his fellow workers around the world, and in particular, Russia, for contributing to the exposure of the frame-up.

Once again, President Wilson made a secret move on the prisoner's behalf. In January, four days before release of the Commissions's report, Wilson wrote again to Governor Stephens suggesting that, rather than haggle over the propriety of the conviction already attained, a new trial be held on one of the remaining indictments.

While the President's act was *sub rosa*, the Commission's was public; the Governor's office was swamped with letters and telegrams, invaded by swarms of people, all beseeching him to order a new trial for Mooney; the press demanded to know how the Governor of California felt about this slap in the face from the Federal government. Stephens mildly murmured that he would do nothing about Mooney until after the California Supreme Court had brought down its opinion on the convict's automatic appeal.

Meanwhile Mooney was gathering the reins of battle into his own hands. From the men's side of the county jail he issued a written statement decrying a move on his behalf of which he had heard — agitation for a nation-wide 24-hour strike. His statement, addressed to his union brothers throughout the nation, first made the point that their target must be the Governor; he saw no possibility of gaining any semblance of justice from the California courts.

"Delay is suicide," wrote Mooney, "and the sooner you demand that justice be done, the better. The Chamber of Commerce hopes to tire you out by this process [legal procedures]. These blood-curdling murderers have no intention of giving us anything, and to hear talk of a 24-hour strike is a huge joke to their ears."

Tom pointed out that workers who tell the boss they will walk out unless given a wage increase do not say in advance how long they intend to strike. A political strike, Tom argued, should be no more fettered by timing than an economic strike; otherwise it would generate no response. He also noted the important differences between a strike threat and an actual strike.

In counseling caution, Tom had higher strategy in mind. Who in authority was his best friend? The Federal government. Who had prime responsibility for bringing World War One to a quick and victorious end? The Federal government. Who would be most embarrassed by any strike action reducing war production? The Federal government. As much as he disliked the war, Tom knew better than to annoy President Wilson.

A slight but significant change had taken place in the thinking at Governor Stephens' office. The Governor let it become public knowledge that President Wilson had been appealing to him on Mooney's behalf. In fact, it was acknowledged that the President had written the Governor for the third time about this most urgent matter.

Like a queen returned from exile, Rena Mooney appeared at the weekly meeting of the San Francisco Labor Council on the first Friday night after her release from jail. The unkind called her entourage a bodyguard, and perhaps in a sense it was, for the delegates were in one of their continuing torments over Tom. This time the issue involved whether or not to hold a mass protest meeting in the City in April, 1918 — barely two weeks away. The Mooney forces carried the vote, and the Council endorsed this demonstration, but by a margin too slim for comfort.

While it might be unfair to say that Rena began to enjoy life again, certainly the manner of her days and nights was now very different than it had been before Preparedness. Celebrity was thrust upon her, and she found it a thousand times more stimulating than sitting in the jail dormitory making lace. She traveled hither and yon around the Western states, often accompanied by Weinberg. She found herself able to stand up before audiences and speak about the frame-up, and felt the satisfaction of arousing sympathy and winning support.

It was springtime; protest meetings were coming up like flowers all over America — Butte, Minneapolis, New York, Chicago, Seattle — but the best took place in San Francisco on the night of April 16. Ed Nolan, Israel Weinberg and Rena were very much in the limelight, but this time the main attraction was another woman — Mother Jones. The Scourge of the Rockies, then in her eighty-eighth year, was still eager to get in a blow against her favorite monsters, the capitalists. The Civic Auditorium seats ten thousand, and it was full that night, including more than a thousand Eastbay union members who came over by a special ferryboat and marched up Market Street with bands playing, flags and union banners flying, and signs held high demanding justice for Mooney and Billings. Mother Jones lived up to her reputation, filling the air with imprecations against those who plotted to take the life of her dear friend

Tom Mooney and to otherwise persecute his wife and the rest of the bombing defendants. Resolutions were adopted supporting the appeals of President Wilson. Finally the meeting came to a standing, roaring climax as Tom's message, hand written and sent from the county jail, was read to the audience. He demanded, as he was to do many times during the months to come, that he be given either a new trial or an outright pardon; no halfway measure like commutation of sentence to time served would do.

(Not all protest events went so well. A man named Morgan, one of a battery of Mooney speakers who fanned out all over the United States, came to the agricultural town of El Centro in Southern California and, while registering at a hotel, was mistaken for Weinberg. A group of vigilantes invaded Morgan's hotel room, forced him out into an automobile, and took him for a wild night ride into the desert. The kidnapped man was found the next morning, unharmed but furious, at an Army camp near the Mexican border where he had found shelter among the soldiers.)

One of the forums in which the Mooney-Billings case was thoroughly aired was the United States Senate. Poindexter of Washington denounced Seattle workers as "treasonous" for planning a May Day strike on Tom's behalf. While Judge Dunne was telegraphing congratulations to Poindexter, Senator Phelan of California, although asserting that Mooney and his companions had probably done the bombing to earn German money, came out in support of President Wilson's plea for a new trial "in order to vindicate the United States and the regularity and fairness of Mooney's treatment." California's other senator, Hiram Johnson, kept silent, but associates reported that, despite a strong personal prejudice against Mooney, he too believed the Oxman exposures warranted a new trial.

Like Senator Phelan, but for entirely different reasons, Tom and his attorney Maxwell McNutt were inclined to think the bombing had been arranged and paid for by Consul General Bopp. The defense had discovered connections between the German Consulate in San Francisco and Fickert, and through Fickert to the local Chamber of Commerce. Thus, the defense theorized that the Preparedness Day outrage served two motives: pro-German and anti-labor. For a time they held this theory in such high esteem that they spent time and money trying to pin the bombing on Bopp, with the thought that they might also succeed in enmeshing labor's local enemy, the Law and Order Committee. However, tantalizing though the clues were, no proof panned out.

In spite of Tom's warnings, the fervor mounted for a nationwide strike as May Day neared. News came of definite preparations in Washington, Arizona, Ohio, and other states; strike talk was everywhere. However, Mooney would not sit back and let the strikes happen. He sent telegrams to all unions known to have made strike preparations asking them, for his sake, to abandon such plans. Also he telegraphed President Wilson, thanking him for his kindly acts — and making sure Wilson knew who had prevented the May Day stoppages. Finally, the strike talk died away, though other protests increased in number and intensity, coming from communities spreading from England to Alaska.

On June 3 Fickert announced his candidacy for the Republican nomination for governor, basing his campaign almost solely on his fight against radicalism — to wit, his prosecution of Mooney. On the following day President Wilson sent a fourth letter to Governor Stephens, suggesting that legal technicalities might be overcome by granting Mooney a conditional pardon for the murder of which he had been convicted, and then requiring him to stand trial on one of the other indictments.

Then, out of the blue, came an assist to the defense that eventually was to prove useful. The youngest man to serve as a juror in Tom's trial, who had since become a lieutenant in the Army Aviation Service, volunteered a public statement: he had voted for conviction on the testimony of Oxman and Estelle Smith; since both had been discredited, he felt the convict deserved a new trial.

This unexpected good news, however, was soon buried under the expected bad news from the California Supreme Court. On July 16 that court swept away the last legal obstacle delaying the execution of Tom Mooney by denying his automatic appeal.

On the evening of that sad day Rena came to the county jail, along with Mother Mooney and a few close friends, to say farewell to Tom. The next morning he was taken to San Quentin, became Prisoner No. 31921, and was lodged in condemned row in a cell known as 220 Stone. The execution was now set for August 23, 1918.

Judge Dunne was not the only Californian to snort at the President's Federal Mediation Commission. There was a general mood throughout the state of distrust, if not open dislike, of almost anything emanating from Washington concerning the Mooney case. The more cautious newspaper publishers expressed their sentiments in print somewhat gingerly, but bold sheets like the San Francisco *Wasp* and the *Los Angeles Times* (in those years a rip-roaring enemy of labor and liberalism) made no bones about their feelings; the government of the United States had no business meddling in this affair. The *Wasp*, a weekly commentary of considerable prestige among California pioneers and their descendants, editorialized that it hoped California officials would not "bow to the will of the President."

The Sacramento *Bee*, liberal on most subjects other than Mooney and Billings, slammed the Mediation Commission, editorializing that pro-Mooney sentiment at home and abroad had been created by "as marvelous a system of thorough misrepresentation and downright lying as has ever been known in connection with any criminal case in any country."

The *Wasp* and several other publications commented on the uncomfortable political position of Governor Stephens, who was asking the voters to return him to office. Whether he moved for or against Mooney's execution, he was bound to incur the wrath of considerable segments of California's population. And the Governor's potato grew hotter as Fickert, campaigning against him, rampaged up and down the state, crying to all who would listen that he alone could deal with mad bombers. Nudging this political clash along, Hearst's San Francisco *Examiner* speculated that Stephens would grant the condemned man some form of clemency, which gave Fickert something more to howl about.

While the Governor must have been having an occasional attack of the political dithers over Mooney, the labor movement was having an occasional riot over the same issue. One such, with police called to quell the violence, took place in the Los Angeles Labor Council when a group of fifty men and women calling themselves the "Mooney Defense League" were refused admission on the ground that they must be Wobblies. A year earlier, some San Francisco labor leaders had thrown in their lot with Fickert, including the Labor Council President, a former shoe clerk turned lawyer, whose private and public insults to Mooney supporters finally cost him the presidency of the Council and his seat as a delegate. This tooraloo, which went all the way up to the executive board of the American Federation of Labor, plus other issues generated by the Mooney-Billings case, brought about debates verging on violence Friday night after Friday night, week in and week out, as the execution date drew nearer.

There was enough political support in New York state to get a resolution introduced in its Legislature requesting Governor Stephens to grant Mooney a stay of execution — but not enough to get the resolution adopted. In Detroit, a mass meeting for Mooney drew 4500 persons who heard speeches in eight languages denouncing the frame-up.

News from the outside trickled into the cell on Condemned Row. Mooney's sense of public relations, quickening as his time grew shorter, caused him to react sharply when he heard of the Germans using his name. He issued a statement repudiating all such propaganda and pledging support to Wilson's efforts to establish "peace through justice" throughout the world. Furthermore, he took steps through Socialist channels to see that his message reached concerned sources in Europe.

Governor Stephens, with all eyes centered on him as the only remaining hope for Mooney's life, still stood mute. The nation's conscience stirred more restlessly as August 23rd, the day of execution, came uncomfortably near.

July 28 was designated as Tom Mooney Day. In the industrial cities of the East and mid-West posters and handbills publicizing the event indicated the makeup of the expected audiences by promising: "Speeches in Italian, Lithuanian, and Yiddish." Speaker of the House Champ Clark agreed to be honorary chairman of the Mooney Day meeting in Washington, D.C. In San Francisco the headliner was to be John H. Walker, president of the Illinois State Federation of Labor — who had helped uncover the Oxman letters and served on the Federal Mediation Commission. Clarence Darrow in Philadelphia, Bourke Cockran in Washington, D.C., and Dudley Field Malone in New York headed a long list of prominent speakers. Letters and telegrams poured into the Governor's office, the White House, and other presssure targets. Tom Mooney had won the sympathy of the American people — except those in charge in California.

Twenty-four hours before Mooney Day, Stephens announced a reprieve for the famous convict until December 13, saying the extra time would be needed to properly consider all the ramifications of the case. Editors, politicians, and labor leaders were quick to note that by postponing the execution until five weeks after the November general election Stephens had sidestepped the necessity of making a politically difficult decision in mid-campaign. Fickert and friends yelled to high heaven that the Governor was timid and spineless; many unionists were almost equally unhappy, calling the reprieve "a sop to labor" which shelved the requisites of justice in favor of the requisites of politics.

The Governor's act did not alter the essential thrust of the Mooney Day demonstrations. In San Francisco six thousand persons jammed Dreamland Rink, three to four thousand more stood outside in overflow meetings, and uncounted late comers gave up and went away. Those who got in heard Walker of Illinois lump together Fickert, Oxman, and the German saboteurs, and top off his suspicions with a war-time analogy: "To fight for Mooney is to fight against the Kaiser!"

In Chicago, Frank P. Walsh spoke to twenty thousand, saying that if necessary Federal troops should be sent into California to save Tom's life. This was strong talk, coming from the man who had been co-chairman (with former President William Howard Taft) of the National War Labor Board.

And the mayor of Butte, Montana showed a little frontier spirit at the Mooney Day gathering there: "Hanging is too good for Fickert. I believe that Almighty God would look down smilingly on a bunch of men who would burn Fickert at the stake!" The audience, mainly copper miners and their families, shouted back in cadence: "Hang him! Hang him!"

The labor press reported Mooney Day meetings in five thousand communities throughout the nation; half a million men stood pledged to strike, if necessary, to save the life of the condemned man. A delegation led by Bourke Cockran including the leaders of many international unions called at the White House to urge the President to persevere in his attempts to save Mooney.

Then came the California primary elections of August, 1918, which gave dramatic indication of a downturn in Fickert's political fortunes: a year earlier, Fickert had won in the San Francisco recall election with 46,000 votes; now he was able to poll fewer than 14,000 votes statewide. Judge Griffin, who according to rumor had suffered undercover opposition from Fickert's crowd, ran for re-election in the City and won handily. Perhaps bolstered by this vote of confidence, Griffin wrote a lengthy analysis of the Mooney trial, showing the unreliability of all prosecution witnesses and sent this to Governor Stephens to support his argument for a new trial.

World War One ended a month and two days before the final, "absolute" date for Tom Mooney's execution. Russians were fighting Russians; the Germans were teetering between Socialists and Junkers. In New York five thousand Socialists, marching up Fifth Avenue to Madison Square Garden for a fund-raising rally in behalf of Mooney and Billings, displayed red flags as a pledge of support to German Socialists in Europe. Sight of the red flags infuriated American doughboys just returned from battle, and while policemen looked the other way many a Socialist was chased and beaten that night by men in Army uniform.

In Oakland a parade of shipyard workers was disrupted by police, who seized a banner proclaiming "Free Tom Mooney" and arrested the man who carried it. The paraders secured reinforcements and marched on police headquarters in such imposing numbers that they got their man freed and their banner back, posthaste and with apologies. In San Francisco a man making a sidewalk speech in which he shouted, among other things, that Mooney was innocent, was taken into custody by Federal authorities on a charge of making seditious statements.

Throughout the nation, labor groups began taking up subscriptions for floral pieces to lay on Tom Mooney's grave.

6

The Providential Presidential Wallop

The correspondence between Governor Stephens and President Wilson
regarding justice for Tom Mooney was kept secret by both parties.
During most of the crucial pre-execution days, except for the postponement from August to December, the Governor did nothing but
sit tight. The man in the White House must have felt a stubborn
reluctance on the part of California officialdom to do anything that
might cheat it out of a hanging.

Early during that anxious time, a man named John B. Densmore
made a quiet entry upon the scene. As Solicitor of the United
States Department of Labor, he had been in San Francisco in
1917, directing a team of immigration inspectors, whose main concern
was the smuggling of Chinese aliens into the country. When the
Wilson administration became interested in Mooney, the Secretary
of Labor had asked Densmore, a skilled investigator, for his assistance.
Densmore and his men uncovered a great deal of information,
which they turned over to the Federal Mediation Commission. Some of
this material had been publicized in the Commission's report, but
quite a bit had been kept secret. Shortly after the report was issued
Densmore had been promoted to Director of the U.S. Employment
Service, but new developments in immigration affairs brought him

back to San Francisco for further investigations. In the course of all this, Densmore had made many contacts with local officials. One day he chanced to overhear a remark that set him ajangle; Fred Berry, one of the assistant district attorneys, was telling Fickert that a friend who was "very close" to Governor Stephens had reported, in confidence: "Stephens is going to let Mooney go to hell; he's going to let them hang him."

Densmore kept a poker face; but inwardly he boiled. As a loyal Wilsonian, he resented the insult to the President. He was also concerned over the broader implications of such an act — disaster for American diplomacy abroad, serious disruption of the war effort, industrial chaos on the home front. He lost no time informing Washington about that confidential remark; soon he received official authorization, funds, and technical assistance to counteract what he felt to be subversion by the men running the State of California.

Densmore had a keen appetite for this particular job, and he secretly put into play a novel and unorthodox [at that time, the FBI was nothing much and J. Edgar Hoover had not yet been heard of] method of exposing Mooney's prosecutors: electronic eavesdropping.

Densmore considered the crusading editor, Fremont Older a man of unquestionable veracity, and it was Older who gave him a lead to one of the mysteries locked within a mystery.

Back in mid-April of 1917, the Mooney defense — piling Oxman upon the Edeaus upon Estelle Smith upon Rigall upon what Ed McKenzie had learned through his brother of Cunha's boasting of jury-fixing — had the prosecution almost literally hanging on the ropes. McKenzie, using the theory he was to cling to for many years, had offered the prosecution a deal. If the defense would refrain from accusing the prosecution of malfeasance, subornation of perjury, and all other crimes, would the prosecution confess innocent error and ask for a pardon or, at least, a new trial? This question came to a head one night in a room where McKenzie, Older and others cornered Cunha and Fickert. At 9 o'clock that night Fickert yielded. Yes, he would issue a statement along the lines indicated. But he wanted to wait until midnight, to catch the final headlines of the morning papers, so no editor would have time to scotch his statement with an angry editorial. There would be no interview that night, no press conference; he would just issue the statement and duck until the next day. It was agreed. Fickert shook hands all around, said he was going right to his office to prepare the statement, and disappeared.

At midnight that night Fickert did issue a statement — a statement blasting Older and the Mooney defense, claiming they had tried to blackmail him into agreeing to a new trial. He revived an old story that Older had been too friendly with Anarchists, and claimed the Mooney people had attempted to intimidate prosecution witnesses. To top it all off, Fickert went before "his" grand jury shortly after midnight and demanded that it probe the Oxman-Rigall affair (Oxman had just been arrested on a defense complaint charging subornation of perjury) with himself as the prosecutor. That grand jury did try to exculpate Oxman, but its members had sense enough to refuse to go along with Fickert's suggestion that he investigate himself.

Hearing this story from Older a year and a half later, Densmore asked himself what could have happened during those three hours. He felt the answers to this question would turn up a towering scandal. He was even more certain the District Attorney's defenses would be difficult to breach. The slightest hint of publicity would ruin the whole venture: what had been done in secret had to be exposed by secret means.

Gradually Densmore's report assumed written form. When it was complete, Older "broke" the story — ostensibly without the consent of Densmore or his superiors — on November 22, 1918, three weeks before Mooney's execution date.*

The report consisted mainly of excerpts from transcribed conversations between Fickert and others for two periods in 1918: the first in June, when the DA was launching his campaign for governor; the second from September 5 to October 26, after he had been defeated in the primary. During both periods, he had been desperately seeking new evidence on which to bring Rena Mooney to a second trial.

Many of the recorded conversations had a sinister ring, accentuated by the nicknames used. Fickert himself was variously known

---

*By this time, Older had left the *Bulletin* to run Hearst's *San Francisco Call*, with the understanding that he could maintain his position on Mooney. While most Hearst papers had by now softened their anti-Mooney stance, the *Examiner* ("flagship" of the chain) often went its own way, particularly with the Mooney case.

as "The Chief," or "Legs," or "Big Fellow." Pete McDonough, bail bond broker and head of a fixing ring, was referred to as "Centipede." Bennie Selig, another fixer, was called "The Butcher," — his actual occupation — and Edward Bryant, San Francisco's tax collector, was known as "Very Good, Eddie." The fixing ring included a couple of police judges, a former U.S. District Attorney, various detectives and secret operatives [labor spies], including Martin Swanson, and a retinue of more or less shabby hangers-on. Louis Ferrari, who had prosecuted Rena and Weinberg (and who later became chief counsel for the Bank of America), was called "The Garbage Man," or "The Little Scavenger" because his function had been "to carry it out." Code words were often used, most of them connected with Selig's legitimate trade, such as "sweetbreads" and "pork tenderloins."

The dictaphone record was replete with references to payments of bribes by which offenders escaped the law. The District Attorney's office was the natural center for such operations, for if the prosecutor came into court and said he did not have sufficient evidence to convict the accused, what could be done about it? Even the most honest judge was practically powerless; so were the police. A man charged with crime had only to hire an attorney who knew the workings of the ring and plunk down liberal sums of money, guilty or not. Two fixing cases depicted most clearly involved a tire and automobile thief and a wealthy citizen who had been caught *in flagrante delicto* in acts of degeneracy.

Summing up disclosures of all sorts of jury-rigging, bribery, and ordinary frame-up, Densmore reported: "The San Francisco District Attorney's office, thrown wide open by this investigation, reveals the public prosecutor not as an officer of justice but as a conspirator persecuting the innocent. . . In the strictest and most literal meaning of the word, anarchy reigns in the office which is supposed to be dedicated to law and order."

The Densmore Report then tied a known fact to one of its most sensational revelations. In her 1917 affidavit Estelle Smith had sworn that Oxman told her the five figure bribe offer came from "those higher up than Fickert." Densmore said these higher-ups were Frederick W. Henshaw, who had suddenly and mysteriously resigned from the State Supreme Court eleven months earlier, and Frank C. Drew, the Chamber of Commerce attorney who later was charged with being his payoff man for another witness. Fickert leaned most heavily on Henshaw; the two were in telephonic communication daily, sometimes hourly.

Henshaw had made a long climb from police court judge to Associate Justice of California's highest judicial body, where he stayed for many years. During all of his career, according to Densmore, Henshaw had consistently served the most unscrupulous interests. Densmore said Henshaw had picked Fickert out of limbo and brought him to the attention of the top men in the United Railroads "at a time when these officials were desperately casting about for a man of straw to put into the office of District Attorney. With Fickert's election, dismissal of graft indictments against those officials was quickly obtained." After the bombing, Densmore asserted, the Chamber of Commerce and utility magnates saw "in this pliable public servant vast possibilities for further usefulness, and it was not long before they were employing him to further their designs against unionism and organized labor in the Mooney case."

Densmore went on:

> In this celebrated affair, as in all Fickert's official acts connected with the graft indictments, Henshaw has supplied the brains which have controlled the awkward motions of the mannikin. He has been the power behind the throne, the chief counsellor and guide, the unseen master of the show. Fickert has reported to him every move, has shown him every exhibit, and has consulted with him daily in regard to prospective witnesses, new clues, general policies, and detailed manner of procedure.

To back up his accusations, Densmore revealed the real reason for Henshaw's resignation. Many years before, contending heirs had fought a nip-and-tuck legal battle over the will of James A. Fair, an estate valued at millions of dollars. By changing his vote at a crucial moment, Henshaw had reversed a State Supreme Court decision in this case. For this, Henshaw assertedly received a down payment of $10,000, with the understanding that if the heirs for whom he was secretly acting were successful he was to receive an additional $400,000. His side eventually did win out, and by devious methods all or nearly all of the $400,000 was placed at Henshaw's disposal.

All this was documented by the written confession of a go-between, a speculator named Dingee, and an affidavit from Dingee's bookkeeper. Fremont Older now published a big picture of the judge, together with a facsimile of a ledger sheet from the bookkeeper's accounts, showing payments of large sums to F.W. Henshaw, and also to "J. Brown," an asserted pseudonym for Henshaw. In all, it was a melodrama of greed, luck good and bad, huge business deals, misplaced confidences, deceit, spite and other ignoble passions — including very clear suggestions as to how to bribe a justice of the California Supreme Court.

Fremont Older had long since heard hints of the connection between Fickert and Henshaw, and had concrete proof of the bribery in the Fair will case about a year before the Densmore Report came out. Older had been about to run the story and ruin this dishonest justice, when Henshaw somehow got wind of the prospective exposure. The justice ordered Older to visit him in chambers. Older declined, but suggested they meet in the editor's suite at the Fairmont Hotel.

Mr. Justice Henshaw kept the appointment in white tie and tails. He was an elderly fashion plate with high, balding forehead, pouches under large wide-set eyes, puffy cheeks and a dewlap that settled luxuriously into his wing collar. At first Henshaw had put up a bold front, maintaining that although a bribe may have been paid, he had received none of it.

Densmore's report quotes Older's comeback as follows: "Quit bluffing. I will show you the absolute, undeniable proof, if you insist."

Just as Henshaw seemed to be wilting, Mrs. Henshaw was ushered into the room. She also was dressed for the evening. The conference was dissolved almost instantly and the pair swept away to a dinner party. As they departed, however, Henshaw, over his shoulder, made an appointment to meet Older again the following morning. Quoting Densmore:

> It is alleged by Older, whose veracity is above suspicion, that on this occasion (the second meeting), Judge Henshaw cast aside all pretense of innocence and sought to throw himself upon the mercy of his visitor. . . He reminded Older that he was fast nearing the end of his life, that he was hard pressed financially, and that nothing but misery could ensue from an exposure of his past misdeeds.

Older's sympathies had always been easy to arouse; he who had seen so much of sin and shame was a compassionate priest at heart. Sensing this mood, perhaps, Henshaw now declared that he thought Mooney deserved a new trial. He offered to resign forthwith from the court, break with Fickert — at least as far as the bombing cases were concerned — and use his influence with the Governor to procure the new trial for Mooney. These promises won from Older the desired response: he would refrain from publishing the story.

Henshaw, according to Densmore, honored only the first of his promises and reneged entirely on the others: "He is still the stage director of the district attorney's miserable tragedy, busily engaged in pulling the wires, shifting the scenes, sounding the tin thunder, and manipulating the demon traps. If he himself is not openly stalking up and down the boards, he is at least secretly coaching the principal actor for his stellar role."

With joy that was almost savage Fremont Older now used the *Call* to smash Fickert and the Henshaw ring and save Tom Mooney's life. The front page of the *Call*, and six inside pages, were devoted exclusively to the Densmore Report — not a line, not a word, mentioned any other subject.

There were wild tales aplenty, including one concerning a Mrs. Virginia Judd, who had come to the attention of police as a possible witness in an unrelated murder case. While talking with investigators, she had remarked that she had noticed a woman in a taxicab at Steuart and Market Streets on the day of the bombing. Densmore reported that Fickert and Henshaw had discussed Mrs. Judd on the telephone. Now, if they could get her to identify that woman as Rena Mooney and set the timing just right. . . .! A plot was evolved: Mrs Judd was young and rather nice-looking, and she lived near Buena Vista Park on one of the city's many hills. A local police detective, a Burns operative from Los Angeles, and other men whose identities never became clear, were enlisted to approach the lady at her home. They claimed to be a motion picture crew from Hollywood, doing some scenic stuff on San Francisco, and wanted to take some shots in the park across the street. A touch of femininity, preferably provided by some pretty resident of the neighborhood, would lend charm and realism — wouldn't she like to step into the park and pose? It would only take a few minutes, and she'd be in the movies. It was a ploy many a girl would have jumped at. She could not know that if she did go in among those trees, she would be frightened or tripped so that for a second she would find herself in the arms of the nearest man. Pictures would be snapped by waiting photographers, and these, the plotters hoped, might be used to secure a monumental piece of perjury from Mrs. Judd.

Fickert loved this sort of scheming, but had the weakness of counting his chickens before they hatched. His conversations with Henshaw about this plot were guarded, but the dictaphone recorded a talk with Cunha about the fact that Mrs. Judd had seen a taxi rather than a jitney bus:

Cunha: "Chief, if you can get a witness who will put Mrs. Mooney at Steuart and Market Streets, I don't give a damn if you put her there in a balloon."

Fickert: "I think I can put her there in a taxicab. It looks as though we had the witness."

Cunha: "If you have, Chief, I'll put that - - - of a - - - - - Mrs. Mooney on trial again and I'll convict her by every rule of the game."

(The dictaphone transcriptions were loaded with oaths and obscenities, uttered mainly by Fickert and those closest to him. Densmore, somewhat Victorian in literary sensibility, reported such language euphemistically, or indicated it by dashes—or merely omitted it.)

Fickert's hopes, however, were soon dashed. When police had first spoken with Mrs. Judd she had been with her sister; consequently, the leader of the "Hollywood crew" was to say he had been sent by her sister. But in the interim the sisters had quarrelled, and were no longer speaking to each other, so Mrs. Judd's suspicions were aroused; she telephoned her husband, and the whole scheme sank away like water on sand. Soon Mrs. Judd, instead of testifying against Rena Mooney, was telling her story to "Scoop" Gleeson — known on official documents (but nowhere else) as Edgar T. Gleeson. A protege of Fremont Older, he had become the editor's right-hand man, keen for the hidden story, the secret scandal, the exclusive shocker that would expose the villains, rescue the heroes, protect feminine or civic virtue — and sell newspapers.

The Densmore Report had much more to tell. The dictaphone showed Fickert proud of his talent for dancing and of his successes as a ladies' man. In addition to a wife and several casual female acquaintances, he had two particular girl friends, roommates who helped each other arrange assignations with the District Attorney. One ran a dancing school, while the other was Fickert's secretary at his private office in the Kohl Building. A married lady at the St. Francis Hotel used to call him now and then and invite him to her room for a drink. Occasionally he received "mash notes" from a woman whose husband was in the Army overseas. Fickert would pass these notes around among his friends and assistants, interspersing lewd remarks with gales of laughter. (Sixty-odd years ago the public took such pecadillos less calmly than in the shock-proof present.)

On one occasion, according to the telltale dictaphone, Fickert asked the dancing teacher to accompany him on an automobile trip into the San Joaquin Valley. Although swearing she loved him devotedly, this girl side-stepped the trip but suggested her room-mate as a substitute. The other girl proved willing, and she and Fickert arranged to meet at the Ferry Building. At this point, Densmore interrupted the dictaphone record to state that an operative had observed the secretary get into the District Attorney's car and ride with him, just the two together, onto the ferryboat for Oakland.

Turning from sex to politics, the report included abundant references to Fickert's scathing opinions of President Wilson, mostly in regard to his passion for justice for Tom Mooney.

Densmore warned that a miscarriage of justice in the Mooney case would inflame the minds of underdogs everywhere "and add to the conviction, already too widespread, that workingmen can expect no justice from an orderly appeal to the established courts." He closed his report with the suggestion that it might be "within the province and privilege of the Federal government" to step in and take charge of the case if the defendants could not be assured of their Constitutional rights by any other means.

The report never pinpointed what Fickert did during those crucial three hours. Mooney always assumed, however, that the District Attorney consulted his bosses and acted according to their orders.

The repercussions came swiftly. Judge Henshaw, immediately disowned by his former associates on the State Supreme Court, went around telling everyone who would listen that he had never taken a dishonest dollar. Fickert and most of the others spotlighted by the report issued formal denials, but McDonough, the "Centipede," merely kept his mouth shut. Governor Stephens refused to comment, and San Francisco Mayor Rolph merely said he was giving "close attention" to these allegations.

Tom Mooney praised the report and urged the Federal government to follow through on Densmore's final recommendation — and quickly; time was short. The taking of strike votes on Mooney's behalf speeded up in many American cities.

Police Captain Duncan Matheson spoke out, declaring that Densmore had told the exact truth in describing the District Attorney's handling of certain cases "a travesty on justice." The Captain also said the report had been "absolutely right" in quoting Fickert as saying, "Matheson is raising hell"; Matheson cited case after case where he had gone as far as a cop could go in complaining that the District Attorney was hampering police and creating unnecessary failures in prosecution.

While excitement rose among the many, and the few tried to maintain stonewall fronts, Fickert yielded to a temptation that overcame him whenever goaded by criticism — violence.

Before, when ridiculed in print by Older for his efforts to frame Mooney and Billings, Fickert had encountered the editor in one of the City's fanciest watering holes, the Palace Hotel bar. There, in front of Maxfield Parrish's famous mural of the Pied Piper, the former football hero had bulled up to Older, twenty years his senior and committed to fighting with the printed word and not with fist or gun or cane, and had smashed the crusading editor to the floor.

Fickert had also jumped upon Selig Schulberg, so tiny he was almost a dwarf, and broken his victim's glasses and cut his face, because Schulberg had been vocal in defense of Tom Mooney and loud in his denunciation of the District Attorney.

Now, Fickert and Older met again in the Palace Hotel, this time in a corridor. Fickert, accompanied by one of his deputies, Fred Berry, rushed up to Older and floored him with one Sunday punch. Berry and another man quickly hauled "the Chief" off the prostrate form, but the story went like wildfire and the reporters came running. Older, nursing a bruised jaw, told them the attack had come without preamble and that Fickert had kicked him several times while he was down, screaming curses but otherwise saying nothing intelligible. Fickert admitted he had punched Older, but denied the kicking. He claimed he had used his fists only after a dialogue in which Older had been "forced" to admit friendship with Emma Goldman and had "refused to deny" that Tom Mooney had cashed a check signed by the editor two or three days before Preparedness. The Emma Goldman accusation was a favorite with Fickert; he had made it repeatedly during the battles he had fought against Older over the Oxman disclosures the year before.

Others came forward as well. Police Detective Tom Furman, who had corroborated Weinberg's trial testimony that Fickert, using a Jewish go-between, had offered Weinberg a bribe if only he would "finger" Mooney and Billings, now got into public print again. Furman cited specific cases where he had made arrests only to have them dismissed by Police Judge Morris Oppenheim, one of those pilloried by Densmore. Oppenheim denied everything.

Also adding to the hubbub was a Berkeley architect, Maury I. Diggs, who had done time in a Federal penitentary for a frolicsome, non-commercial violation of the "white slave" act. Speaking before a union meeting, he declared that while in prison he had come to know C.C. Crowley, a man convicted of performing sabotage for the Germans. Diggs said Crowley had told him: "They got the wrong man. The man who did that job (the Preparedness Day bombing) is in Mexico."

Diggs' story set off a quick flurry of detective work by the Mooney defense, for Fickert and Crowley had been friends and collaborators. The District Attorney had even supplied Crowley, (a known bomber,) with misleading credentials for use as he traveled around the United States on sabotage errands for German Consul-General Bopp.

There were several other side-effects of Densmore's report. The president of the Oil Workers' Union at Martinez resigned under fire because the dictaphone showed he and another member were in league with Fickert to frame a suspect in an industrial case. An assistant United States District Attorney quit suddenly, saying he had quarrelled with one of Densmore's aides who had threatened to shoot him.

As soon as he knew his report was to be made public, Densmore took the train for Portland, Oregon where he told reporters, "A man has no chance if they start to get him in San Francisco. They jostle a man off the street, kill him, and have a dozen witnesses testify he pulled a gun and started the fight. I have been in nearly every city of importance in the United States, and San Francisco is worse than any of them."

The San Francisco Grand Jury ordered that Densmore be returned for questioning and issued subpoenas for two men suspected of doing the wire-tapping. Densmore retorted by giving another interview in Portland, declaring that the jury which acquitted Oxman had been fixed — no question about it.

Charges and counter-charges flew. Densmore was called a crook; he said Fickert should be tried for sedition. Densmore was denounced by the San Francisco Downtown Association for slandering the City. During all this hulabaloo the public — but not Tom Mooney — almost forgot about that man in Sacramento, the only one who could halt the hanging.

Five days after publication of the Densmore Report, at 7:20 p.m. on Thanksgiving eve, the Governor's private secretary left his office with a sheet of paper in his hand and walked to the press room in the State Capitol. That piece of paper contained a short, simple statement: Mooney's sentence was being commuted to life imprisonment.

Defense lawyers and labor leaders lost no time in denouncing this act as a further miscarriage of justice, but it was twenty-four hours before Tom's reaction became public. The delay came because Warden James A. Johnston feared for his job if Mooney was permitted to have his full say against the Governor. The statement that finally passed the warden's censorship was in two parts. The first, addressed to Governor Stephens, declared: "I demand that you revoke your commutation of my death sentence to a living death. I prefer a glorious death at the hands of my traducers to a living grave."

This may have sounded well in print, but it had no meaning: a condemned man cannot refuse commutation to life imprisonment. The potentially powerful part of his statement was his call to the working class for struggle. Declaring that the only hope for him and Billings lay in the solidarity of organized labor, Tom said: "I now appeal to you to act, and the sooner the better."

But no matter how fierce the anger of labor and the liberals, Governor Stephens' act, in the broad, public sense, was like the lancing of a boil. The Densmore Report had not given justice to Mooney and Billings, but it undoubtedly helped save Tom's life.

It also had another effect, albeit with a longer fuse. In 1919 when Fickert came up for re-election he was easily defeated by Police Judge Matthew Brady.

Densmore had put an end to Fickert's public career.

Ed Nolan, Machinist Union official, and wife.

Loneliness

As soon as the official notice of commutation was received at San Quentin Prison, No. 31921 was removed from Condemned Row and put to work, like most other inmates, in the jute mill.

Tom Mooney was alive, and this made it possible to continue the fight. Instead of Rena's becoming a widow she became a prison widow — a vast difference, as she was to learn during the long, busy, lonely years to come.

Tom Mooney was not content to suffer silently while his lawyers and his defense committeemen functioned or failed to function according to their own ideas. Defense groups such as those that emerged to help Mooney and Billings are usually composed of leftists of one category or another. Leftists, by nature disputatious and doubting, are likely to disagree among each other more viciously than Republicans do with Democrats; with American leftists hope for power was visionary, and therefore agreement and compromise had little immediate practical value. Tom's original charge d'affairs, Bob Minor — who abandoned a career as a nationally known cartoonist to become a revolutionary — had been forced out of the Mooney defense by factional rows in the International Workers' Defense League. The next man up, Ed Nolan, came to differ so intensely with Tom on defense procedure that he quit — and burned all correspondence, lists of supporters, and other valuable documents in the process. The connecting link between changes of the guard had been Rena, and the time came when, by force of necessity, she became the chief — and sometimes the only — defense functionary.

In a *cause celebre*, the defense secretary must first of all be an organizer, a person who lays out the program, wins acceptance of it from those concerned, and then locates and energizes the people who will carry it out. This person must be skilled in extracting money from the pockets of supporters, rich and poor, for a defense mechanism cannot function simply on perusal of a citizen's rights. The defense secretary must be deft in the arts of propaganda (or know how to find and use a good propagandist) to keep interest for the cause alive, must be politically above suspicion, and a meticulous bookkeeper — always able to show where the money went. And this many-sided human must be something of a schemer to discover and forestall opposition moves; a prognosticator, who can sense trends early on; and a diplomat to soothe hurt feelings and repair the rifts that bedevil the activities of men — even those of good will. Finally, he or she must be a drudge, able and willing to work at high tension eighteen hours a day, seven days a week, with little or no pay, plenty of brickbats, and once in a blue moon a word of praise.

Rena Mooney was simply not up to the job. Tom had plenty of time for planning. He laid out the program; he directed the writing, chose the pictures, the layouts, selected the type, even picked the printer for his defense literature. He decided which creditors should be paid and which would have to wait. All this might have taken a great load off Rena except that Tom, caged in stone and steel, was a frustrated, driving man with no one to drive but her. Rena visited him every week, and each time she was dismayed to find that he had thought up more things than even the most able and adept person could do single-handed in twice the time. At every visit, Rena made a list of things he wanted done; at every visit the list of things done wrong or not at all grew longer and longer. Prison life was changing Tom from loving husband into a testy, short-tempered inmate. Rena was apologetic, then tearful, and finally defiant.

As penologists know, the most certain way to ruin a marriage, even the happiest, is to incarcerate one of the parties for a long period. The more prolonged the separation the more certain the breakup.

While these problems were moving slowly toward crisis, Tom was befriending a short-termer named George Sayles. A pleasant man with a journalistic background, Sayles seemed to share many of Tom's ideas, particularly in regard to the political aspects of class struggle. Sayles was an alcoholic, but Tom did not learn of this: prisoners don't drink. Tom had proven helpful in lining up jobs for convicts upon their release (a solid job prospect was a prerequisite for parole). Sometimes the job would be with Mooney's defense committee; that was all right with the parole board. Sayles was becoming eligible, and Tom was eager to get out a news and propaganda sheet that might reach California voters; he felt this would be money better spent than in continuing tangles with the courts. The two men came to an agreement: Sayles was paroled to defense employment and soon began publishing *Tom Mooney's Monthly*. The small tabloid carried pictures of Mooney and Billings on its masthead, the latter captioned "the silent partner."

As a matter of course, Rena and Sayles were in daily contact. She found him a nice person to have around. Although almost the same height as Tom, he seemed much smaller, probably because he was lean — literally skinny. Unlike her dark and hairy husband, his complexion was light, his eyes were small and blue, and he was almost totally bald, with a greying fringe that must have been blond when he was younger. A small flask of whiskey was always in his hip pocket; but, for a "sipper," he was remarkably reliable and conscientious. He talked entertainingly, had a warm smile and a sympathetic manner, and soon was making a special effort to be kind to Rena on her return from those weekly trips to San Quentin. So many things not done; so many new things to do; such a scolding from Tom. Weeping and woebegone, she needed comforting. Sayles would pull up a favorite chair for her and pat her arm and pour her a little something from his flask.

She would take a nip, and then another, and she did forget her troubles. The progression was simple and fairly rapid: first she took George Sayles into her confidence, then to live in her home, and finally into her bed. She acquired something in addition to this lover — a master, alcohol.

Tom found out. Those closest to the Mooneys said that Mother Mooney got wind of the scandal and went straight to San Quentin with the tale — an educated guess, for she was known to watch after Tom's welfare with a love that could be ferocious. But however he learned, Tom ordered Rena to visit him forthwith. When she came he bluntly put the accusation to her. She had never been good at duplicity; she confessed. From that moment on, even though an occasional endearment passed between them, the marriage was at an end as far as Tom was concerned.

This was not a clean cut ending, however. Tom asked Rena to get a divorce, but she refused. He was hamstrung; he could not publicly announce to his millions of supporters that he had turned his back on her. So he chose to wear his horns in private; anything else would have been a grave error in propaganda.

For her part, Rena seemed to feel that Tom was overdoing it; her actions indicated a hope that he would get over this upset. The morality of her situation was not, to her, of such great moment as her need for protection from loneliness. Tom had no right to ask that she go on and on without companionship and affection, with only one life to live and that shortening day by day. She felt no less devoted to the prisoner; she was giving him as much as the circumstances allowed. She would be his again, to the fullest, the moment he became a free man.

Furthermore, Rena had become accustomed to the role of heroine. The terror and dreariness of jail, the mental torment of the trials, the endless labor of defense work, all caused her to feel she had some right to be a celebrity: to stand under spotlights at the podium and tell the frame-up story, to have a guard of honor when she went to meetings on behalf of Tom and Warren, to hear the applause and feel the warmth of outstretched hands, had become a tonic almost as important as the sip from George's flask. She was an integral part of the Mooney-Billings case. Why should the question of a sleeping partner endanger this position?

But there were repercussions. Tom fired George Sayles forthwith, which brought *Tom Mooney's Monthly* to a halt. Rena abandoned day-to-day defense activity and returned to her best-loved occupation, teaching music. She still took speaking engagements whenever invited; she went now and then to visit Tom, acting as if nothing had gone wrong. Sometimes he made a limp effort to join in the pretense, but usually any gesture of affection from her revolted him. For one thing, she had not turned her back on George, a fact that brought many a stinging remark from Mother Mooney and Sister Anna. John, the bachelor brother, commented to Tom that now he was gladder than ever that he had had nothing to do with "them": presumably women. Tom felt that Rena's refusal to continue with the chores he had heaped upon her constituted a double desertion, and made little attempt to hide his bitterness from his intimates.

The rift soon brought on a difficulty that grew increasingly exasperating to No. 31921. The further Rena moved away from the day-to-day defense work, the less familiar she became with Tom's strategy and tactics. Rena began to make serious mistakes when speaking or acting on his behalf. Without her husband's sense of the dangers of public relations, Rena was simply over her head. But she was entirely unaware of any deficiency, and spoke right up as Tom's wife and partner whenever she sensed the spotlight. One blunder that shook Tom to his foundations came from a stunt dreamed up by a Los Angeles newspaper. Fickert was struggling to make a living at a private law practice in that city. Accompanied by reporters, Rena invaded his office and shouted insults at him. Rena could not be aware of it, but Tom had been courting the former prosecutor through the mails and felt he had just moved him into a position where he might drop his opposition to the prisoner's latest pardon petition!

Never knowing when Rena was next going to put her foot in his mouth caused Tom endless worry. He pleaded with her to keep out of his affairs; he commanded; he threatened. He wrote a stream of warnings to those who had taken over the defense to keep her out of meetings at all costs, and frequently managed to forestall or disrupt her speaking engagements. One of her most aggravating tendencies came to the fore whenever she helped plan defense meetings: if allowed, Rena would fill at least half the program with performances by her most talented music pupils. Injecting such non-sequiturs into the struggles of men fighting framed murder charges brought many an angry outburst from Tom.

Matters reached such a pitch that at the larger rallies he had guards set to prevent her from attending, even as a member of the audience. If she did manage to get in — which she always did, for who would keep Tom's wife out of any defense affair? — Tom's secondary instructions were to bar her from any seat up front or on the stage. Thus many embarrassing, tight-lipped conflicts ensued between Mooney adherents and this woman, frequently half seas over, who refused to be rejected. She was dauntless; the most direct rebuff brought no sign of anger or humiliation; she merely persisted. More than once Tom told her in the most unmistakable terms that he was through with her; she stuck tight, his wife by right, his helpmate by public acclaim.

One day, after a long visit from Rena, Tom wrote a letter to his sister Anna. In regard to his latest pardon petition, Tom wrote: "Rena has just one concern, 'When will he act?' Not that she is interested in bringing that date forward any sooner by her efforts — on, no! But she wants to have her dear friend George dispatched shortly before I get out, so the way will be clear for my reception — the house painted, and all; even the beds, etc. Ain't that nice? How lovely it will be. How lucky I am to have such a wonderful reception awaiting me!"

Anna and Mother Mooney kept supplying information that infuriated Tom the more. After one such session later on, he wrote Mary Gallagher, then his defense secretary, a bitter comment on his domestic prospects if and when freedom came: "I am almost tempted to want to remain. If it were not for the cause that the case represents, I am strongly inclined to think I would choose that course." In another letter Tom told how Rena, thinking him on the verge of a pardon, had twice talked of having her kitchen painted to celebrate his homecoming. He commented bitterly: "I am still here, however, and if music lessons will get me out I sure will be out soon."

Into the breach came Belle Hammerberg. She was more handsome than her sister Rena; she was also much more practical — publicity and applause and speechmaking were not for her. The sisters got along well, and after Belle's divorce they shared a large house on Pacific Avenue. For a number of years Belle also got along fairly well with the caged man in San Quentin — although she did not approve of his treatment of Rena. But aside from love of her sister, Belle helped Tom because of deep hatred for the wrong. She knew Tom had been unjustly convicted; thus she could overlook her growing dislike and give him vital assistance.

When Belle took over, the defense was stagnating. Tom's propaganda mill was shut down; the office was little more than a mail drop with no regular staff. No corps of speakers toured the country shouting against the rape of justice in California. These doldrums were caused partly by dwindling resources and partly reflected Tom's new strategy. Political pressure for a pardon had failed; he had not been able to sway the various Governors. Tom was now taking a quiet, deliberately unspectacular tack. He had set out to compile such a massive and compelling pardon petition that no Governor with any claim to human decency could refuse.

The keystone of this new effort, Tom decided, was to be a complete reversal of opinion by the trial judge and the jurors who had voted to convict him. With Judge Griffin and the youngest juror already won over, the prisoner set out to convince the other jurymen that they, too, should publicly confess a change of heart. There were nine of these men still living, and Tom's goal was ten letters to the Governor asking that Mooney should be pardoned. (This was not the first attempt to use the Mooney jurors. When Fickert reneged on his agreement to support a new trial, Cunha promptly circulated a statement for the jurors to sign, declaring they would have voted to convict Mooney even without Oxman's testimony.)

Tom and Belle worked on these nine men as a team, like a hunter and his bird dog. They found out everything they could about each man: his circumstances and personality, age, occupation, family, friends, business and social associates, psychological traits and personal preferences. They concentrated on one man at a time, and when he knew that man as well as Belle's investigations could picture him, Tom began writing, one letter each day. At first, the letters would dwell on the jurors who had already written the Governor. Another series would discuss the Oxman disclosures; then on to Estelle Smith. For weeks Mooney might write of nothing save prominent Americans' views of the conviction. The ramifications of the frame-up were virtually endless, so Tom did not lack for material. At intervals the barrage of letters would be interspersed with personal visits from Belle; she was most helpful in changing the minds of set old men, for her face was open and honest, and her certainty of Tom's innocence impressed the most stubborn. Gradually Belle and the prisoner worked this campaign until only one juror remained alive and unsigned. He was a San Francisco hardware merchant named John W. Miller, and a lesser man than Tom Mooney would have given up on him. It took five years to turn the hardware man around. During this long tussle, Tom at one point considered asking Mother Mooney to approach Miller's mother: if Mother Mooney convinced Mother Miller that Tom was innocent, then she would be morally bound to convey this realization to her own son; if he was a good son, he would take the maternal advice and write the Governor. Whether or not this scheme was carried out, water dripping on stone will eventually leave its mark; Miller slowly, slowly changed his mind. At one stage he conceded doubts about Tom's guilt, but told Belle it was not his policy to write letters to the Governor on behalf of anyone. Belle then nudged him into agreeing that she could write the Governor announcing that John W. Miller had told her he thought Tom Mooney should be pardoned. She wrote such a letter, and for a long time things rested thus; Tom had the support of the trial judge and nine and one-half of the ten living jurors. Finally — Tom never knew exactly why — John W. Miller completed his about-face. On December 2, 1929, he wrote his letter to the Governor, and that phase of the pardon application was now ready.

Belle accomplished much more for Tom. She got a letter asking for a gubernatorial pardon out of District Attorney Matt Brady, the former police judge who, in 1917, had held Oxman to answer for perjury. Brady had readily agreed to write the letter; the real task was persuading him to find (and give the defense) a document, sequestered by the prosecution, which shed further light on the spurious nature of Oxman's testimony. This document had a most spectacular history:

In the closing months of 1916, Fickert, hot on the trail of witnesses for the bombing trials, heard that an Oregonian named Oxman was telling people he had seen the placing of the bomb in San Francisco on Preparedness Day. The D.A. learned Oxman was enroute to Kansas City, shipping a herd of cattle to market, and hired the Burns Detective Agency to have its Kansas City office look for Oxman. The local operative found the cattleman, got his story in written form and had it sworn to before a notary public. The affidavit was sent to Fickert, direct contact was made with Oxman, and the game was on.

As any criminal lawyer knows, a man's statement taken at first blush, before he knows exactly what may be expected, is more likely to be accurate than later statements made after hearing any particular theory. Immediately after Oxman left the witness stand in Mooney's trial, Bourke Cockran, chief defense attorney, had demanded the right to see the Kansas City affidavit. Cockran asked both Fickert and Cunha for it, and Fickert promised to produce it. However, the transcript of Tom's trial failed to show any such request or dialogue; whereupon the defense claimed that if the record was silent on that point, it must have been doctored.

For years the defense had tried mightily to locate that statement. Tom had written the Burns Detective Agency; he had appealed directly to Matt Brady, after he became District Attorney; in early 1924 Tom had tackled Fickert himself. The results had been zero. Tom had even accused Brady (intermittently one of his supporters) of deliberately withholding the document.

Finally Belle Hammerberg had a long talk with Brady; she must have been persuasive, for he put his clerks to an all-out effort and they found a paper purporting to be a copy of Oxman's Kansas City statement. From this, the defense had traced the notary public who had taken Oxman's affidavit. This man had long since moved to Chicago and much effort was expended to find him — but it turned out to be well worth the trouble. The notary, William C. Crowe, made affidavit that the copy shown him was, to the best of his recollection and belief, a true copy of what F.C. Oxman had sworn to in the stockyards in 1916.

Comparison of that stockyard affidavit with Oxman's testimony in court was most revealing:

In Kansas City:	*In court:*
Oxman placed himself at Washington Street near Front, which intersect eight blocks from the bomb scene; [his streets seemed to fit downtown Portland, Oregon better than downtown San Francisco.]	Oxman placed himself at the southwest corner of Steuart and Market Streets, within a few feet of the blast.
From pictures shown him by the operative, Oxman identified Weinberg as the driver, and Mooney as the man sitting beside him in the front seat, but	Oxman said Mooney was holding the bomb suitcase on the car's running board; Billings and the unidentified man got out of the back seat where they were

described him as of medium build, about 5 feet 6 inches, 155-160 pounds, light complexion, blue eyes, age 25 to 27. He said "Mooney" did not leave the car and made no mention of holding the suitcase on the running board.

Oxman said that as the two men who placed the suitcase returned toward the car, he heard them conversing in a foreign language he could not understand. The unidentified man did not get back in the car or speak to Mooney.

sitting with Rena and took turns carrying the suitcase. Mooney got out of the car, very excited, and watched Billings place the suitcase.

Oxman said Billings and the unidentified man, after placing the suitcase, joined Mooney in a doorway; he heard Mooney say to Billings: "Give it to him and let him go. We must get away from here; the bulls will be after us." Billings handed something to the third man, who then disappeared.

Belle's gentle persistence brought many things. Police Captains Matheson and Goff did not write requesting a pardon without many visits. But Belle was not an organizer; only those things were done that she could find time to do herself. As with Rena, Tom verged on the tyrannical; he grumbled and Belle grew weary. His scoldings did not hurt her as they had Rena, for her involvement was much more impersonal. Nevertheless the continual overloading and sparse appreciation wore Belle's idealism down to the point where she quietly dropped out.

Warren Knox Billings, a New Yorker of English-German stock, arrived in San Francisco in 1912. He was 19, and thought he was en route to Mexico to join Pancho Villa and become a revolutionary. His concept of revolutions was dim, but he knew they involved excitement and danger, conditions that fascinated him. So small was he, so immature in appearance, that he could have passed for a lad of 14.

He wore his shock of reddish-gold hair high off his forehead, pompadour fashion, and he had a penchant for big stiff collars that swallowed up his neck and emphasized his tinyness. His manner was easy and he was blessed with an infectious grin, but his life, from infancy, had been far from easy. He was already familiar with the thrills and pains of taking chances.

His poverty-stricken family had lived in the semi-rural fringe of Brooklyn under the domination of a surrogate father, a Brooklyn cop who had taken the place of Billings' real father, who had died when the boy was two years old. The cop, the husband of Warren's grown sister, was tyrannical and grasping, and forced the boy to perform arduous chores with no reward — except escaping the all-too-frequent thrashings. The punishments became increasingly severe and the growing boy became increasingly rebellious, until one day he fended off an impending belting by grabbing a loaded rifle. From then on tyrant and youth kept a surly distance, with the tension easing somewhat when Billings began to find jobs. He worked most frequently as a leather cutter in shoe factories; in slack times he found temporary employment as a streetcar conductor. There he quickly learned the art of pocketing an occasional nickel without getting caught too often by the company stooges who were always riding the cars. He also acquired a set of burglar tools, which he claimed he never used but which got him into serious trouble at least once.

With this rugged schooling Billings developed a cool stubbornness that kept him steady when confronted by danger, no matter how violent. Still, he could change in an instant from iciness to silly giggles, even when his circumstances were anything but funny. Long before he left Brooklyn, Billings had become cynical about schoolbook moralities such as honesty, chastity, and respectability. In the world he knew such codes seemed to have slight value.

Life got complicated in Brooklyn and wanderlust seized Billings; Pancho Villa was much in the news those days, and Billings thought the Mexican leader could probably use a young Gringo lieutenant who knew how to handle a gun. He took off across the continent, lacking money but loaded with dreams; he rode the rods or the blind baggage, occasionally sneaking into the luxury of a boxcar. He made the acquaintance of a host of hoboes, including articulate men aware of life and its perplexities, men who made good talk while cooking a can of mulligan beneath a railroad bridge. Billings met cops here and there and a deputy sheriff or two, and saw the inside of several jails. Sometimes he earned a quick dollar; then he paid for his meals and slept between sheets. Sometimes the grub was good and the girls were kind — but mostly it was quite the opposite.

Luck in stealing train rides took Billings to the northwest, not toward Mexico. Arriving in Oregon in the winter of 1913, still determined to join up with Pancho Villa, Billings headed south. Riding blind baggage over the Siskiyous into California, he nearly froze his fingers off. The burglar tools got him into trouble in Sacramento, but he talked his way out and finally reached San Francisco. He had been on the road nearly a year.

It was easy to find a job, but no sooner had Billings gone to work as a leather cutter in a shoe factory than the place was hit by a strike. This brought the nineteen-year-old wanderer into contact with a black-haired, beetle-browed labor organizer, nearly eleven years older, named Tom Mooney.

Tom quickly hatched up a scheme to occupy this daring young man. Let him work behind the picket lines in the struck shop, spying for union labor. Cutting leather as a front, he could report to Mooney who the scabs were, getting names and addresses wherever possible, so union "educational committees" could call on the scabs and persuade them to mend their ways. Such educational attempts could be peaceable, or they could end up in brawls depending on the truculence of the scab. If possible, Billings was also to spy on the foreman and the manager in hopes of giving the strikers clues as to their prospects for victory.

This assignment fitted Billings' style exactly, and he put himself vigorously to his new task. Occasionally Mooney encouraged him with small sums of money, and this also tickled the lad's fancy. It was delightful, taking in the cash with both hands.

It was not long, however, before Billings came to grief. One night a serious act of sabotage took place in the struck plant, ruining hundreds of pairs of shoes. Billings felt he was under suspicion and decided the time had come to quit. While he was waiting for his closing pay, a company guard began plying him with questions. Billings grew resentful, the guard persisted, and the two got into a scuffle for possession of the young worker's gun. (There was nothing unusual about his carrying a weapon; men working under strike conditions were supposed to be prepared to protect themselves.) An onlooker jumped into the fray to help the guard, and all three grabbed for the gun. It fired, the bullet ripping the tip of Billings' left thumb and permanently damaging the nail, then hitting the interloper in the foot.

Billings was arrested and charged with assault with intent to commit murder, but the case — tried in front of Judge Dunne — was dismissed for lack of evidence: no one could be sure whose finger had found the trigger.

Not long thereafter a protracted and violent struggle took place between the anti-union Pacific Gas & Electric Company and the electrical workers' union. Mooney was making himself useful to the strikers in many ways.

Billings hung out in a saloon near the union's strike headquarters. It was a good place to pick up "moonlighting" jobs, some of them interesting and well-paid. But here Billings' luck began to turn sour; he let someone talk him into carrying a suitcase by train from Oakland to Sacramento — the job that landed him in the clutches of Martin Swanson and the PG&E and, in due course, in Folsom Prison.

A year and a half later, out on parole and finding no work in San Francisco, Billings hoboed his way to Denver. There his youthful appearance and ingratiating smile won him a job with an employer who was kindly and had a religious turn of mind. Soon this man invited his new employee to join a men's Bible class — a little odd, maybe, for such a hard little nut as Warren K. Billings, but the class brought back some pleasant childhood memories of Sunday school. Billings, then twenty-two, found himself being treated hospitably by "nice" chaps his own age, and their kindnesses disarmed him. He was unable to sneer when they spoke of God, a personage he had heard put down as either the figment of overheated imaginations or as king of the finks. He began to think seriously of giving God and Jesus and the Holy Ghost another try, particularly after evenings spent in the homes of his Bible classmates, chatting with their sisters, eating their food and telling his tales of a sad, misspent youth and the cruel brother-in-law.

They convinced him: he might hope for a better life if only he would bare his breast to God and his fellow man and purge himself of sin. He thought privately of this purging business, wondering how one did such a thing. The answer came unexpectedly at a class banquet. His employer got up and posed a practical question: he had caught a young man attempting to pass a forged check, and the culprit was pleading for a chance to make good. As a Christian, should he grant that plea, or should he turn the miscreant over to the police?

Billings jumped to his feet and pleaded for the second chance, saying what a terrible thing it was to send a man to prison. He blurted out that he spoke from experience, having done time in prison. Billings saw at once he had made a terrible mistake. The faces of those nice young men fell and fell until they could fall no lower. As the banquet broke up, some of the class members cut him dead; the smoothest could muster no more than an embarrassed "Goodnight."

Before that evening ended Billings had reconverted; he was The Kid again. He knew of a saloon where the bartender believed he was of age and would sell him a drink. He hastened there, putting the Holy Bible and all the characters in it behind him forevermore. Soon he was back in San Francisco's Mission District, living at a rooming house where the landlady had a fancy for young men, working on and off as a mechanic's helper, doing little jobs for striking unions and running errands for Tom Mooney.

1930 - - - -

Thirteen years had gone by since Mooney and Billings had had any contact other than through correspondence or verbal messages carried by visitors. When Billings was sent to Folsom Prison, they had trusted each other completely. Recognizing that Mooney was the leading spirit and had the better case (he had no prior convictions and his judge and, eventually, jurors had come out in favor of a pardon) Billings had been willing to be "the silent partner" while Tom fought tooth and nail for pardon. If Tom won freedom, surely Billings could not long be denied.

Thirteen years, however, can become an eternity to a man in prison, and Billings began to get restive. There was talk that he might be willing to accept parole — a proposition Tom still fought as vehemently as he had fought the death sentence. To the man in San Quentin, release on such terms would be freedom in name only. It would force him to knuckle down to lawmen who would be only too glad to return him to custody as a parole violator if he should take a stand on any labor or political controversy. And accepting parole would be tantamount to a confession of guilt, in Tom's view.

It had been in the usual order of things to incarcerate one man in San Quentin and the other in Folsom, for "Q" was intended primarily for first-timers and Folsom was the *oubliette* for supposedly hardened criminals. And from the prosecution viewpoint the separation had also been clever. James Brennan, the deputy district attorney who had prosecuted Billings, had always thought that, given time, The Kid would reveal the true story of Preparedness Day; and Brennan was not alone. If there was ever to be such a revelation, its time was coming, for thirteen years had dimmed the magnetism that had once bound The Kid to Mooney.

The rift was deepened by Paul Scharrenberg, secretary of the State Federation of Labor and originally a valued supporter of both Mooney and Billings. Tom had sensed an insidious change in Scharrenberg's support as early as 1926, when C.C. Young, a man of somewhat liberal reputation, had been elected Governor. In the 1922 campaign, Tom had issued defense literature supporting the man who won, and had got nothing for his pains. In this campaign Mooney kept hands off, even though friends told him Young might be expected to grant a pardon. Scharrenberg, on the other hand, had done everything possible to help elect Young, marshalling union voters, securing endorsements, putting up labor money, and otherwise working himself into the personal orbit and esteem of the candidate.

When Young won, Scharrenberg (appointed state Director of Industrial Relations) doubled in political stature overnight and, in Mooney's opinion, became a sycophant seeking always to earn smiles from the new Governor. Thus, when Young temporized on labor's most important case, Scharrenberg temporized; when Young caused delay after delay, Scharrenberg failed to press for action. When Young hinted that he could not pardon Mooney but would be delighted to let him out on parole, Scharrenberg went about the California labor movement beating the drums for parole.

When Fremont Older and other influential supporters began to lean toward the parole idea, Tom was like a monarch facing a palace coup; he gave the rough side of his tongue to anyone who tried to discuss the subject with him. It was a thunderclap to Tom's ears when he heard Billings might take the easy way out; and there was another ominous rumble from up Folsom way: Billings was beginning to think he could make better progress through Scharrenberg and men like him than by taking Tom's course — appealing to lesser labor leaders and public figures and trying to inflame the radical sensibilities of rank-and-file trade unionists. Irate letters passed between the prisoners; emissaries traveled back and forth, seeking to placate Tom and Warren. No. 31921 prevailed, and the notion of parole faded away.

There remained, however, the problem of Billings' attachment to Scharrenberg, whom Tom thought more dangerous than an avowed enemy. Billings had a volunteer secretary named Madeline Weiland, and who also performed secretarial work for Scharrenberg for pay. Tom saw this woman as a regular link between the little man in Folsom Prison and the hated AFL hierarchy.

For a time, however, there were other and more pleasing prospects. Governor Young had been most gracious with a labor delegation that came calling on Mooney's behalf. The Governor visited Fremont Older and gave the impression that the Mooney-Billings case would soon be settled — and settled right.

Tom yielded to this new mood to the point where he visited the prison tailor shop to be measured for his "going-away" suit. Rumors of an impending pardon grew so strong that many Mooney adherents slackened their efforts, particularly in the most sensitive area of fund-raising. This brought scoldings from Tom who, although remaining outwardly diplomatic toward those on high, saw no sense in dissolving his defense apparatus before the pardon was actually in hand. Tom reminded his friends and helpers, as he always did when they displeased him, that "I am the man who is doing the time." In other words, Tom was more than the prisoner. He was the brain and heart and soul of labor's most famous case: the boss!

Still, there were several sectors of the battleground beyond the control of any man shut up in a cell. Governor Young — prompted, Tom believed, by the Scharrenberg-Weiland-Billings cabal — came to Fremont Older with a proposition: since the cases of Mooney and Billings were inseparable, he could not in fairness pardon the one without pardoning the other. Billings, according to the law governing recidivists, could not be pardoned without first winning a formal recommendation from the California Supreme Court. Young suggested that Billings ought to apply for such a recommendation.

Mooney instantly saw the hook and its barb. He sent sizzling letters to Billings and Older, pointing out there was no reason to believe the justices would be any more favorable to the Mooney-Billings cause than they had been in the past, and were almost certain to refuse the recommendation, leaving the Governor free to ignore both prisoners.

Billings, like Older and many others, could see neither hook nor barb. They were dazzled by a rumor that the State Supreme Court justices would vote four to three in favor of pardoning Billings, and stood as firm as though the opinion had already been written and published.

The Kid's wish to come out of oblivion struck sympathy throughout the defense team. For thirteen years the hue and cry had centered upon Mooney, with Billings little more than an addendum. Now many liberals began to feel Billings was entitled to end his self-effacement; perhaps Tom Mooney deserved rebuff.

Just as a blind man develops other senses to overcome the deprivations of sightlessness, the imprisoned Tom Mooney had grown remarkably sensitive to the moods and trends of the times. Although very much aware of the dangers of Billings' move, Tom was stung by such criticisms. He could not agree — but neither could he risk mutiny in his own camp. Never let it be said that Tom Mooney was blocking Billings' freedom. Therefore, Tom let himself be pushed into reluctant agreement. Word was passed privately to Governor Young that his proposal would be welcome; Young made public the proposition he had suggested privately to the newspaper editor; Billings promptly filed his application with the State Supreme Court.

The story persisted; four of the justices favored Billings. Older believed it; Rena told Tom it was a certainty; many others were also convinced. But Tom cancelled the order for his "going-away" suit. He knew the State Supreme Court all too well, and he had lost all faith in Governor Young.

The news came out on July Fourth, 1930, making a splendid holiday headline. The court decided six to one against Billings, the lone dissenter being Justice William H. Langdon, the man who in earlier days had preceded Fickert as District Attorney of San Francisco and had done his utmost to rid The City of corruption.

Three days later all those patient years of work by Tom Mooney and Belle Hammerberg, all those letters from officials, trial jurors and others involved in the case, all the marshalling of facts proving that Mooney and Billings had been convicted by perjured testimony, came to a sudden zero. As Tom had predicted, Governor Young denied his pardon application.

Belle Hammerberg, Madeline Weiland (Billings' cousin), Mary, John and Anna Mooney at courtroom hearing.

8

The Syphilitic Waiter

The twin actions of the court and the Governor had several offshoots, some of which provoked unexpected, dramatic reverberations.

Rena wept, telling reporters: "I had planned to have Tom home for the holiday. It would have been the day after our wedding anniversary."

Mother Mooney, now age 82, was too old for tears. "Sure, and it is the will of God," she told the press. "The innocent must suffer, often enough, and the Good Lord in His wisdom knows why. . . Mind, and I don't go to carry courage to Tom. It's him who's always been the brave one and kept up the faith of those on the outside."

Tom was permitted to hold an interview in the warden's office, and he minced no words: he denounced the Governor for "political trickery," and called the court's decision "one of the crudest and most unscholarly documents I've ever seen. True Californians should hang their heads in shame over it."

This outburst brought the warden to his feet, shouting: "That's all, Mooney! I'm not going to let you turn this prison into a political headquarters."

Once again, Fremont Older voiced his feelings in his newspaper, stating that in the past year Governor Young had told at least three prominent Californians that he intended to pardon Mooney. There was a single plus for the defense: in the Governor's rather lengthy denial he dismissed Oxman as a "romancer." Older connected this with a statement made a couple of years earlier by William McNevin, foreman of the Mooney jury, who had told Young face to face in 1928: "Without the evidence of Oxman there would have been a hung jury, and without the evidence of MacDonald, Mooney would have been acquitted." How, asked Older, could the Governor ignore such a declaration?

The most important offshoots of the decision, however, were sparked by two independent concurring opinions in the six to one decision against Billings. One, written by Justice John Shenk, stated that it might have been advisable to examine the whole Mooney-Billings case rather than relying solely on Billings' trial record. This, it was later disclosed, referred to a hint the court had thrown out to Billings during its deliberations: if John MacDonald could be located, the court might be interested in whatever he had to say.

This feeler was apparently based on a minor sensation that had occurred nearly a decade earlier in 1921. MacDonald had suddenly surfaced in New Jersey with an affidavit swearing that all the testimony he had given in the bombing trials had been false. His perjury, the waiter declared, had been committed under the specific instructions of Fickert. The defense had brought MacDonald, desperately ill and expected to die at any time, to California — but for naught. The foreman of the San Francisco Grand Jury bluntly told the tottery waiter that if he made formal admission of perjury he would undoubtedly be indicted for the crime and probably end his days in prison. His story untold except in the press, MacDonald had slunk back East.

Billings had scotched the court's hint by writing a letter to the seven justices saying he wished his application to stand upon the material he had presented; nothing more. The court had assumed this meant Billings was apprehensive as to what MacDonald might reveal. Actually, Billings and everyone else — including the justices — assumed that the sick old derelict had long since died. On this assumption, Billings was opposed to delaying action on his application with a wild goose chase after a ghost.*

---

*As a reporter on the *Oakland Tribune* and the son-in-law of the Chief Justice of the State Supreme Court, I was privy to both personal remarks and intra-court

The other independent concurring opinion against Billings was written by Justice John W. Preston, who had been United States District Attorney in San Francisco at the time of Preparedness Day. He denied Billings' application primarily on the ground that the prisoner had brought forth nothing that might lead to the actual perpetrator of the crime. This set up a legalistic hullabaloo. The defense said Preston was subverting the principle of American jurisprudence that holds the accused innocent until proven guilty. The other side argued that in this case, that principle had already been carried to conclusion: Billings had been proven guilty. After conviction, Preston held, the convict could escape penalty only by pinning the crime on some other suspect.

By this time, Mooney and Billings had become something of a cause in American journalism. Support for the two had been the policy of the national Scripps-Howard chain of newspapers since shortly after the bombing. Now Scripps-Howard bet cash and resources on the outside chance that John MacDonald might still be alive, and able to call the State's bluff. All papers in the chain carried front page stories on the hunt for MacDonald, with photographs front and profile, offering $500 for information leading to his discovery. "John MacDonalds" popped up all over the United States, either directly or through identifications made by reward seekers, but the general opinion was that this was nothing more than a newspaper promotional stunt.

It took only four days for the snickers to die. The real John MacDonald, still alive and still in poor health, was found operating an elevator in a Baltimore apartment house. He readily agreed to return to California and repeat the story he had told in 1921. He now had virtually nothing to fear, for the passage of time had given him the benefit of the statute of limitations. "I am anxious to tell the truth," he told the world through interviews arranged by pro-Mooney men who rushed to guard him — no chances were being taken with this frail weather vane.

Now it was Governor Young's turn to squirm. The August primary elections of 1930 were nearing, and Young was anxious to win the Republican nomination — at that time tantamount to reelection in California.

---

gossip of California's highest judicial body. I learned that the justices agreed with Billings on only one thing — the assumption that MacDonald was safely dead.

Young's first move was to announce that "to keep the case out of politics" he would not grant MacDonald a hearing until after the primary. Mooney publicists in the East told Scripps-Howard writers that the former waiter had better be heard quickly, lest he never be heard at all. The Governor, dodging brickbats from several directions, did a quick turnabout and offered MacDonald an immediate hearing with travel expenses paid by the State.

Again public interest in the fates of Mooney and Billings grew red hot. Again Mooney warned against any further testing of the State Supreme Court by Billings. Again Billings ignored the warning; he let Ed McKenzie, now his attorney, file a petition for rehearing, asking this time for a decision based upon "facts obtainable from any source."

MacDonald became a celebrity overnight. He traveled westward with a retinue of lawyers, reporters, and labor officials. Interviews with the press were staged in every major city his train passed through. Daily progress bulletins were issued, for his physical and mental ability to withstand the journey became matters of common concern. These bulletins asserted that although MacDonald had left Baltimore in feeble and gloomy condition, he seemed to improve the nearer he got to California.

Furthermore, defense supporters were making a major effort to offset a sarcastic comment, made by the justices in the majority opinion denying Billings' pardon, that MacDonald's 1921 affidavit must have been motivated by the fact that "he failed to receive the reward which he claims to have been promised." Defense lawyers promised an armful of affidavits proving that the derelict had been spurred to recant his trial testimony not by greed but by a guilty conscience and fear of imminent death. In one of these affidavits, the man who had been MacDonald's employer in 1921 swore that all who heard and saw the waiter's accusations believed they were witnessing a deathbed confession.

MacDonald was described as sporting new clothing and a straw hat. Fancy raiment, however, could not hide his staggers, or his inability to smile, or the difficulty he had in uttering an audible sentence. He had a crushed appearance that betrayed the personality living somewhere within that wispy shell.

Coming West with the man of the moment was Frank P. Walsh, the famous attorney who had always believed in Mooney's innocence.

Years before he had taken on the job of chief defense counsel in a scene made to order for the finest Irish dramatist. The old orator, Bourke Cockran, had labored as long and as hard for Mooney as any one could, and when he lay down to die he had summoned to his bedside that other great Irish lawyer, Walsh. In passing the defense baton on to his younger friend, the dying Cockran exacted a sacred promise; Walsh would do all in his power to set Tom Mooney free. Walsh was accompanied by a coterie of lawyers, coming West like him at their own expense to do what they could to right the great wrong the State of California was imposing upon innocent men.

With perfect timing, MacDonald arrived in San Francisco on the anniversary of Preparedness Day. Reporters and defense figures, including McKenzie, met the MacDonald group and proceeded directly to the State Building in San Francisco's Civic Center for a private audience with the Governor, which Young stressed was not a hearing. The session was brief and distasteful to the defense. The Governor, speaking only to the attorneys and ignoring the old waiter, proposed that the State Supreme Court should examine the witness before Young heard MacDonald. Reporters outside could plainly hear Walsh's shouted protests; the proposal would reverse the natural sequence of events and imperil the interests of Tom Mooney. However, the Governor had spoken, and his wishes prevailed.

During the brief interval while the stage was being set for Billings' rehearing, Mooney made a new plea for a pardon, direct to the Governor. Meanwhile in New York City three thousand persons attended a rally in Union Square, sponsored by Socialists, to hear famous Americans such as Rabbi Stephen S. Wise, newspaper columnist Heywood Broun, and lawyer Dudley Field Malone denounce justice as practiced in California. Malone, whose reputation extended far beyond the confines of America, called the men who graced the highest judicial posts in California "country lawyers and Tories who don't know how to act on the bench."

In examining MacDonald, to meet legal technicalities the justices decided to constitute themselves as a special judicial commission to the Governor, rather than a court. And the justices appointed Fred Berry (the former deputy district attorney — and Fickert's companion on one of the occasions when the latter had used Fremont Older as a punching bag) "to represent the people." This caused lifted eyebrows, notably among defense counsel; objections brought the judicial explanation that Berry would not act as a "prosecutor"; the justices themselves would examine the witness or witnesses.

The hearing opened amid pomp, circumstance and excitement. The courtroom, semi-circular and draped in dark blue velvet, normally held not much more than a hundred persons. Since the justices were acting as a special judicial commission, they sat on the same level as the spectators, leaving the bench vacant. The witness chair was elevated one step, centering attention upon its occupant and also helping MacDonald's weak voice carry further. Admission was by special tickets issued by the court. Six detectives stood guard in the courtroom, while four policemen guarded the elevators, shoving back all who could not show tickets. Mother Mooney, who assumed she had the right to be present in all matters pertaining to her son, came empty-handed. The old lady stood back, impotent but imploring, until a reporter noticed her plight and wangled a ticket for her. A makeshift press room was set up on the floor directly beneath the courtroom with a battery of telegraphers to service writers from important newspapers and magazines all over the world.

Cops were scattered throughout the corridors and stairways of the building. Crowds pressed up the broad front steps, struggling to see, to hear, to enter; more crowds gathered under the trees in the park across the street.

Through this gauntlet on the opening day of the hearing came Charles Fickert. He had arrived from Los Angeles, announcing his intention of facing his traducer, the syphilitic waiter. As he mounted the steps of the State Building, a surge went through the crowd, raising the noise level by several decibels. A drunk shook his fist, shouting curses until cops hustled him away. From the day Ed McKenzie returned from Chicago with the Oxman letters, Fickert's star had declined, becoming a dramatic slide after he lost the race for governor. Out of office and discredited, he had become an object of pity among his most faithful associates of better times. Tom Mooney was speaking more and more openly about his ancient adversary as a wine bum, sunk so low that he went from speakeasy to speakeasy, begging for drinks among men once honored to be in his company. The reporters were kinder than Mooney; they described Fickert as gentle and rather bumbling, with an awkward gait, a man with his fires drawn, resigned to vicissitudes of life.

The seven justices agreed among themselves that, because of his previous experience as a U.S. District Attorney, Justice Preston would take the lead in questioning MacDonald. Preston hailed from Tennessee and was in full vigor, with a voice he could snap like a bull whip and the temperament to make full use of it — a lion to MacDonald's mouse. Preston also enjoyed unusual advantages because this was not technically a court of law; although he was playing the role of prosecutor, he was still Associate Justice of the Supreme Court of California. Ordinary courtroom procedures did not apply: no counsel represented the syphilitic waiter; no judge restrained Mr. Justice Preston. To make the situation even more lopsided, MacDonald came to the witness chair confessing that he had lied under oath; his hands were unclean.

MacDonald began to talk. In essence, his story was that at the direction of Fickert, Cunha, and Police Sergeant (now Captain) Goff — but primarily Fickert — he had given sworn testimony based upon a single shred of fact: he had seen someone put a suitcase down at or near the point of explosion. Never again, to his knowledge, had he seen that man — or those men: he seemed uncertain now whether he had seen one man, or two men.

Justice Preston lost little time in tearing into MacDonald, and within minutes the one-sidedness of the contest became all too apparent. After half a dozen questions the old waiter was in tears, cringing, trembling, his answers so low that the justices had to strain to make them out. His big white handkerchief came into play, and more often than not his face was hidden in it.

If he lied under oath when he helped condemn one man to life imprisonment and another to death, had he not also lied, and was he not lying now, when he said that Fickert had prompted him in perjury? He was obviously not addicted to truth-telling. Did not the preponderance of known facts indicate him to be an habitual liar? What caused him to lie? Money? Where had he acquired such a bad habit? How could he prove that he could lie one year and tell the truth the next? Thus Preston lashed MacDonald, demanding in a hundred different shouts and pleadings to know which if any of MacDonald's stories might be worthy of belief.

"I was in the clutches of Fickert and couldn't get out," was MacDonald's most coherent answer.

While this verbal mayhem was in progress, a sideshow was

developing outside the courtroom. Some years earlier, following the lead of Duncan Matheson, Captain Goff had written the then Governor of California expressing his doubts as to the validity of Mooney's conviction and saying he felt the prisoner deserved a pardon. While Goff's letter named only Mooney, in practical terms he had also spoken on behalf of freedom for Billings. So matters had stood until MacDonald named Goff as one of the officials who had prompted him to commit perjury. Overnight this had cost the defense the support of Captain Goff. Publicly he denied MacDonald's accusation; privately he began passing the word that new information had caused him to think Mooney and Billings may have had something to do with that bombing, after all.

As MacDonald's hearing got under way, Goff was in a frenzy searching for a lost document. Goff recalled that he first met the sickly waiter on the Monday after Preparedness Day. MacDonald had come to the Bomb Bureau and had made statements that had been put into writing by Officers McCullough and Hughes. Shortly thereafter those original statements had disappeared. The defense knew of their existence and had made official request to see them during the Billings trial — but they had never been produced. Fourteen years later, Captain Goff suddenly became as anxious to see those missing statements as defense attorney Maxwell McNutt had ever been.

The lean, hawk-faced policeman had only the faintest recollection of the statements, but felt they might contain something that would help disprove MacDonald's charges. Police files on the bombing cases had gotten out of hand. Material had continued to come in, year after year, and the whole accumulation was now a mass of documents in various stages of disintegration, piled ceiling high and wall to wall in one of the basement rooms under the Hall of Justice. Finding the needle in the haystack could not have been much more difficult.

Goff took his problems to Chief Justice Waste, thinking the court would also be interested in MacDonald's original statements; also he asked other public officials for help. As a result, court clerks, police clerks, and deputy county clerks dug away in that haystack for several days.

While this search went on, Justice Preston continued his dismemberment of MacDonald. Had he received money from the prosecution? Once Fickert had paid him $20 directly, the waiter answered, but mostly the money had come through the Chamber of Commerce attorney, Frank Drew. "He paid me every time I went there," MacDonald said. He also told of being sent to a farm near Tracy to keep him safe between trials, where he had been paid a farmhand's wages but had never done a lick of work.

It was not very long after his first visit to the Hall of Justice, MacDonald related, before he began meeting regularly with Fickert. "A whole pack of lies bumped into my head."

Preston: "A pack of lies that bumped into your head. When did you begin to pack those lies into your head?"

MacDonald: "I did not pack them into my head."

Preston: "Who was the first man that started putting them in your head?"

MacDonald: "Mr. Fickert."

If MacDonald scored on that exchange, Preston came right back with a double score. In 1921, shortly before making his "death-bed" affidavit, MacDonald had written Duncan Matheson offering to repeat his testimony of 1916 and 1917 if there should be a new trial for Mooney. In this letter he had reaffirmed a statement made under oath against Billings: "As God is my judge I am telling the truth."

Had MacDonald written such a letter? No answer. "Are you sitting there now with God judging you to be a liar?" The waiter took refuge in his handkerchief. Eventually, however, Preston wrung from him the admission that he had written the letter. His motive? "I was hoping to keep a piece of the reward."

With the financial motive established in terms of MacDonald's relations with the prosecution, and with the implication that similar considerations had turned him toward the defense, Preston urged the witness to discuss the business of lying in greater depth. What about Mr. Cunha? This was the man, MacDonald responded, who had caused him to set the time [when he claimed to have seen the bomb suitcase being placed] earlier in the Mooney trial than he had in the case of Billings.

Finally all this questioning reached the crucial point. Preston: "You don't know which is the truth and which isn't?" MacDonald: "Yes."*

---

*While this interplay was taking place for the record, in the evenings among relatives

Just as it appeared that Preston had wrung from the old derelict every damaging admission the State of California could desire, a very pleased Captain Goff entered the courtroom. The missing statements had been found! Preston virtually snatched them from the policeman's hand.

The statement witnessed by Officer Hughes: MacDonald had claimed to have seen a man placing the suitcase. He was 25 or 30 years old, five feet seven inches tall, weighed about 145 pounds, smooth shaven, and wearing a dark suit and soft brown hat. The second man, described by MacDonald as having met his confederate at a nearby saloon door, had been put down as 25 to 30 years old, five feet eight inches tall, weight 145 pounds, medium build and complexion, smooth shaven and wearing a dark suit and a fedora hat.

The statement witnessed by Officer McCullough: The man with the suitcase was 30 to 35 years old, five feet seven or eight inches tall, weight 145 to 150 pounds, dark complexioned, wearing a brown hat. The second man had been described as 25 to 30 years old, five feet eight inches tall, weight 145 pounds, of medium complexion and a dark blue serge suit and a grey fedora hat.

Two fairly consistent descriptions — but neither was consistent with the appearance of Billings or Mooney: Mooney, the older and taller of the two, was five feet ten inches tall, and a hefty 190 pounds, fair but with dark brows. Billings was 22, but looked much younger, fair complected, and short and slight at five feet four inches, 122 pounds.

Justice Preston used the statements to rattle the witness into utter helplessness and then dropped him, finished.

It was Ed McKenzie's turn. From his questions it appears he was intent upon the final ruination of the whimpering thing in the witness chair; he gloated over those original statements as much as, if not more, than Goff and Preston.

Billings' attorney had one of the most famous exhibits in the bombing trials set up in the room: a picture enlarged 25,000 times from a snapshot taken on the roof of the Eilers building — over a mile from the site of the bombing — during the Preparedness Day

and close friends, Chief Justice Waste was having a high old time describing the scene and the reactions of the participants. He remarked that Preston was playing it "pretty rough," but that his performance was a pleasure to watch.

Alibi photo hidden for years by the prosecution. Tom in light suit, Rena standing on roof of building where Rena had her studio. When greatly enlarged, sidewalk clock (white dot on lower left) shows time as 2:01. Explosion was a mile away, five minutes later.

parade. This was the building which housed the Mooney's living quarters and Rena's music studio. Practically everyone in the seven story structure had gone to the roof that afternoon for a grandstand view of the marchers and bands and flags coming up Market Street. A clerk in the ground floor music company, Wade Hamilton, had taken photographs of this rooftop assemblage and some of them clearly showed Tom Mooney, dressed in a light-colored "ice cream" suit, leaning over the parapet, with the face of a big sidewalk clock on the street below setting the time at 2:01 PM, exactly five minutes before the bomb went off. When Hamilton saw the developed snapshots and realized he had photographed a bombing defendant, he turned the pictures over to the police. However, Mooney had vaguely recalled someone snapping pictures on the roof that afternoon, and this quickly led the defense to young Hamilton and then to demand that the prosecution make these invaluable alibis available to the defense. Finally, after the issuance of court orders and fierce wrangling, the police had produced Hamilton's films just long enough for the defense to get prints from them. After that the films disappeared, gone forever.

Now, with the best enlargement set up on an easel, McKenzie directed MacDonald's attention to Mooney and asked the witness to say what color the suit was. MacDonald had forgotten his glasses, but he took a long, careful look and said the suit was dark. This caused a buzzing among the justices, some of whom rose halfway from their chairs and peered at the picture as if to make sure their own eyes had not tricked them. Chief Justice Waste could be heard saying to his colleagues: "You can plainly see that it's light."

McKenzie then proceeded to tie together four established facts — MacDonald's timing as given in his original statement to police, the time shown by the sidewalk clock, the dark suit MacDonald had said Mooney was wearing when he came out of the saloon, and the light suit he was wearing when watching the parade at 2:01 PM Assuming that the waiter's first statements were credible, McKenzie pointed out, Mooney would have had about five minutes in which to travel 4066 feet up Market Street and climb seven flights of stairs in the Eilers Building. (The elevator was not running; the operator, like everyone else, was on the roof watching the parade). And somewhere en route, Mooney would have had to change from the dark suit to the "ice cream" suit.

Up to this point, nobody had officially questioned the *bona fides* of the alibi pictures. But while sifting documents in the Hall of Justice basement, a police detective had noticed a strange difference between the street scene as shown by the 1916 pictures and the same scene, viewed from the Eilers roof, in 1930. That sidewalk clock seemed to have moved a half block down Market Street. The detective whispered to his boss, Captain Goff. Goff whispered to Mr. Justice Preston, and the court launched a secret investigation to determine whether some darkroom wizard had doctored the alibi pictures.

In the courtroom, unaware of any doubts about the picture, the defense was still pounding away at MacDonald. McKenzie elaborated on discrepancies other than the color of Mooney's suit, particularly the difference between MacDonald's original descriptions and the actual appearance of Mooney and Billings.

McKenzie established that MacDonald had been penniless when he first went to the Hall of Justice. Had he read about the $5000 reward? MacDonald couldn't remember. Was it true that Goff had pointed The Kid out to him and said, "This is Billings?" Yes, that was the way it happened. And had MacDonald known when he identified Billings that this was not the man who had placed the lethal suitcase alongside the brick wall of that saloon? Yes, he had known it.

McKenzie's next move was in keeping with the strategy he had first formulated in 1917, when he had tried to woo Cunha and Fickert into agreeing that Mooney should have a new trial. The defense lawyer now hoped to achieve exculpation of the District Attorney and police by getting MacDonald to say that he had been mistaken in accusing Fickert, Cunha and Goff of subornation of perjury, to maneuver the witness into conceding that his perjury had been the product of his own mind and his own volition.

McKenzie sought to ease the witness into this reversal and make it palatable to the judges by harking back again and again to the "as God is my judge" statement. Had this letter not been more truthful than his "deathbed" affidavit to the defense three weeks later? No, sir! McKenzie tangled MacDonald in a new maze of confusions, contradictions, and tears; that was easy. But McKenzie could not make the derelict absolve Fickert, Cunha and Goff. Although reduced to a weeping blob, MacDonald stuck to that story. Finally McKenzie turned to the justices and said; "I stop with a sense of futility."

Goff replaced MacDonald on the witness stand. Very much at ease, he denied coaching the old waiter or otherwise framing the defendants; he also admitted disagreements with Fickert, saying he had considered him a "personal enemy" at that time.

Would Captain Goff care to join Duncan Matheson (now Treasurer of the City and County of San Francisco) in the opinion that there had been something fishy about the bombing trials? No, not exactly. Had Captain Goff changed his mind about advocating a pardon for Tom Mooney? No, not exactly that, either. Mooney, he thought, probably deserved pardoning, but Billings did not.

McKenzie then turned to the electronic surveillance that had laid the basis for the Densmore Report. Goff, it developed, had helped plant dictaphones on Fickert and given explanatory information as government stenographers took down the telephone conversations. During this highly secret operation, Goff had rubbed shoulders with the government operatives. While working with these men, had Goff remarked that MacDonald was a dissolute, drunken bum, utterly unworthy of belief? Goff replied that at the bombing trials MacDonald had seemed much more reputable, and it had been easy to take his word. When, then, had Goff changed his mind about MacDonald? Later, the Captain declared, when the waiter changed sides and made the "deathbed" affidavit.

Goff made a smooth and affable witness until McKenzie inquired how he could have failed to notice the discrepancies between MacDonald's original statements and actual appearance of the suspects. Or, if he had noticed, why had he not dismissed the waiter then and there? Goff shouted that he had searched for and found the missing statements of his own free will. Having discovered them, he could have destroyed them had they contained information he preferred to hide. Certainly he had noticed the discrepancies, but few witnesses can tell a person's exact height within four inches. Though women, he added, were different in one respect — clothes. Give a woman one look and months later she can accurately describe what another woman was wearing. A ripple of laughter swept the courtroom.

Now came the face-to-face between Fickert and MacDonald. If the former District Attorney had anticipated that he could emulate Justice Preston and make an easy conquest, he was very much mistaken. Fickert in his prime had never been capable of good courtroom performance, and his prime was now far, far back along a rocky road.

Possibly MacDonald felt that Fickert had sunk to his level and that they met as equals; perhaps the waiter now felt himself superior to the former District Attorney. At any rate, an amazing change

MacDonald, the derelict waiter who changed his story many times.

came over the witness as Fickert began to question him. The derelict's body expanded; his spine stiffened; he sat up in the witness chair. His voice strengthened so he could be easily heard throughout the courtroom. When Fickert glared at him, he glared back.

Fickert did his best to get MacDonald to retract his statement that he had met eight or ten times with the District Attorney for coaching on his Grand Jury testimony. In reply MacDonald shook a long, bony finger at Fickert, shouting, "You remember that!" Fickert tried a few more questions, but obtained nothing other than tart contradictions. When Fickert gave up and sat down, MacDonald would have gone on quite gladly.

"I was getting mad," he later told reporters, complaining that Fickert had quit too soon; MacDonald had been just about to tell how his one-time mentor had given him the exact height and weight of Mooney and Billings and instructed him to stamp those figures deep in his memory.

As soon as Fickert subsided, MacDonald's flush of manhood passed away. A letter written by him to Fremont Older in April, 1921, was introduced into evidence; in it he detailed some of the revelations he had intended to make until dissuaded by the threat of prosecution for perjury. One of these revelations concerned a coaching session between himself, Fickert, and a secondary witness named Crowley about their testimony on Billings. In this letter MacDonald claimed Fickert dictated the exact language, profanity and all, he wanted Crowley to use in backing up MacDonald's claim that he had seen Billings place the lethal suitcase. Another item in MacDonald's letter quoted Mrs. Edeau as confiding to him that Cunha was coaching her and Sadie.

Justice Preston was up with a question. Did MacDonald have the "mentality" to compose such a letter without aid? "Yes, sir." Preston next tried to pick up the thread of theory left dangling by McKenzie, asking:

"Wouldn't your conscience feel better at this time if you admitted that your identification of Mooney and Billings was just an honest mistake, if you absolved Fickert and the other officials of all blame?"

"Yes, sir, I think it would."

This was more than McKenzie could take. He leaped up to demand of the witness whether he had not just testified that Goff had coached him, and that he had lied because he was "in the clutches" of Fickert.

"Yes, sir."

Again McKenzie turned toward the justices, his hands aloft. "You see, it all depends on who asks him last."

Exit MacDonald to the sound of soft laughter, half pity, half disgust.

9

Billings Front and Center

Fremont Older had a reputation as one of America's great crusading editors. He had been kidnapped, stalked by gunmen, honored and vilified. Tall and slender, with a hawk nose, piercing eyes, and a full, dark moustache, he was anathema to The City's mossbacks. They condemned Older as an uncomfortable sort of fellow, too militantly liberal, too pro-labor, too impatient of hypocrisy and pretense. And too damned good at smelling out scandals.

Every type, style, and variety of human conduct had been exhibited in Fremont Older's office, a shabby, bruised room, littered with papers, photographs, files and junk. This editor believed, like Portia, that the quality of mercy is not strained; with that sentiment uppermost he had shaken hands with pimps, whores, preachers, murderers, society women, burglars, generals, and prosecutors.

Ever since the Mooney-Billings case became his baby, Older had been fascinated by an odd couple, Billings and the woman who had testified she had seen The Kid, posing as a photographer, at 721 Market Street on Preparedness Day.

Older knew that, earlier in life, Estelle Smith had been arrested in a raid on a Los Angeles house of prostitution, that she was not known for truth and honesty, and that Los Angeles police had an extremely low opinion of her. These troubles paled, however, compared to the mess she got into when she became the live-in lover of her own half-brother, a man named Bohannon. He took to cheating on Estelle with a woman named Irene, so openly that people in their circle looked upon Irene as Bohannon's common-law wife.

This stirred Estelle's turbulent nature until one day in 1913, when she told her troubles to her mother's brother, James L. Murphy, and the two of them went calling on Irene. This meeting ended up with Irene dead on the floor from a gunshot wound and Estelle and her uncle under arrest and charged with murder.

The defense and Fremont Older assumed Estelle did the shooting and Murphy took the rap. At any rate, charges against her were dismissed and Murphy went to San Quentin for a 12 year term on second degree murder. Older and others always assumed there was some connection between these facts and the affidavit Estelle gave defense attorney Tom O'Connor in 1917, for that document contained nothing directly damaging to Fickert — in sharp contrast to the charges and confessions in her second affidavit, made in 1929. Very shortly after the 1917 statement, James L. Murphy left San Quentin, his sentence commuted to time served.

While the two 1917 events might have been mere coincidence, something about Murphy's release whetted Older's suspicions. In granting the commutation, Governor Stephens ordered that Murphy leave California forthwith, never to return, and that this departure should take place only when "arrangements shall have been made satisfactory to Warden James A. Holohan for the transportation of the said James L. Murphy out of the State of California."

Older had developed the idea that something beneficial might come out of a confidential meeting between Estelle and Billings. Both had been in trouble with the law; both had known sordid poverty. A spark of sympathy might be struck up between them. And before Billings was committed to Folsom, the editor had in fact arranged such a meeting, but the net result had been zero: she cooed at The Kid and sympathized over his recital of a sad life, but he would have none of her story of the goings-on at 721 Market Street.

The patient Older remained in contact with Estelle, however, figuring that if one gambit failed another might be more productive; and on March 20, 1929, his efforts were rewarded. Older had

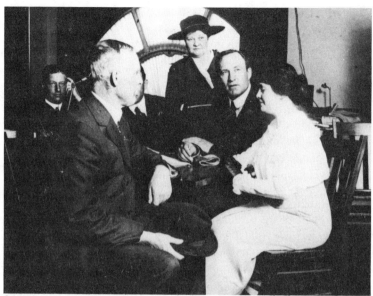

Getting the story "right." Police captain Matheson, Wade, Mrs. Tredwell, District Attorney Fickert and Estelle Smith.

another scoop to add to his string of Mooney-Billings sensations.

Estelle's second affidavit, after going into detail about happenings in and on the roof of 721 Market Street, on Preparedness Day, went straight to the point — Fickert. She *had* seen a man with a suitcase who had gone up on the roof, all right, claiming to be a newspaper photographer. When she saw Billings' picture in the papers, she had remarked to her boss, a Dr. Shane, that the picture looked like the man with the suitcase. Thus began her involvement in the case. But when Fickert and Swanson had found her uncertain and reluctant to testify that Billings and the stranger were one and the same man, the District Attorney and the detective had yelled at her, threatening to send her to prison unless she went into court and did their bidding. So Estelle said in the 1929 affidavit.

And that is not all she said. Her affidavit contained the following sentence: "At this time I was a morphine addict." She named the private sanitariums and hospitals where she had been treated during

August, 1916 — a month before Billings' trial — and the doctors and nurses who had attended her. She said her bills for this care had been paid by her employer, Dr. Shane, a dentist; during one spell that August she had had to be restrained in a straitjacket. When she testified against Billings, she was still taking tablets containing morphine; had them in her purse, right on the witness stand. She also recalled that Dr. Shane had given back-up testimony at that trial by swearing she was honest and trustworthy, even though he knew of her past and her drug addiction. She declared: "Had I been normal I would never have identified the man as Warren K. Billings."

One year and four months after having signed the 1929 affidavit before a notary public, Estelle Smith entered the Billings hearing — on the side of the prosecution. She arrived at the State Building with a typical flourish, dripping tears upon her ample bosom, gesticulating to the crowd around the entrance and shouting that this time she would tell the whole truth, so help her God! A woman reporter asked Estelle to pause for a picture. She slapped the reporter and got slapped in return.

In the courtroom Estelle's performance was only slightly more restrained. She had diarrhea of the mouth; the more she tried to dodge embarrassing questions, the more she had to say — most of it irrelevant. Her story, as nearly as it could be discerned amidst her spew of contradictory verbiage, absolved Goff, Cunha and Fickert of all accusations about coaching witnesses, put a cloud on Fremont Older for having exerted a strong personal influence over her, and claimed that in 1929 she had merely been talking to Older while a reporter took notes. She said she had signed the resultant affidavit without reading it, and repudiated outright her accusations against Fickert and her admission of addiction to morphine.

She told the justices that although Older had persuaded her that she might have been mistaken about seeing Billings, now that she was free from the editor's influence all doubts had been removed. She *had* seen The Kid at 721 Market Street! She *had* picked up his suitcase, which weighed 40 or 50 pounds. She claimed to be expert at judging weights because since childhood she had made it a habit to frequently test her strength by lifting heavy objects. She regularly exercised by raising a 50-pound weight with her little finger.

She babbled her way out of one embarrassment after another,

resorting in the most difficult spots to semi-hysteria. Even Justice Preston could not coax or force her into giving any direct answers. Justice Langdon questioned her for two hours and finally held up a hand to stop her flow of words, saying: "Madam, I have been endeavoring to ascertain your state of mind for some time, but frankly I have been unable to get it yet." Ed McKenzie, for the defense, had no better luck.

Yet for all the air of tawdry farce, Estelle Smith struck one blow that changed the entire tenor of the hearing. For 13 years, in court and out, Billings had told an innocuous story of his doings on the afternoon of Preparedness Day, but had produced no supporting witness or other evidence. Now she gave the clue to what he had really been doing on that fateful afternoon. She claimed that Billings had confided in her in that jailside conference which Older had arranged in 1917. He admitted, she now told the justices, that he had lied at 721 Market Street: his suitcase had actually held not photographic equipment but cans of acid which he had been squirting on fancy automobiles in the hope it would help automobile mechanics, one of five groups of workers on strike in San Francisco on Preparedness Day. Estelle declared that Billings described to her how he had jotted down the license numbers of sabotaged cars in a book of cigarette papers, and said he had emphasized his story by handing her that very book.

According to Estelle, she had reported this revelation to the authorities and had turned the book of cigarette papers over to Police Captain Duncan Matheson.* Her account had a point that needed clarification: did Billings actually admit he had been at 721? She replied that she and Billings had "talked as though it was understood he had been there."

Rena, Mother Mooney, and Belle Hammerberg looked ill; the defense lawyers turned grim. The sabotage part of Estelle's story was true.

---

*Matheson, who had gone East on business after testifying for the defense, telegraphed the justices and the press, indignantly denying Estelle's claim.

Those were relatively happy days for Billings. Press stories described the little man going about his work at Folsom Prison with beaming countenance and a cheerful word for everybody. Tom Mooney, on the other hand, was said to be full of gloomy forebodings — "sulking," one paper wrote — in his cell at San Quentin.

The night after Estelle pulled her big surprise was a busy one for three men. In the courtroom that day, among others, were H.L. Carnahan, Lieutenant Governor of California and chairman of the Governor's Pardon Advisory Board and the State Parole Board; and Court Smith, Warden of Folsom Prison. As soon as the woman finished her story of the sabotage, Carnahan called Warden Smith and Ed McKenzie into a huddle. He asked for an immediate interview with Billings so he could get the prisoner's version before Billings learned of the courtroom revelation through normal channels. Smith telephoned the prison, ordering Billings to be kept out of his cell that night. Otherwise, time locks would have prevented contact with the prisoner until the next morning.

Driving to the prison, McKenzie reached an understanding with his companions. Before the interview began, the lawyer would be granted a minute alone with his client so that he might advise Billings to be completely frank and hold nothing back from Carnahan.

On arrival at 11 PM they found Billings in the office, waiting for he knew not what. The warden and Carnahan hung back while McKenzie briefed Billings on Estelle's disclosure. The prisoner readily agreed to talk freely; then Carnahan moved in. Billings was questioned for three hours, and his statements were direct and positive. He had never told the story to Estelle. He had, however, given it in strictest confidence to Fickert when the former District Attorney visited him in prison four or five years earlier. He had ruined the paint jobs on several cars with acid, and jotted down their license numbers on a cigarette paper. Upon his arrest he had rolled that cigarette paper into a smoke, lit and smoked it, thinking to tell no one about the sabotage. However, during the trials, Defense Attorney McNutt had learned of it from Ed Nolan, and had asked permission to use it, believing it would strengthen The Kid's alibi. Mooney, Nolan and Billings discussed the idea, but with the latter finally deciding to keep silence; coming so soon after that terrible bombing, they felt that the true story would only inflame public passions against all the defendants. Over the years the tale had become something less than a secret: Fremont Older knew it; the defense attorneys were keenly aware of it; the yarn had gone the rounds at Folsom and was well known in the warden's office.

Billings now explained the thinking behind his actions. In 1916, certain high-priced automobiles were sold with a year's guarantee against any damage or defects, including paint jobs. Repainting cost $300 to $400, and it was reasoned that if enough purchasers of 1916 models piled into the local repair shops with ruined paint, the dealers might feel the pinch and decide it was better to do business with the Machinists' Union. Billings said he had originated the scheme and Nolan had agreed to it. The Kid bought a can of varnish remover and poured some of it into a half-pint flask. From this he drew the liquid into an egg-shaped rubber syringe with a pointed nozzle, small enough to fit in the palm of his hand. After squirting a car he would enter the nearest saloon, buy a beer, and then refill his syringe in the wash room. The cars he was supposed to sabotage were Haynes, Cadillac, Oakland, Chalmers and Hudson, and he had managed to spoil the appearance of five or six that afternoon.

The interview ended at 2 o'clock in the morning, and during the long drive back to San Francisco the Lieutenant Governor remarked to McKenzie: "There isn't a chance but that the story told by Billings is absolutely the truth."

Billings' rehearing had been started on the premise that John Mac-Donald would be the only witness, but it spun out beyond all expectations; a wide variety of witnesses, including Cunha, Fickert, Matheson and Fremont Older were heard. With the proceedings broadening so, defense attorneys pleaded for the right to bring the famous convicts into court to clarify the record. Walsh demanded the presence of Tom Mooney on the ground that the sabotage story was just as damaging to his interests as to Billings'.

The Mooney request was denied out of hand, but the justices decided to hear Billings. At first it was planned to bring The Kid to the courtroom, but suddenly someone discovered that since the justices were not sitting as the California Supreme Court, they did not have the power to issue an order bringing the convict out of prison; *ergo*, the justices would go to Folsom and question Billings within the prison walls. Because serious disturbances were not unknown at Folsom there was a fear of a possible attack upon the justices, so it was decided to hold the special hearing at night, after lockup.

On the night of August 10, 1930, Billings was ushered into the directors' room at Folsom to face six of the seven justices. The Kid had made good use of his years in captivity, and his earlier deeds had become little more than a stubborn memory in the back of his mind. As the warden, with pride, told the justices at dinner preceding the hearing, Billings ranked as the seventeenth best chess player in the United States. He had groomed himself with care. His white shirt was laundered to perfection, his black four-in-hand was neatly knotted. His shoes shone, his pants were pressed to a razor's edge, his reddish hair had been brushed until it gleamed. He spoke excellent English, better than that used by the average man — he was respectful but not cowed.

He started by making a number of admissions. He had possessed burglar's tools, but the nearest he had ever come to an actual burglary was to pry open a box car for a free train ride. He had stolen and transported dynamite. When the Shoe Worker's Union went on strike, he had taken a job in the struck plant, ostensibly as a scab but in reality as a spy for the strikers. In the past, "for matters of expediency," he had sometimes avoided telling the whole truth.

All that, however, was far back in the past, Billings asserted. His opinions of right and wrong had gradually changed; if pardoned, he intended to become an upright, law-abiding citizen. To prove his sincerity, he was willing to tell all.

Again Justice Preston did the bulk of the questioning; he harped and harped on that shoe strike. When Billings was hired, why hadn't he told the company he intended to spy for the union?

"Well," the convict answered, "if a man accepted employment as a spy in any movement, for any government, he wouldn't naturally tell his opponents he was a spy."

The justices rewarded Billings with polite laughter; encouraged, he frequently larded his replies with a dry wit that amused his listeners. He sensed he was arousing judicial sympathies, and his confidence grew noticeably.

Preston asked if Billings' change of heart had caused him to embrace any religious faith; the answer was that Billings had always had a religious faith, but had backslid for a number of years. Preston edged closer to the core of the matter; what about the PG&E strike in 1913? Yes, he had done little jobs for unions during layoffs from the leather-cutting trade. Mooney had put him in touch with people at the Electrical Workers' Union, and he had done some investigating to determine how closely company guard patrolled certain transmission lines.

And who was the union official who had hired him to do this investigating? The prisoner hesitated. McKenzie prompted: "Tell him." Billings told; the man was John Wilson, secretary of the union.

And on that ill-fated trip to Sacramento with the suitcase full of dynamite — who had hired him to do that job? Again the balk; again the nudge from McKenzie. The name passed Billings' lips: Edgar N. Hurley, a leader of the Electrical Workers' Union who had gone on to become a State Senator from Alameda County and was at that moment up for reelection.*

And who had sent Hurley to him? Billings replied: "It may have been Mr. Mooney or it may have been John Wilson. . . I have been informed that they recommended that I be hired to carry .he suitcase."

Pressed for every detail of that Sacramento episode, Billings said he had been instructed that a man would meet him at the railroad station and tell him what to do next. The man was to make himself known by putting out his hand and saying, "Hello, Kid, how are you?" And had that assignment been fulfilled? It had. Preston asked Billings to describe the man. Short and heavy-set: "Stout, I might say."

"Was it Tom Mooney?"

"No, sir, it was not."

Justice Preston expressed incredulity at this answer, so Billings repeated it. In fact, he declared, he had been told Mooney would play no part in the Sacramento end of the scheme. This would not go down with Preston, who kept up a tattoo of questions.

(It was Mooney, all right; he told me about it twenty-six years

---

*The naming of Hurley caused a sensation: Hurley was defeated at the polls shortly after the disclosure.

later. He was to meet The Kid at the Sacramento railroad station, tell him where to take the dynamite, and then — following a round-about route — rendezvous with Billings and representatives of the strikers at the saloon. Tom failed to make this rendezvous because a traffic jam delayed him. "The luck of the Irish was with me that day," said he.)

Finally, Preston took another tack. When Mooney was tried for complicity in the Sacramento matter, Billings had been brought from prison but, on advice of his attorney, had refused to testify. Why? Billings could not recall the reason given by his attorney. Nor could he bring to mind anything Mooney might have told him about the boat incident in the Carquinez Straits later that year.

Preston next asked Billings about his employment at the San Francisco Cadillac agency during the machinists' strike. Had he been spying for the union at that time? Yes; on the quiet, he had been working for Ed Nolan. And what had his wages been? Three dollars a day from the agency as a mechanic's helper, and $2 a day from the union.

Preston: "Had you turned away from the Lord then, or was [sic] you doing His work?"

Billings: "I certainly was not doing His work when I was in an occupation like that."

Only once, said Billings, had he stolen dynamite: eighteen sticks, from a quarry in the San Francisco Mission district, to help the electrical workers in their 1913 strike. For this he had been paid $5.

Had he ever told fellow workers that he got $50 for every box of dynamite he stole? Oh, no, sir.

Preston: "You are quite capable, are you not, of stringing fellows along with stories that are not true, when you desire?

"Well, yes."

With that admission under his belt, Preston returned to the question of spying. If Billings betrayed one employer, the business man, might he not also betray his other employer, the union?

Billings came out with a firm "No." Taking this to mean the prisoner felt an obligation to "the so-called labor movement," Preston asked if that might be the reason why Billings had never asked for parole although he had been eligible for the last six years.

Billings explained that he had taken sides in the war between employers and unions. His deeds on behalf of unions had been motivated by loyalty to the working man, not solely for money. The cash came in handy, of course, but it had never been the controlling factor. As to parole, he felt that to apply would be an admission of guilt — too high a price to pay.

"Liberty would be everything, whether you were innocent or not, wouldn't it?" asked Justice Preston.

Under his present philosophy, Billings replied, such reasoning would not apply. And what would that present philosophy be?

"The Golden Rule and the truth," replied Billings.

The prisoner had a few relatively comfortable moments as Preston sought his opinions on war and preparedness. Yes, he had attended the anti-Preparedness Day rally two nights before the parade and bombing, had heard the Mooneys and others talk against preparedness, and been influenced by them. However, he had been swayed even more strongly by President Wilson and other great Americans who at that time were arguing that the United States should remain neutral.

Justice Preston exhibited little concern for Wilson's position.; he wanted to know if Billings had been acquainted with Anarchist Alexander Berkman. Yes. Emma Goldman? Well, he had heard her lecture on "Modern Tendencies in Art," but they had not actually met. What about Miss Fitzgerald? Yes, he had met Fitzie at the Dolores Street apartment. And he had met other anarchists here and there, at labor meetings, in saloons, and such. Yes, he had heard that Berkman published some kind of paper, but he had never read *The Blast* and was unaware that Mooney had written an article for it.

Since he had associated with such people, Preston wanted to know, how could Billings help but realize their aims were revolutionary? The prisoner replied that at that time he had merely been "a hired mercenary." Aside from anarchists, what other associates had Billings had? Oh, saloon keepers, gamblers, "and other obnoxious characters of that type," he replied. "It wouldn't be any great credit to my character at that time to mention who they were."

Preston: "And following this so-called slimy trail . . . you sit here and want us to recommend a pardon for you and are not even asking for a commutation or parole, is that right?"

Billings' reply was to ask for honest justice.

If given complete freedom, did he not intend "to get on the lecture platform and to try to tell how you were framed and corrupt officials prosecuted you, and all that sort of stuff?" Billings had just gotten a "no" out of his mouth when Preston shouted that the convict had accepted an invitation to speak at the Labor Day program of the Chicago Federation of Labor two weeks hence, should he have obtained a pardon by that time. Was that not so? Yes, it was.

In the next phase of the hearing McKenzie's strategy showed plainly. Billings declared that he knew of no deliberate plan, concocted by corrupt officials, to put him behind bars. How, then, explain his arrest and conviction, Preston inquired; was he not implying, out of his own mouth, that he had been guilty as charged?

Not at all: "Those who have been induced to participate in my trial and conviction were under mistaken opinions as to what the facts were." Billings was following McKenzie's instructions to the letter. The defense lawyer believed this sort of testimony would swing wide the gates for Billings.

Justice Preston next took up the abortive street car strike shortly before Preparedness Day. Had Billings not pulled the emergency cord on a trolley car, tying up virtually all downtown San Francisco traffic at the rush hour? Yes, Tom Mooney had asked him to return from vacation to do that job.

"You were daring enough and had an abandoned heart to the extent that you were willing to do that, were you, at that time?"

"With nine men around me," retorted Billings, deprecating any imputation of bravery. The nine had all been members of the carmen's union.

"What was working on your soul when you was [sic] doing that?" asked Preston. Did Billings have any personal grievance against the traction company?

No, nothing of that sort; nor had he received any pay for his act. He was willing to help Tom "out of sympathy for employees, strikers."

"Do you think it was safe for a man of your ideas at that time to be at large?"

"At that time, no," replied Billings.

Preston ticked off Billings' numerous anti-employer activities and asked for a comparison of the two jobs, sabotage as against spying: "Was it a more odious one or a more laudable one?"

"A more odious one," said Billings. "It was an act of vandalism, although I did not think of it in those terms — at that time."

"Don't you have a real pity for your former self?"

"Not a pity; no, sir."

"What is it?"

"A disgust, I imagine," replied Billings.

Preston asked how old the prisoner was; thirty-seven. "With a wasted, ruined life lost. Does it not strike you as a sad commentary on human existence?"

"In a way I imagine it is; yes, sir."

Preston: "You were just simply 'agin' the government? . . . . Against law and order or against business of almost every kind, weren't you?"

"I was against capitalism —"

"Are you now in favor of capitalism?"

"Capitalism can be good or bad, like anything else. It can be benevolent or it can be despotic."

Had Billings ever been in sympathy with communism? No, never; he was for unionism, and not for any other kind of ism.

A few nights later, Chief Justice Waste gave his account of the evening hearing to a family gathering: he felt Billings had tried very hard to be slick and shrewd, but Preston had made mincemeat of him — a wonderful job!

Thousands and thousands of working people could have agreed. Billings' admissions hurt. Militant union members might understand the need for spying and sabotage, but not the general public. And those who could best appreciate Billings' acts as a striker were most likely to be infuriated at his unforgiveable sins: he had "sung" on his brothers-in-arms. His crawling before the justices, his acceptance of Justice Preston's every nasty innuendo, left a bad taste in the mouths of liberals. Was that any way for a convict to prove he deserved freedom?

Billings followed his attorney's advice. Prior to the rehearing, McKenzie thought he had a gentleman's agreement with the court: a pardon recommendation in exchange for the defense abandoning charges of frame-up. Whether someone deliberately deceived McKenzie, his wish was apparently father to his convictions — a state of mind shared by Fremont Older and many others, but *not* by

Tom Mooney. The hearings ended August 20. In their six-to-one denial on re-hearing, the majority opinion of the justices made a good thing out of Billings' attempt to absolve Fickert & Company of wrong-doing, arguing that Billings' statements were tantamount to an admission of guilt.

The single member of the California Supreme Court who had consistently believed in the innocence of Mooney and Billings, Justice William H. Langdon, wrote a bristling dissent to the denial on rehearing — one that made a juicy bit of judicial and public history.

It seems that Justice Preston, (probably acting upon the tip-off from Captain Goff) had raised questions about the alibi pictures in his opinion denying recommendation for pardon in Billings' first petition, heard earlier in 1930. Could it be possible, he had asked, that the position of the hands on the face of that clock had been altered? A clever darkroom man could work miracles. This question was asked in public, but what followed was kept tightly locked among the court's secrets. Very hush-hush, the court sought the aid of science to answer Justice Preston's question; and very hush-hush the court kept the answer thus obtained to itself.

Langdon's dissent ripped away this cloak. The alibi pictures showed shadows cast by the sun on various objects and structures. They could be measured, and the time they indicated could be checked against the times shown in the pictures. The orientation of the shadows could be established definitively because the Market Street car lines, shown in the pictures, were known to run true east and west. Two engineers and two astronomers from the California Academy of Sciences had examined the picture using the most reliable timepiece known to man — the sun, and showed the clock was accurate to within four minutes. As Langdon wrote in his dissent: "The report of the experts . . . definitely establishes the authenticity of these pictures . . . "*

---

*The mystery of the moving clock was resolved years later when a new defense attorney, George T. Davis, thought of calling up the people at the jewelry store which kept the clock as an advertisement in front of its place of business. The store, clock and all, had been moved 365 feet east on Market Street during the intervening years.

Langdon's dissent, which went around the world in thousands of pamphlets demanding more struggle on behalf of Mooney and Billings, also made short work of all the splutter about John Mac-Donald's veracity. Langdon cut this knot by pointing to the original statements, so painstakingly produced by Captain Goff. Langdon said no one reading MacDonald's first descriptions (plus his initial estimates of the time) could have "reasonably" attributed the crime to Mooney and Billings.

None of this left Mooney feeling triumphant; he had been hurt by Billings almost as badly as Billings had injured himself. Tom referred to Billings' venture as "a tragic blunder," and heard with dismay of his one-time friend's plans to keep on going it alone. Tom wrote to the printer who put out most of the defense literature warning that someone speaking for Billings might seek to have printing done on credit, and went on to say the Folsom prisoner did not have the personal ability or organizational background to make a strong fight, "and his recital before the court has placed him in a very unfavorable light."

After thinking things over still further, Mooney wrote a statement excoriating his co-defendant on six counts:

1. Telling the court he no longer believed he had been framed.

2. Identifying Ed Nolan as the man who had hired him to sabotage automobiles.

3. Naming State Senator Hurley as the person who had engaged him to transport dynamite to Sacramento.

4. Implying that Mooney had guilty knowledge of the dynamite transportation scheme.

5. Painting himself as "a mercenary of the lowest type rather than heralding himself as an idealist of the highest type."

6. Thinking to better his lot by joining with Scharrenberg and other labor leaders who had aided the prosecution and resisted the pardons; a "foolish notion."

With the defense now divided into two camps, suspicion replaced confidence, old friends became new enemies, and unions — with divisive problems of their own—had to take sides, Mooney supporters against Billings' men, in competing for defense donations. Believers in the Mooney-Billings cause were disheartened and confused, for the fratricidal row was much more difficult to explain than the stark facts of frame-up.

To compound these difficulties, the Great Depression was beginning to take full effect. Daily, men by the thousands were losing their jobs. The breadlines grew longer; apple sellers appeared on street corners. Stock market speculators had quit jumping out of windows, but new hoboes appeared everywhere, hunting for dinner in garbage cans. Bills went unpaid; mortgages began to be foreclosed. Husbands threw up their hands and deserted wives and children.

For causes like that of Mooney and Billings, it was harder to get a dime than it had been to get a dollar before the crash.

10

The Hard Sell

One of the many feelings that swept over me when I first laid eyes on Tom Mooney was surprise: he looked so much healthier, so much younger, so much more vital than I had expected.

If ever the populace was blanketed with pamphlets, leaflets, booklets, and other forms of appeal for justice in a particular case, No. 31291 did it. It must have been a rare citizen in the United States who had not seen some of this deluge of propaganda, most of it containing a pitiful picture of an aging man: hair grey and almost gone, staring eyes, cheeks hollow, face gaunt, wrists bound with handcuffs. He looked as though death was not far distant.

This picture was not entirely malarkey; there was just enough truth behind it to send the San Quentin warden up the wall of his office whenever he caught sight of it. The prison diet had, at one time, come close to killing Tom.

To all who visited him, all who worked with or for him, Tom Mooney gave countless dissertations on the nuances of publicity. He argued constantly with members of his defense committee, and with writers, photographers, cartoonists, printers and others versed in the use of words and pictures. He strove always for the right approach, the best subject matter, the most appealing ideology in preparing defense literature. He showed great concern for the facial angles and expressions photographers should try to catch: No. 31921 should be made to look determined but not grim; he must show suffering without revealing weakness.

Tom warned against pictures that were printed too dark. Light prints, he felt, made him look more youthful, less "savage." In every picture, his logotype had to be clearly shown: prison number 31921. Half the world already knew it by heart; Tom wanted the other half to learn it as well. In actuality, the numbers on his prison shirts were not large and showed up poorly in his pictures. This meant retouching the negatives, a subject over which he wrote many letters of instruction to his staff. The hands alone could be of great importance — fist clenched or fingers spread; hand cupped or put out flat; wrists garlanded with "bracelets" or left free.

Well-wishers sometimes asked if picturing Tom in handcuffs wasn't stretching the truth a bit. Everybody knew prisoners were not handcuffed in prison, unless they were extremely unruly. And was it strictly kosher to take his false teeth out before posing, so his cheeks would sag in, his jaw fold tighter, giving him that gaunt, hollow, aged look? Or his hair; he really had more of it, and darker, too, than his pictures showed; the magic airbrush added a quarter of a century to his years. Wasn't this bamboozling his public, just a little?

Tom argued sharply against such ditherings. Handcuffs! Sure, there had been years when his wrists had not felt the touch of cold steel. But, on those rare occasions when he had been taken outside the walls for court appearances or special hearings, the bracelets had been snapped on more often than not. As Tom often explained, all wardens, sheriffs and guards who had ever dealt with Tom Mooney knew it was absolutely unnecessary to restrain him; the San Francisco sheriff, for one, publicly declared that if you wanted No. 31921 to go somewhere, all you had to do was to give him the nickel fare and tell him which streetcar to catch. But, since that portion of the public which believed Mooney should have been hanged long since either did not know or stubbornly overlooked this fact, the wardens played it safe; they wanted no adverse publicity on such a tendentious question.

Tom was wont to say: "I'm certainly not about to spoil my whole case by trying to escape — not at this late date."

"After" picture of Tom Mooney, following lengthy hospitalization.

As to the false teeth, the hair, and similar questions, No. 31921 also had a stock answer. The State of California and its minions had chosen to burden himself and Billings with a thousand outright lies, a towering fabrication complete with fixed juries, biased judges, perjured witnesses and dishonest prosecutors; if he found it helpful to fight fire with fire, even a glowing match against a roaring blaze, who was to say him nay?

"I am the man who is doing the time!" This was Tom Mooney's reply to any and all criticisms.

Always looking for some new device to catch the conscience of the world, Tom saw a great opportunity when he learned that Los

Angeles was to be the site of the 1932 Olympic Games. He sensed the historical, almost mythical significance of those games; he knew they whetted the hopes and passions of people from almost every land. And Tom was well aware that ever since those Games had begun in Greece they had been used for political and propaganda purposes. He proposed to make use of them himself.

Tom began long before the athletes arrived in California. First he tried for a foreign boycott of the Games, on the grounds that California was a shameful place, unfit for honest competition between honest men and women. The Swedes seriously considered this, but the movement did not gain momentum and the Swedes had no desire to be unique, so the idea fizzled. But another idea came swiftly: at Tom's instigation, young workers in many an American community got up races and field events, calling them "Tom Mooney's Olympics," and had fun competing against each other. The official name for such events was "Counter-Olympics," and the honorary chairman, of course, was No. 31921. He planned large, envisioning a continuing organization of workers' sports clubs that would provide healthy entertainment and might help unify Labor and the Left in the United States and throughout the world. The thought took hold; plenty of workers were keen for this type of sport. A State-wide meet was held in Fresno: later, competitions with teams from other states climaxed with an affair in Chicago billed as the International Workers' Sports Meet.

Though this event did not rate much space on the sports pages of the commercial press, it provided an important propagandist prelude to the real Olympics, which opened in Los Angeles shortly afterward. There Tom pulled an electrifying stunt which has come down to posterity in the rebellious prose of a radical newspaper, the *Western Worker*:

> It was August 13, the final day of the Olympics. The last event was apparently concluded. Everything went smoothly and peacefully. In the huge stadium at Exposition Park athletes from all over the world, agents of imperialism, . . . Governor James Rolph, Jr., Tom Mooney's jailer, sat in the stand. Herbert Hoover was honorary chairman, but was probably fishing at Rapidan. Rolph was dispensing his harlot smiles . . . .
>
> Tom Mooney was peeling potatoes and onions at San Quentin. The sun was beginning to set. Suddenly there was a stir. Four boys

and two girls who sat quietly in the front row jumped to their feet, doffed their outer clothing and leaped over the railing onto the track. Underneath their clothes they wore athletic suits. On the front and back of their shirts blazed in crimson letters, "Free Tom Mooney." Shouting "Free Tom Mooney" they dashed around the track.

The six were members of the Young Communist League. Two of the boys carried a ten-foot banner with their slogan blazoned on both sides. While they circled the track, supporters in the stands tossed thousands of Mooney leaflets among the international crowd. As the runners passed the reviewing stand the cops moved in; the six were arrested and led off the field in handcuffs; in moments their banner was in shreds.

The *Western Worker* reported: "Mooney sympathizers cheered. The Fascists booed . . . Three hundred correspondents from all over the world kept cables busy. The story circled the globe."*

The six were first charged with "suspicion of criminal syndicalism," but this was later reduced to disturbing the peace at a public meeting. They were tried and convicted, and all drew six month jail sentences. Leo Gallagher, a prominent liberal lawyer, was fired from the law school faculty at Southwestern University for defending the six. (This did not deter Gallagher, a tiny, white-haired Irish Catholic who later went on to become one of the defense lawyers for Georgi Dimitrov in the Reichstag Fire trial which signaled the opening of the Nazi regime in Germany.)

Although the story of the pro-Mooney stunt was warmly received by the foreign press, most American editors, particularly in California, filed it in their wastebaskets. Tom did not take such silent treatment quietly. He asked the reporters and foreign correspondents who had witnessed the incident for their written versions of the demonstration. Most responded, on the pledge that their names would not be revealed. Tom then had his writers weave these varying

---

*Nearly fifty years later in a radio interview, Meyer Baylin, who was one of the six, recalled: "I knew the risks and I was willing. I did six months in jail, and I've always been glad I did it. The feeling of being useful in such a cause made it all worthwhile." And Elaine Black told of being beaten with brass knuckles by men from the Los Angeles "Red Squad" when trying to stage a Mooney defense rally in a downtown theater. It took courage to act for Mooney in some parts of California, even sixteen years after Preparedness Day.

accounts into a special press release to be issued as soon as the demonstrators' trial concluded. He instructed his supporters to form delegations, as large and influential as possible, to try to convince newspaper editors that reader interest demanded publication. Tom's orders were carried out in several communities fringing Los Angeles, but with spotty and slim results. Some papers ran a couple of lines from the release back among the advertisements; other editors temporized politely with their visitors but did nothing; a few sneered pointblank.

Another propaganda stunt, also originating in Los Angeles, began when Socialists rigged up a hearse, complete with coffin, for purposes of their own. When they were finished with it, Tom saw its possibilities and took it over. He had the hearse motorized and adorned with signs saying "Justice Is Dead In California," "Free Tom Mooney — Innocent," and the like. The driver was an articulate true believer, always ready to stop and answer questions or make a speech, and with an assortment of pamphlets, most featuring that picture of Tom at his worst, under the caption "From A Living Grave." Thousands — probably hundreds of thousands — of hands reached out for the pamphlets. In Northern California the reception was most gratifying. In Sacramento the hearse was driven around and around the State Capitol to bedevil the Governor and educate the legislators. In other states the hearse antagonized virtually nobody. In fact, it did so well throughout the West that Mooney ordered a second hearse prepared and sent on a leisurely journey eastward; it reached Washington, D.C. and paraded in gloomy portent around the nation's capital. Lawmakers looking out of Capitol windows could not help but see it, nor, at certain times, could those entering or leaving the White House.

Tom recruited powerful helpers who had keys to the press. Had it not been for three reporters of national prominence, Max Stern, Laurence Todd, and Gardner Jackson, the public might never have known of the third Federal investigation of the Mooney-Billings frame-up, the Wickersham Report. It was a shocker.

"I myself could hardly have put it any stronger," Tom used to

Second hearse, used to plague Sacramento officials and educate the public.

say, "and the real reason they tried to withhold it from publication is well known. It was such a terrible indictment of President Hoover's home state, California, that he didn't want anyone to know about it. In fact, I wrote a letter to Wickersham, making that charge right in his teeth."

George W. Wickersham, a former United States Attorney General, was chairman of the National Commission on Law Observance and Law Enforcement, appointed by President Hoover. This commission was to survey the country's laws and the practicality of their application, with special attention to prohibition, enforcement of which had become a national joke. As a side effort, an investigation of the Mooney-Billings case was conducted by a sub-committee headed by William S. Kenyon, Judge of the U.S. District Court in Iowa. Serving with him were Newton Baker, Secretary of War under President Wilson; Walter H. Pollak, Thomas Halleran and Carl Stern, New York lawyers; and Professor Zechariah Chaffee, Jr., of Harvard Law School. Professor Chaffee was the actual author of the sub-committee's lengthy report.

The report blasted Fickert & Company for a multitude of sins: blindly following Martin Swanson's lead without making any independent effort to track down the bombers; violating California law in many ways — making arrests and raids without search warrants, holding prisoners incommunicado; manipulating identification of suspects; stirring up prejudice against the defendants by planting daily stories in the press — mainly the Hearst press; using witnesses known to be of very doubtful credibility; coaching witnesses "to a degree approaching subornation of perjury," making wild charges before the juries without bringing in an iota of supporting evidence; and much, much more.

Judge Kenyon and most of the members of his sub-committee wanted the report included in the full report of the Commission, but they were out-voted by Wickersham and the majority of the commissioners.

Someone leaked the sub-committee's report to the three reporters, and they got busy with press attacks on the Commission — which caused that body to insert a squib, a reference of about two hundred words under the heading of "Criminal Procedure" in the final, full report.

"Shocking to one's sense of justice" was the quoted catchline that led most of the stories that poured out of Washington on the suppressed portion of the Wickersham Report, stories which made headlines in virtually all the nation's newspapers. (Despite much pressure from Tom and his friends, government publication was never accomplished. However, a commercial firm did publish the section a year later.)*

Of the countless ploys used by Tom in his quest for freedom, his master-stroke came next — his use of Mother Mooney to carry the story of mother love for an innocent son halfway around the world.

---

*In all the years when I had intimate knowledge of the thoughts and acts of Chief Justice Waste, I never heard him use a profane or vulgar word—except once. It was to quote, with approval, Justice Preston. Waste told intimates that Preston had dismissed the Wickersham Report with the comment: "Wickersham is nothing but a damned horse's ass, and everybody knows it."

11

Mother Mary Mooney

Mary Mooney bore five children, three of whom lived to adulthood and to survive her. Tom was always the gifted one. Without him the Mooneys might have been the stereotypical Irish working class family, lovingly engaged in brawls at home, but ringing defensively around Mother whenever attack threatened from without.

Because of Tom, brother John and sister Anna found themselves swept into situations too difficult for them to master. This was not the case with Mother Mooney, who had fought time and again against tragedy — including the deaths of two babies and untimely widowhood. Faith had always been a precious thing to Mother: in early life she had placed her trust in the Catholic Church; later her faith centered on the innocence of her oldest boy. Every person, every incident, every meeting, every newspaper article, Mother measured in two dimensions — for or against Tom.

Tom reciprocated. His was not simply conventional sentimentality over motherhood. He remembered her on all the holidays and anniversaries, and on every other day as well. They were forever in each other's thoughts.

Tom often cursed John and scolded Anna in terms so biting that many another sibling would have dusted his hands and walked away. And they did grow tired of having their failures described so often. Mother, however, never failed Tom. If she did, he never saw it; or if he did see it, he smoothed it over. Where Mother was concerned, Tom purred as smoothly as the finest diplomat.

Mary Mooney was heavy of bone and flesh and she had bequeathed this solidity to Tom and Anna; John was taller and on the slender side. For a time before 1916, her family raised somehow, Mother had enjoyed comparative ease. Like his father, Tom became so busy trying to improve the lot of the working class that he himself worked not too steadily — but no Mooney slighted him for that. There were the quieter, steadier ones; John the streetcar conductor, an easy-going bachelor who spoke only when he had to; Anna, the plump and pleasant waitress, rather pretty in her own hefty way. They scraped together the money for a modest, two-flat home "south of the slot" in the Mission District, where San Francisco's Irish clustered in those times.

The arrest of Tom and Rena had not unnerved Mother. Tom had been in trouble before; it was part of the price to be paid for doing what needed to be done. Mother understood and was proud of her son. But the hysteria and the hate, the neighbors taking sides and the pestering reporters and photographers and the crowds and the cops! The trials had been a terrible strain, leading to the darkest day of Mother's life, the day she heard the jury say that Tom must hang. She had bought flowers for the house, so confident was she that Tom would be home that night. She had sat in the front row where she could see and hear everything. On hearing that word "guilty" she had run up and thrown her arms around her son.

Fourteen years later she gave an interview in which she described that moment of stress: "Tom was taken away from me and I went out into the street with my son John. The newsboys were running around with papers screaming, "Mooney to hang! Mooney to hang!" I grabbed a kid and says, "'It's a liar you are. My boy will never hang!" She straightened up and laughed. "Sure, I was right. He hasn't!"

Until the day of her death Mother visited Tom faithfully every

Tom and Rena Mooney

other Saturday, while he was in Condemned Row.

"They brought me inside the jail wall and set me in the office, waiting," she told the interviewer. "Then I see Tom coming out of the condemned cell to see me. But my boy wasn't afraid; he walked straight and proud-like. He came right to where I was and put his arms around me and kissed me."

Mother Mooney had given her son great courage and a stocky body. They also shared a history of frequent, disabling gastric disturbances. The starchy, monotonous prison diet magnified this tendency into bleeding ulcers which sent Tom to the prison hospital several times and came close to finishing him off. These experiences made Tom extremely solicitous of his mother's health — often he wrote John, who lived with the old lady, urging that he be properly watchful over her. To her he described the diet he had found most soothing and the beneficial effects of sun baths and strictly controlled food intake. Milk, milk toast, raw eggs and beef tea, prescribed by the prison physician, had worked wonders for Tom — but only after his illness had gone so far that the State of California had to decide whether it could afford to execute its most celebrated prisoner by dietary torture.

Tom's worries about his bodily weaknesses and those of his mother were sharpened when he learned that bleeding ulcers brought an early death to Rudolph Valentino, great romantic star of the silent movies. Even in his small and crowded cell, Tom found room for several books on health: Dr. McCoy on *Diet: The Quick Road to Health, The Lazy Colon,* plus a physical culture cookbook and similar tomes. He felt well equipped to give advice on such matters.

To John he wrote: "John, I hope Mother is feeling better. Give her my wholehearted love, and you be good to her. Have a kind word for her on rising in the morning and before retiring in the evening, and try by some act of yours during every day to show her that love she longs for and is her just due from her own offsprings. Comfort her always."

Aside from tending to Mother, John had to run countless errands for the family celebrity, who demanded more service than any ordinary mortal could provide. John found it difficult to work ten hours a day as a streetcar conductor and then make the rounds of Bay Region union meetings in the evenings. Sometimes he was able to describe the latest Mooney-Billings developments to two or three union audiences in a single night, but this required agility, luck, and more energy than John normally had to spare.

That left Anna, bound, like John, to attempt whatever No. 31921 demanded, but in this regard the least capable to the Mooneys. As for Mother, nearly blind and often ill, her duties were necessarily limited. She kept house for John and attended meetings and hearings involving Tom and the case. If she went to the Labor Council and heard a man speak against Tom, she hated that man then and there, and could be heard cursing him many seats away. Sometimes she would be asked to speak in her son's behalf; such efforts produced more tears than words. But it mattered little what she said; her work-worn body, her face lined with strength and sadness, was appeal enough. She made people feel that if she was Tom's mother, Tom must be a good man.

One of the deficits of Tom's imprisonment was the bad blood that sprang up between his womenfolk — Rena on the one hand

and Mother and Anna on the other. Without the beneficent presence of the man who was husband, son and brother to these three women, the mingling of their lives became a grating necessity. If Rena did not or could not do enough, if Tom expressed displeasure with her or she complained of him, Mother's mind locked instantly in antagonism to her daughter-in-law; Anna was almost as rigidly loyal. Still, for years Tom managed to keep his dear ones more or less at peace with one another. He knew his relatives were not saints — once, in a controversy that did not involve Rena, he wrote a defense secretary that the members of his family had "flea minds"; please excuse them. But after their falling out over George Sayles, Tom made little effort to protect Rena from those of his own blood. When the chips were down, Mother counted most.

The prisoner's attitude toward his brother and sister was not consistent: he played them against each other, praising first one, then the other. He was especially critical of John, however — John didn't do enough defense work, he made stupid mistakes in judgement; he liked "the jug" too well. Worst of all, Tom was convinced that John lacked proper filial devotion. He constantly berated John about Mother, but never as searingly as in a particular very lengthy letter:

> I do not want you to read this letter to your mother, nor do I want you to mention one word of it to her; for if you do, I will consider it a breach of your honor, an affront to me and direct, deadly injury to your dear Mother.
>
> I want you to . . . meditate on what I have to say, and if you will not be too hasty in blurting out your noise . . . you will say Tom is right, I must be more careful and change my ways so that no act of mine will hurt Mother or cause her grief — worry and innumerable troubles of the mind and body . . . . I don't want you to feel that I have taken it upon myself to lecture you — to ball you out — or more especially how bad you are and how good I am . . . . This letter has but one purpose, our Mother's best welfare, her good health and happiness, and that can come only in some small measure through your efforts, for Anna is out of the question . . . .
>
> John, you are good at heart . . . . but you are so coarse and crude and to some people who hear you talk to Mother, cruel to her at times in your language commanding her to do this and that and the other thing . . . and your balling her out all the time . . .
>
> Just one illustration: a short time ago you caught two mice. Do

you remember what you said when you displayed them in front of Mother? John, that is a downright shame for you to do such. You know that all women fear mice, and such a small matter could have been the means of causing your mother's death — her weak heart to stop beating . . .

I think often of the desperate struggle Mother put up for us kids . . . . When she worked out in homes, if they gave her an apple she would not eat it; she would bring it home and divide it between us. She wanted us to have what she never got, a chance to read and write, at least . . . . And above all, her devotion during these . . . . past years — what a beautiful thing that is! . . . .

John, I would lay down my life for you or Mother. I would not do that for Annie — you know why . . . . With my warmest brotherly love, I am, Tom.

A few months later Tom changed favorites:

"You remember what I told you with respect to my value of John's opinion. Well, in light of what Anna told me, I am willing to give two of what I said . . . . As time passes you will better appreciate what I have had to contend with, the staggering obstacles I I have had to hurdle through life and especially since my entombment. My kingdom for a real Brother!"

The prized item in the rude furnishings of Tom's cell was a Victor Grafonola, the gift of some supporter. On it he played, over and over, a record which always brought tears to his eyes: "Baby Your Mother Like She Babied You Back In Your Baby Days."

For all the sentiment, however, Tom was canny whenever money entered in. He did not encourage use of defense funds for the support of relatives, either his or Billings', and when he authorized sending $50 apiece to the two mothers he did so with the warning that he would not permit his defense to become a "collecting agency" for such purposes. He was ever alert to protect his defense from attack on the handling of donations.

Money! It always had Tom in difficulties — between the defense and the public, between the defense and the donors, between the defense and enemies in the labor movement, between the defense and Tom's family, between his family and his wife, between John and Mother — and sometimes between Tom and Mother, though these disputes were always tender, for Tom never failed to get his way with her.

Trouble arose when the Mooney relatives were entrusted with defense funds, not because of any tendency to squander or misappropriate, but because each one had strong ideas as to what should be done with that kind of money. If Mother happened to be the recipient, she guarded it with her life. No defense employee could talk her into letting go of it. Money was to be saved, not spent — and it mattered little who the real owner of that money might be. More than once Tom had to intervene to pry the needed dollars away from Mother. On the other hand, when John happened to to take in defense money and the family and defense staff were feuding, his idea was to establish a separate bank account. This drove Tom frantic because it created all sorts of technical difficulties and dismayed the staff; also it worried Mother, who evidently trusted John's judgment no more than did Tom.

Another problem was John's voice; he was something of a singer, with just enough ability, Tom said, to make a "conceited ass" out of a streetcar conductor. Difficulties arose between Tom and George Kidwell, one of his most powerful supporters in the California labor movement, because this Teamster official was always encouraging John to cultivate his voice.

"Kidwell used to kid him, saying if he'd only develop his voice he could sing me to freedom," Tom complained. Such talk was "rot"; it took John's mind off the main job, which was to get out among the unions and hustle for his brother — but not always as John proposed. At one point John planned to attend the annual State Federation of Labor convention as a delegate from the Window Washers' Union, where he had many friends and much influence, rather than from his own Carmen's Union. Tom could visualize the scene if John had to explain this to the credentials committee at the convention. The convention would be controlled by Paul Scharrenberg, and if John should actually attend under false colors, Scharrenberg could cause great embarrassment for Tom and his defense. Knowing Scharrenberg to be "foxy," Tom could imagine him allowing John to be seated as a delegate so as to give him maximum opportunity to be "ridiculously harmful."

Tom was reminded of an earlier state labor convention when one Communist with more zeal than brains cooked up a resolution which was pro-Mooney in intent but so worded that it could not possibly gain approval. The Communist, proud of his idea, had visited Tom and let him read the resolution. Tom pleaded with the man to drop the whole thing in the nearest ashcan.

Whereupon the Communist joined the legion of those who knew better than Tom how to free Tom Mooney, went to the convention and put his resolution into the hopper. When it reached the floor the Communist sought to speak, but was howled down because of his known political coloration and also because of the extreme nature of his proposal. Then Scharrenberg rose to his feet and made a spread-eagled speech pleading the right of every delegate to say his piece. The Communist regained the floor and gave his argument while Scharrenberg sat back, gloating.

"He knew his [the Communist's] talk was ridiculous, and that the best way to hurt me was to permit him to talk," Tom said in reminiscence. "That is the way Paul will fight us."

When John proved stubborn, Tom threatened to send emissaries to the superintendent of the San Francisco Municipal Railway to block John's application for the necessary leave of absence, and warned John bluntly that he might get himself flattered into doing things "suicidal to my defense." Finally John yielded; he did not go to that convention.

Anna got her lumps when the inevitable changes in defense secretaries occurred; there were interregnums when she had to be and do all things on behalf of her famous brother. Anna received telegrams from San Quentin like this: "Stop stupid blundering follow instructions. If you cannot accomplish it, I will place Rena and Belle in charge. [As if either of those women would ever again do Tom's bidding]. Wire me your results immediately."

Anna's use or comprehension of the written word was hazy, and while her brother was hardly a word-master, he was always willing to raise the roof over her gauche errors. One phrase Tom favored in referring to his sad condition was "in durance vile"; when Anna mangled it as "endurance vile" his screams could be heard clear across the Golden Gate.

Sometimes Tom did not approve of the company his sister kept. She made friends with a married woman; they became so close that often this lady spent the night at Anna's. She told Tom that this was perfectly fine with the husband, but the prisoner worried, just the same. He advised Anna: "Now just get off your foot on the cooperation with L's husband. That is out of this matter altogether

— get that right now — and from this time forward sleep alone if you want to handle my work. That's for both of them. I am frankly suspicious. Keep your eyes open and look wise."

The depression was doing more than make it difficult for workers to dig into their pockets for money to free Tom Mooney. Borne on the winds of hunger and desperation, a mood of revolt was sweeping America. Farmers were banding together, using their hunting rifles to prevent bank seizures of their homes and lands; tenants blockaded hallways when sheriff's deputies tried to evict the unemployed. As fast as the furniture of the poor was moved out onto the sidewalk, the poor moved the stuff around to the back and right up to the rooms it had come from. Men who had never thought of joining a union went in search of leaders to organize them. There was talk of cleaning the crooks out of Wall Street and outlawing stock swindles; of banking regulations to protect the widow's mite; of insurance to tide over the unemployed; of social security to comfort the aged and infirm.

One yarn redolent of the times bears retelling: New York City; tenants organizing into unions in fever heat against greedy, negligent landlords; finally a group armed with banners and signs catches one of the worst landlords alone on the street, backs him up against a wall, and forces him to listen to their complaints. Finally, he shouts: "All right, all right, already: I'll fix your toilets; I'll get new garbage cans; I'll paint your kitchens and bathrooms; I'll have the plumber in. But one thing you want is beyond me; I can't free Tom Mooney!"

For one thing, Tom made peace with the International Labor Defense, a Communist organization he had battled in the past, feeling that its efforts in his behalf had been solely a front for its own organizational purposes. He now told confidants that he was convinced the ILD's "rule or ruin" policies had been eliminated. It was now possible to work with them; if they used the Mooney-Billings case to further their own ends, so did every other leftwing organization which might help. The ILD did ask one concession: Tom must yield at least a little from his ironclad position that the Mooney-Billings case should not be put before the public intermingled with any other cause. Grudgingly, cautiously, he consented — but he insisted, come what may, that ultimate approval remained with the Tom Mooney Molders' Defense Committee; in other words, with Tom himself.

With these arrangements taking shape, what had once seemed out of the question now seemed at least possible — the use of Mother Mooney as the stellar attraction in a great campaign to make America responsive to the rights of the poor as well as to the wishes of the rich.

The decision was not easy to make. Tom knew his mother would make any sacrifice he asked. But in this instance, that sacrifice might be her life. The doctor said so. She had recently recovered from a severe heart attack. She was 84 years old, almost blind, incapable of saying more than a couple of dozen words at a time, and liable to drop dead at any moment. The prescription for her was definitely not travel, crowds, speeches, interviews, changes of diet and climate and exposure to excitement.

But the people behind the tour promised so much; they practically had Mother wrapped in cotton batting, snug as an infant in the cradle. There would be strong arms to lift her, hands to steady her, eyes to see for her, voices to speak for her. Every step, every stop, would be a triumph that would warm her spirit and make her tired old heart pump better than ever.

As always, Mother had her ear to the ground and soon knew every detail of the proposal. It excited her, and bad cess to the doctors! With the eagerness of a girl forever young, she wanted to go. The plan developed and she got the consent of her son, who must have felt a mixture of self-interest, pride, and deepest love. To hell with fear! Mother Mooney went.

Of course, Tom had a multitude of instructions. If, as contemplated, Mother should visit the Soviet Union, they must buy her, in New York, very special underwear and extra warm outer clothing. He had heard about Moscow winters, and he did not want her to catch pneumonia as she walked up the Kremlin steps to call on Josef Stalin.

Tom also asked that Mother be given a dollar bill every day. Gifts of money were always welcome to her, they gave her a sense of security. As another small attention, Tom wished Mother to have her "smile" — the Mooney euphemism for a shot of good whiskey

— every morning and night; and also once or twice during the day, should undue fatigue set int.

The entourage included a Black orator to carry the main speech-making load and talk about two famous cases, Mooney-Billings and the Scottsboro Boys, a group of young Blacks wrongfully convicted of rape. There were companions to make travel easy, and an advance man to go ahead and make certain there would be a welcome from some city official (preferably the Mayor) at each stopping point. There would be roses in Mother's suite in the best hotel — usually donated by the management — and a car for Mother to ride in, right behind the band, in the short parade that led townspeople straight to the meeting hall where Mother was to speak.

The advance man was Frank Spector, an ILD official who had done time in San Quentin for "criminal syndicalism"—in his case, an attempt to organize the lettuce pickers of Imperial Valley into an agricultural union.

When Spector arrived at San Quentin, he and Tom were ideological enemies. Though they had never met, they had battled at long range for years; Spector had written and distributed leaflets critical of the Mooney defense, had heckled Mooney speakers, and otherwise made himself and the ILD a thorn in Mooney's flesh. On his part, Tom had written diatribes against Spector and his activities.

During his first recreational period in the prison yard, the new "fish" approached San Quentin's most durable celebrity, stuck out his hand and expressed admiration and friendship. Such a man could not be denied — one of the many examples of Tom's versatility in dealing with those he thought could please or help him.

Soon Mooney was busy politicking to help Spector obtain something he very much wanted — a cell to himself. Tom understood this need. A radical reads and writes and thinks a lot, and requires more privacy and room than can be had in any two-man cell. A single cell meant moving from the modern part of the prison into the oldest cell block, built of brick in gold rush days. Most prisoners would have shunned such a move, for this section was reserved for homosexuals, loners, and others unable to get along with their fellows. Aside from the social stigma, the physical discomforts were appalling. The bricks sweated moisture, and chill damp usually overwhelmed the faint suggestion of warmth that seeped from an inadequate heating apparatus. Tom knew all this, for he lived in this section himself. Spector was finally granted similar accommodations directly across the corridor from Tom; they could see each other through peepholes. They never reached full political agreement; their friendship persisted in spite of frequent, heady arguments. When Tom was working on one of his most controversial pamphlets, "Labor Leaders Betray Tom Mooney," Spector and some of the other criminal syndicalism prisoners in "Q" taxed No. 31921 with focusing too exclusively on his own case. They argued that the labor leaders Tom was attacking betrayed a great deal more than Mooney and Billings: they betrayed the members of their unions, they were faithless to the working class, they put their own selfish interests above all other considerations. Tom agreed, but could see no reason to discuss the broader aspects of labor betrayal in his pamphlet. Let others do that, said he; his job was to get freedom for himself and Billings. If this were accomplished, the other ills of the labor movement and the world might stand a better chance of cure.

Spector served two years, and upon his release Tom provided him with a defense job. He went around the country organizing local Mooney defense committees with resounding success. The workers were ripe for this sort of thing. Mother Mooney's trip was now in the works, and soon Spector was sent out to pave the way for her. The result was nothing less than triumph — even though discordant leftist factions gave forth faint outcries, and here and there a nose was lifted as someone took offense at the radical aura surrounding Mother Mooney's tour.

In New York, the Socialist Party announced a pro-Mooney rally for February 24, 1932, only to find that the Communists had scheduled a similar affair for the same night at a much larger hall. The Socialists promised that Mother Mooney would speak via long distance telephone. A letter announced the speakers, including the famous novelist Fannie Hurst — and also let a very large cat out of the bag. An addendum said: "Some confusion has been caused by a wide distribution of leaflets stating that Mother Mooney would appear in New York at a Communist meeting on that same evening. These statements are entirely untrue, however, as Mother Mooney is ill at present and will speak by long distance telephone to the bona fide Tom Mooney meeting. . . ."

Despite the Socialists' fulminations, however, Mother Mooney did appear at the Communist-arranged meeting. Sixteen thousand persons stood up and roared their greeting as she was helped onto the stage, trembling with excitement, barely able to walk, and so overcome that all she could do was stand at the podium and smile at the sea of faces, the thousands upon thousands of fluttering hands. When the welcome died away, a Black man named B.D. Ames read her written-out speech for her — but this was anti-climactic. The job had been done by the weary, wrinkled face peering out of the spectacles, and by the message, FREE TOM MOONEY, on the red silk sash draped from shoulder to hip across her ancient bosom — her "platter," Tom called it. At some of her meetings she managed to utter a sentence or two in her brogue, thick as potato soup, but this night was too much; she could not open her mouth. Featured speaker of the evening was Dr. Corliss Lamont, assistant professor of philosophy at Columbia University and son of one of the J. Pierpont Morgan partners. Lamont called the Mooney-Billings case "the fruit of the rotten tree of capitalism," and urged the audience to help "bury capitalism in the deep, deep grave where it belongs."

(The Socialist meeting also took place as scheduled, with 800 in attendance to hear Fannie Hurst describe the Mooney case as "one of the foulest judicial conspiracies in the civilized world." If Mother Mooney spoke to this meeting by telephone, it was not mentioned in the press.)

On the other hand, Mother got the Presidential snub from Herbert Hoover. He could not spare a few minutes, though he found time that day for a pleasant chat in the Oval Office with Jean Harlow. This displeased Tom mightily, for he thought Mother a thousand times more attractive than the most glamorous movie star that ever came out of Hollywood. However, Tom managed to stifle this particular burst of indignation lest he offend the actress's husband, Paul Bern. Bern, one of Hollywood's most prominent producers, had been a cornucopia of financial support for Mooney and Billings, putting thousands of dollars into a radio network broadcast on the case, and backing a play, *Precedent*, about the frame-up.

In less exalted places, Mother was treated like visiting royalty. A newspaper account of her arrival in Youngstown, Ohio, in July, put it this way:

Two hundred cheering, singing friends of Mary Mooney . . . greeted her today when she alighted from an Erie train to speak tonight at Central Auditorium in behalf of her son. Partly blind, the aged crusader is able to carry on only through her tremendous will power and determination to carry the fight 'to the finish.'

Several times she has collapsed on the road. This is her fortieth city and the excessive heat of the past few days has drained her strength. Dramatically she raised her right arm and clenched her fist as she recalled a stormy session with police in a Michigan city. . .

Mrs. Mooney is stooped and bowed by age and her many troubles. Her face is seamed by many wrinkles. Her hair has been cut short for comfort on the long trip. When she got off the train she looked for all the world like somebody's mother coming for a vacation visit and she peered out anxiously and even a bit frightened as the crowd closed in around her.

The cheers brought smiles. Richard B. Moore, New York labor leader, and Anna Reynor of the Tom Mooney Defense Committee took her arms and guided her through the crowd . . . Crowds lined the streets as her car led a parade of workers down Phelps Street, over Federal Street, and around Central Square.

While in Chicago seeking an invitation to appear before the Republican national convention, Mother suddenly put her hands to her face and cried out: "I can't see! Oh! I can't see!"

She was hospitalized. Her trouble was temporary, brought on by nervous strain, and after a few days of bed rest she was up and ready to hit the campaign train once more.

In Milwaukee Mother spoke over radio station WISN prior to her personal appearance at a big hall for a Mooney rally. Brogue and all, she started off bravely:

"I'm here today for my son, Tom. I know he is innocent, but he's been in jail for sixteen long years because he fought for the working people. . . ." There her voice broke; she turned from the microphone, unable to say more; but she had been effective. On occasion she would admit she could pray for Tom more easily than she could "talk out" for him. She vowed: "I'll go on praying for him until my dying breath."

One of her fears was that she would die before Tom went free. She often spoke of it. Yet she still hoped that her son might be allowed to make good his promise to take her back to County Mayo so she could see the green fields of her girlhood again. There had been optimistic times when she thought Tom might be buying the tickets for that journey any day; but so many days had come and gone, so many hopes had died, and Tom yet in San Quentin.

When criticism came, the source was not always the "capitalist" press. Cincinnati, Ohio, was headquarters for more than one international union founded by Socialists, including the Molders. A A labor paper, reporting on a Mooney rally there, headlined: "Mother Mooney Paraded By Reds For Propaganda." The story said:

> Mother Mooney feebly marched into the packed auditorium of the Odd Fellows Temple one night recently as five hundred pairs of toil-worn hands acclaimed her. Amid a pandemonium which might have greeted a conquering hero, old Mother Mooney . . . took her seat on the stage . . . The International Labor Defense introduced its star orator, Richard B. Moore. Moore, a British West Indian, is the head of the Negro section of the International Labor Defense, a subsidiary of the American Communist Party. While the huge throng simmered in a temperature of 95 degrees, Moore used his eloquence, the Mooney case, and the Scottsboro case to inflame the audience against the 'blood-thirsty capitalists'. . . It was a pathetic sight to see the aged Mrs. Mooney sitting behind the vain and cunning Moore while he used her presence and the tragedy of her son's life to swell the membership of the Communist Party.

After the Chicago collapse, plans for a venture overseas were shelved temporarily but Mother regained her strength and seemed remarkably well — and the trip was a grand success, on the whole. An organization called the International Red Aid was about to hold a convention in Moscow; an American delegation would attend. People suggested that Mother should go along.

This revived one of Tom's pet dreams, and he sat up all night in his cell writing a letter of thanks to the Russian workers for having saved his life. He proposed to send this letter to Stalin; the messenger would be his mother, representing the millions of people enlisted in support of freedom for Mooney and Billings.

At that time the United States had not yet recognized the Soviet Union. Still, the American authorities made no difficulty for Mother Mooney and the Red Aid delegation, and Mother set sail for Europe in October 1932. There was another woman passenger of renown aboard the liner *Europa* — Dorothy Parker, one of the wittiest humans ever born. She had plenty of opportunity to study the delegation.

Anything that engaged Miss Parker's interest was likely to find its way into print, and in due course a piece signed by her appeared in the leading newspaper of Holyoke, Massachusetts, the Mooneys' old home town. Miss Parker wrote:

The best person on this ship, and I wish that were higher praise, is traveling third class. Her name is Mrs. Mooney; she has a son, Tom, back in America. She is a big woman, though not tall and not stout, and her eyes are still laughing at old jokes none of us know. . . She is out on deck all day long, and at 84, with the worst sorrow of all sorrows upon her, she has the spirit to sport an emerald green scarf and hang a string of shiny green beads around her neck. She has the manners queens ought to have — she makes you feel of value. The way she thanks the steward for bringing her a cup of tea clouded with milk, and the way she blesses your heart and tells you you're looking fine — "Courage," Ernest Hemingway once said, "is grace under pressure."

Miss Parker was not so taken with the other members of the Red Aid delegation. They held almost daily meetings in the third class dining hall, and she looked in on one. She found the discussion acrimonious, the jargon unpleasant, the speakers cocksure and self important. She described the delegates: "They were stocky young women with strong teeth and short, springing hair; dark young men with insistent beards; a couple of tall, serious Negroes with gold-rimmed glasses. . . Mrs. Mooney is no damper to their voyage. Mother, they call her. Well, so would you."

The old lady was asked to make a little talk at the meeting Miss Parker attended: "So there she stood, after all those angry words and phrases, a broad old lady in a green scarf and an unfortunate woolly sweater. And she spoke in pure Synge. 'It's seventeen long years,' she said, 'they've had my boy in the dungeon for something he didn't do.' Then she stopped. Suddenly she made a good Irish gesture, as if she gave the back of her hand to fools. 'Sure,' she said, 'he was miles away when they threw that bomb. And they put my boy in the jail.' She didn't say anything more."

After the pleasant voyage came a rebuff: British authorities slammed the doors of their country in Mother's face. But the British Home Secretary discovered that his say-so was not enough to bar Tom's mother from the "tight little isle." One Saturday, while Mother was holding court throughout Europe, members of the

House of Commons were startled by bits of paper fluttering down from the galleries — leaflets describing Great Britain's insult to this remarkable mother and demanding swift remedy. Mother deserved the most gracious hospitality the English could offer, the leaflets noted; should this be withheld, the unions would be heard from.

The British visa did come through — the day before Mother was due to sail from France for New York. It was inconvenient to change plans at the last moment; there was a suspicion that the visa had been delayed just long enough so Mother might be unable to visit England. Mary Mooney made up her mind to go; if there were people in England who wanted her that badly, she would come.

Meanwhile there had been the journey to Moscow. Newspapers reported her arrival and the pleasant treatment she was receiving; she was said to be arranging to meet Stalin and deliver Tom's letter. Suddenly, however, this project got lost behind a veil of silence* In all probability the meeting never took place.

Mother landed in New York, homeward bound, a couple of days before Christmas, 1932, and was besieged by newsmen. How had she found traveling, at her age? What did she think of Bolshevik Russia? Well, those were easy questions: she was getting a little old to be traveling, "but I'll never be too old to work every day to get my boy out of prison"; and as for Russia, she wouldn't care to live there. Too cold.

Before Mother could head for California Tom wanted her to seek an interview with the new President-elect. Wilson, a Democrat, had done his utmost to aid Mooney. Roosevelt would be the first

---

*This silence was partially explained by a letter sent to a California friend by Millie Bennett, a prominent San Francisco newspaper reporter who covered many aspects of the Mooney case and who happened to be in Moscow at the time of Mother's visit.

The two women had met many times, and were happy to see each other in that faraway land. According to Millie's letter, the following colloquy took place:

Millie—"Have you seen Stalin yet?"

Mother—"Who?"

Millie—"Stalin; you know, Joe Stalin."

Mother—"Who's he?"

Millie (aghast)—"Josef Stalin; you know, the top man here, the great Red leader of the Russians."

Mother (vaguely)—"Oh, yes. I think Tom told me something about him."

Democratic President since Wilson's time. What suited one Democrat ought to suit another, Tom thought.

As responsive as ever to Tom's call, Mother proceeded to Albany, New York, and asked to see Governor Franklin Delano Roosevelt. At the meeting, which lasted only a few moments, the man who was about to become the nation's leader listened with seeming interest to Mother's plea which closed with the phrase: "My boy is a good boy."

He responded: "I feel sure, because so many people believe he is innocent, that there must be some reason for believing his innocence." There would be a brief period, after retiring from the Governorship of New York and before assuming the Presidency, when he would hold no public office. During that period, he promised, he would write California Governor James Rolph about Tom Mooney.*

Roosevelt kept his promise to Mother, but not vigorously: he merely gave the Governor of California *pro forma* notice that he had been apprised of the case; nothing more.

The trip West was as busy as the earlier journey East. In Memphis, Tennessee, the local newspaper took Mother to task for her Russian adventure. It editorialized: "But there are conditions under which even mother love defeats, by the manner of its expression, the very thing it would attain. A fine example is furnished by the campaign for the release of Tom Mooney that his mother has been conducting in Russia, and this fact of itself will be anything but helpful to her son."

More difficulties arose, more from ignorance than from lack of good will, however. By the time Mother and Richard Moore reached Kansas City, Missouri, Frank Spector had arranged an interview with the editor-in-chief of the Kansas City Star. This man was most gracious. A cameraman took pictures; a scribe was called from the city room to listen to Mother and write a glowing piece about her, including mention of the time and place of the Mooney mass meeting. Spector asked if it might also be possible to secure time on a radio

---

*Others also hoped Tom might benefit from the good offices of the incoming President. Henri Barbusse of France wrote Bertrand Russell of England asking him to join in an international appeal to Roosevelt on Mooney's behalf. Russell replied that since President Wilson had been powerless under American law, Roosevelt would doubtless use that fact to avoid the issue. However, Russell expressed great sympathy for Mooney, and willingness to help in any way that might have impact.

station owned by the newspaper. Definitely yes. The editor called in the radio station manager and ordered him to find out what Mother wanted and act accordingly. In the station manager's office they discovered that he knew nothing about the case; he had only a vague recollection of the name, Tom Mooney. Mother and her helpers launched into a quick "educational," which the radio man interrupted: "Why, you don't need time on a radio station! What you need is a good lawyer!" He suggested the names of several famous attorneys and shooed the visitors out; whereupon they went right back to the editor-in-chief and told him their troubles. The editor then made sure that his manager got the message, and that night Mother and Richard Moore went on the air for fifteen minutes at prime listening time.

There never was a better tonic for an old lady than Mother's exultant campaign. She was all smiles and laughter and tears; the business of making the grand entrance into the best hotel, the bowing manager, the suite of rooms with the big bowl of flowers on the table, the bottle of whiskey placed discreetly in a closet; and usually the whisper of good news — all accommodations courtesy of the house.

Prohibition, however, was still the law of the land, and sometimes the "smiles" were not so easy to procure; as when they came to Great Falls, Montana. This was a mining town, a union stronghold since the days of Big Bill Haywood's Western Federation of Miners; a place where a man who thought poorly of organized labor was likely to be unlucky. The train was late and it was midnight when Mother and her companions reached the station. It was a work night, but the whole town was there — the Irish, the politicians, the non-Irish, a couple of communists and a whole pack of Wobblies, all the anti-Wobs and anti-Reds, and hundreds of plain, ordinary citizens of Great Falls.

The town did not boast of much in the way of meeting halls, Spector found a movie house, shut down for a year or two, and called upon the townspeople to help make it suitable. They responded en masse, and by the time Mother arrived that movie house was as neat and clean and decorated as could be, fit for Her Royal Highness; and all without the outlay of a penny.

But that night, on reaching the hotel, a miscue developed: there was no "smile." Mother was tired; she'd come a long way, and without a "smile" it was easier to be just a weary old lady than to be the belle of Great Falls.

Spector, as usual, had at his elbow a localite who knew everybody and everything. Spector whispered to this man, who went into deep thought for thirty seconds. Then he took off for the Sheriff's office across the street. Learning of Mother's need, the Sheriff grabbed his keys, unlocked the evidence cabinet, and handed over a bottle of said evidence, the best he had. If they lost a prohi case for lack of that bottle, so what? Great Falls had saved its reputation.

Mother always said she had the gift of second sight, and as she passed her eighty-sixth birthday that gift began to worry her. Something kept saying that Tom would never be able to take her on that promised trip to County Mayo. She was back home in the flat on Clipper Street, cooking for herself and John on the old coal stove. Life was quieter now, but it was never dull. She prayed to God for strength to wait for Tom's release; on her better days she had real hope. "He's giving it to me," she'd say to friends. But behind that hope lay the knowledge that her time was coming.

It was 1934, in San Francisco a great time for rebels and union men. There was this longshoreman named Harry Bridges, raising Ned the way Tom had done when he was young; only different, because Bridges had pulled a great general strike, and won. Tom, most always, had been on the losing side. But the two were alike, for the bosses hated Bridges just as bad as they'd ever hated Tom. Mother admired the longshoremen; they had stood The City on its ear — and all the other Coast ports as well — so they could have an honest union and make a decent living.

She had not been idle; she was doing what she could to get Upton Sinclair elected Governor. One of the planks in his platform was to free Tom Mooney the minute he was inaugurated, and that was enough for Mother. And here were the Communists begging everybody to vote for Sam Darcy, who had not the faintest chance. She and Tom had shaken their heads together over that one. The Communists had been a great help to Tom, sure, but was voting against Sinclair going to help? It was enough to make an angel swear.

Then came another fight in the San Francisco Labor Council — this time not about Tom but about Mother. Next Monday would be Labor Day, and it was to be the biggest celebration ever, what with the longshoremen's victory and Labor feeling its oats. This time the longshoremen in the white caps and hickory shirts would march up Market Street eight abreast with flags flying and bands playing, not grim and silent as when they — and fifty thousand men from other unions — had formed the funeral procession after police killed two and shot four hundred on "Bloody Thursday," the day they tried and failed to break the strike.

All this had happened only a few weeks before; the memories were still fresh. Prospects for Labor Day had a delicious tang for Mother: there was be a splendid float, "Free Tom Mooney," and she and Tom had planned that she should ride on or near it. The workers would like that. But, as so often where Tom was concerned, there had been opposition. The labor skates said it would be bad for Mother's health — as if a woman who had appeared on platforms across the world couldn't stand one tiny Labor Day parade! But no. Instead of a ride where she could smile and wave at everybody, they had fobbed her off with a front seat in the reviewing stand on the steps of City Hall. She felt deprived.

A friend drove Mother to San Quentin on the Saturday before Labor Day to visit Tom; Mother talked a great deal to her son about dying that day, saying she would like "a worker's funeral," open to the public. Her goodbye kiss was the saddest she had ever given him. On the way home she said to her driver, "I feel I'll never see Tom again."

That afternoon she went to a beauty parlor to be "prettied up" for the big parade. She spent the night with Anna, who was living at Mooney defense headquarters. Although Mother complained of feeling tired, she went home on Sunday, carrying a chicken to cook for John when he returned from his streetcar run. As dark was falling neighbors heard a feeble cry and rushed upstairs to find Mother on the floor with a heart attack, latest in a long series. She died a moment after admittance to the nearest hospital.

Tom and John scheduled the funeral for the following Sunday in San Francisco's largest hall, the Civic Auditorium. As soon as the date was set, a new fight broke out: Tom wished to attend, and his desire was backed by so many thousands of Mooney supporters that the warden and the Governor were forced to think twice. They took refuge in the law; no prisoner could be released except under certain stated conditions — expiration of sentence, pardon, parole, commutation of sentence to time served, or under court order for appearance as a witness. Privately, the warden also pointed out that if Tom Mooney were allowed to attend his mother's funeral, half the convicts in America would come up with maternal fatalities requiring their presence at graveside. However, Warden Holohan got such a deluge of letters and telephone calls that he offered No. 31921 three days "off" to spend as he liked — in San Quentin. Tom would have none of such a piddling compromise, and peeled spuds and carrots on the day of the funeral, as on any ordinary day.

If Tom could not come to the funeral, friends decided, the funeral would be taken to Tom. On Sunday, a hearse containing the coffin, together with a small cortege of cars, went by automobile ferry across the Golden Gate to the prison gates. In the cars were John, Anna, Rena, a friend of Rena's named Ellen du Freyne, Elaine Black of the International Labor Defense, and Harry Bridges. The windows of the Officers' and Guards' Mess overlooked the main gate and its approaches, and the reporters accompanying the cortege assumed that Tom Mooney looked up from his eternal potato peeling and saw every move of the drama played out below.

John and Anna got out of the lead car and went into the warden's office to plead with the warden's secretary, Clinton Duffy (later warden himself), for permission to take the hearse inside the gates so Tom could look at Mother for the last time. The answer was firm: not a chance.

"He saw his sister sway and clutch at his brother, John, as she was led, weeping, back to the funeral car," wrote a *Chronicle* reporter.

There seemed to be nothing for it but return to San Francisco. But wait! A man came running, hand upraised. A corpse had been brought into Marin County. The cadaver had come within the official jurisdiction of the county coroner, and could not be removed from said county without the permission of said coroner; all in accordance with Ordinance Number Umpty-Ump, adopted by the Board of Supervisors on such and such date forty or fifty years ago. This meant loss of nearly an hour while the cortege went to the coroner's office in San Rafael and pacified the bureaucrats.

At the San Francisco Ferry Building, the funeral procession was met by a group of the faithful and a small band. The hearse and the band, followed by about 1500 persons, moved in slow-step up Market Street, displaying the traditional sign, "Free Tom Mooney." The public paid slight attention; those who stared seemed more curious than partisan. Civic Auditorium, however, was packed with those who had come to mourn Mother and honor her imprisoned son; the funeral came alive. A banner stretching across the stage promised: "We'll finish the fight, Mother Mooney." On one corner of the platform stood an enlarged picture of Mooney as a young man; on the other the current official photograph showing the haggard and greying prisoner, in the center, a gracious likeness of Herself.

The *Chronicle* reported: "Without benefit of the church in which she was reared, she was the unwitting protagonist in one of the most amazing funerals the Bay District has ever seen."

There were tributes to the dead and demands for justice to the living from a list of speakers including Harry Bridges and Henry Schmidt for the Longshoremen and Leo Gallagher, the Los Angeles lawyer who had already put his career on the line in defending Mooney sympathizers in Los Angeles. Gallagher, a devout Catholic, made forceful comment on the fact that no choir sang a funeral dirge, no priest led the assemblage in prayer:

> But let the churches question themselves why Mother Mooney is buried without religious services. For eighteen long years Mother Mooney has seen the churches stand silently by while her innocent son languished behind the walls of San Quentin. How often have the churches and their leaders been appealed to, to come to the aid of Tom Mooney, and how often have these leaders in cowardly silence turned not a finger?

When the speech-making was over, John and Anna took places at the head of the bier as the audience filed by, taking a final look at that militant old face and shaking hands with Mother's free children. Then the coffin was put back in the hearse for a third trip across the Golden Gate. Burial took place in a non-sectarian cemetery high on the eastern slope of Mt. Tamalpais, overlooking the yellow walls of San Quentin.

Since he could not stand by the open grave, Tom sent a letter to be read to Mother before the coffin was lowered. He said, among other things:

"You have enshrined yourself in the hearts of all true workers. A wonderful place awaits you in working class history. Nothing can rob you of that, or the warmth that will always be in my heart for you.

"Again, Mother dear, for the last time, I bid you a last fond and loving farewell forever.

"Your loving and grateful proletarian son,

"Tom Mooney, 31921."

But it was John who had the last word. In spite of Tom's poor opinion of him, John had his feelings about Mother and on that day found tongue to express them:

> You have been sunshine to the workers all over the world. Your place is in the sun. Mother, nearly all the capitalistic lackeys who have prostituted justice and crucified your son have gone down the road ahead of you; but they are down in a fog and it would be a crime to place you alongside the prostituted lackeys, down in the fog! Your place is in the sunshine. That is why we brought you to this beautiful spot where the sunshine will always be upon you. Your son told me yesterday morning; he said, 'I want my mother near me, where she can always look down upon my living tomb'. . . . Your work for Tom is done; my work for you is done. But Mother, I want to tell you before you go on your last restful and peaceful repose that where you leave off the struggle, I'll take up the cudgel, and I am ready!
>
>   And now, friends, let us all raise our right hand and say: We will finish Mother's life work to free her son!

12

Mea Culpa

At just about the time when Tom Mooney was thrown into jail, I fell in love with the girl who sat in front of me in Miss Webb's Latin class at Berkeley High School. In due course, this led me to become the son-in-law of William Harrison Waste, who was rising swiftly from the Superior Court bench in Alameda County to the District Court of Appeals, and thence to Associate Justice of the California Supreme Court. About five years after I married his daughter he reached the pinnacle, Chief Justice of the latter court.

My father did not oppose my marriage, but he made it plain from the start that his social contact with the Wastes would be as minimal as possible. The gulf between the life styles and thought patterns of the two families was simply too wide to be bridged even though I thought I could make the jump. So my wife and I spent most of our social life under the aegis of her family, and I encountered ideas and opinions and reactions to current events utterly at odds with the atmosphere in which I had been brought up.

Take the Mooney case, for instance. To my father-in-law, Tom Mooney was, at best, a contemptible, troublesome, dangerous man who deserved to be kept under lock and key for the safety of society; at worst, he was the Devil incarnate. To my mother-in-law,

Mother Mooney was "a horrible old harridan" who went around cursing policemen and judges and other decent people.

Try as I would, I could not convince myself that these people and their friends were right. However, it was obvious that if I stood on the fundamentals instilled in me from birth, I had an excellent chance of losing that which I had come to consider most precious, my wife and my own growing family. Therefore I kept silence.

While I do not say that the treatment of Tom Mooney was the main cause of the inevitable divorce, it had something to do with it. Shortly before my wife and I came to the final parting of the ways, for instance, we took our political differences to the polls in the 1932 Presidential election, she voting for Hoover, I for Norman Thomas.

Suddenly I was free from the conservative influences with which I had struggled to live in peace for so many years. At first it was a sad, sick, lonely freedom. Then not quite so sad, not quite so lonely, on and up. I also discovered some most unpleasant things: the Oakland *Tribune* on which I had been a loyal reporter and rewrite man for several years, flagrantly reversed the figures of a campus poll on the 1934 election to show that Berkeley students favored the incumbent governor, Merriam, over the socialist challenger Upton Sinclair. That was an outright lie, and when I said so to my managing editor, Leo Levy, he replied it was done "out of necessity."

My education continued when I was put in charge of a seven-man team that covered the San Francisco general strike in 1934. This was an angry protest over police efforts to smash the longshore strike, during which the cops killed two men and wounded four hundred on the infamous "Bloody Thursday." I saw pundits from New York, men with famous by-lines and open expense accounts, walking the long weary miles from the airport to town, carrying their own suitcases. One ferry, no cabs, no streetcars, no busses, no gasoline, no automobiles, food only in very few downtown beaneries allowed to function by the strikers, where the hungry stood in line for hours waiting to buy a sandwich. (Though, if you knew the password, there were a couple of bootleg restaurants where food was served behind locked doors and drawn shades.) I had my cameraman take pictures of foreign seamen, most unable to understand a word of English, being forced to run a police gauntlet while a double line of cops beat upon defenseless heads and shoulders, supposedly because the men had huddled in a hall said to be controlled by the Reds. Those pictures never appeared, and I was told that Leo Levy, the managing editor, scooped up not only the prints but the negatives as well and sequestered or destroyed all of them. By now I knew better than to ask Levy why.

I saw "vigilantes" (cops in plain clothes) running wild on the streets with loaded shotguns. My father's front gate was decorated in the middle of the night by a red rag, hung there by a deputy district attorney who had once been one of my fellow newsmen. At that time I had no front gate, just a cheap room; and so avoided the red rag treatment.

Wages were going down; mine dropped from \$55 to \$40.50 per week. Many dared not complain; a man was lucky to have a job. So I joined the fledgling American Newspaper Guild and helped form a unit of which I was soon elected chairman. As soon as news of this honor reached my employer, I was fired.

I quickly landed work on another newspaper, but I lasted only two days. Later my colleagues told of seeing my former publisher, Joseph R. Knowland, making the rounds of his colleagues. It was obvious he had put the squitch on me — I was on the blacklist.

Under the circumstances, I had no option but to inform my father-in-law that I might not be able to send through him the \$75 per month I was obligated to pay for child support. He offered to go to my former boss and plead for my job, if only I would forget the union foolishness. This I refused to do. Then he announced that the job of bailiff was open on the California Supreme Court, and I could have it. I took it.

I was soon nicely settled into a double life, doing nothing in elegant surroundings during the day, grabbing hasty dinners and attending meeting after meeting by night to help organize the newspaper union. Then Tom Mooney filed application with the California Supreme Court for a writ of habeas corpus. This idea had originated with John F. Finerty, a prominent Irish-American who had made his name as legal representative of the American Association of Railroads, but had also worked for civil liberties causes, including the Sacco-Vanzetti case. Finerty had conceived a theory: if it could be shown that the prosecuting officials had connived at perjury, and that this fact did not appear in the record, the conviction could be challenged under the Fourteenth Amendment to the Constitution as a deprivation of due process. He had discussed his theory with U.S. Supreme Court Justices Holmes and Brandeis and had aroused the compassionate interest of these famous liberals.

He persuaded Frank P. Walsh that a hearing on habeas corpus would permit a review of the entire Mooney-Billings case and allow the defense to use all the smelly disclosures that had come about during the years. But this application could be brought to the United States Supreme Court only through the California high court, and although the latter was almost certain to deny the writ, it was the doorway through which the defense must pass. Tom was far from enthusiastic about the idea, but reluctantly agreed to let his lawyers have one last fling at the courts.

Reviewing all the accumulated evidence on both sides would obviously be a monumental task, one which would take all the court's attention for months, if not years. In view of this, the court appointed a referee who would hold hearings, report to the court when necessary, and finally bring in a recommendation.

Thus came the day, May 6, 1935, when Thomas J. Mooney, No. 31921, flanked by his famous lawyers and guarded by a deputy sheriff, walked into the courtroom where I performed, alternating as bailiff and phonographic reporter.

I realize now that at first sight of the prisoner I was seized by a strong sense of guilt, a need to expiate the sin of attempting for so many years to bury the social consciousness that dwelt within me. Offering my hand to Tom Mooney was my way of asking forgiveness for having kept silence. Tom Mooney had followed faithfully the path his father laid out for him. I had deviated from the path my father laid out for me, and I ached to find my way back to it.

The hearing on habeas corpus took place in various vacant courtrooms in the old Hall of Justice on Kearney Street, most often in the very room where Mooney had been tried and convicted eighteen years before. The referee appointed by the court was a rather impecunious lawyer who had been a classmate of Chief Justice Waste in law school. His honorarium was a handsome (for that time) $50 for each official hearing day; perhaps for this reason he did not try to rush matters. In all, the hearing took thirteen months.

The legalities required that Mooney be present at all times, so he was released from San Quentin in the custody of the Sheriff of San Francisco, who happened to be a good union man and an admirer of Tom's. The court had not originally intended to bring in Billings, but Tom put up such a howl, claiming that the presence of The Kid was essential to his case, that the little man also got the long "holiday." Differences between the prisoners had been papered over, with Billings slipping back into his secondary role; even Ed McKenzie had been forgiven, and contributed mightily to the Mooney presentation on habeas corpus.   Although Mooney and Billings had to spend their nights in the county jail and their days in the perpetual company of deputy sheriffs, one to each prisoner, they were comparatively free men: anything was possible provided the deputies were willing — occasional trips to the movies, the right to telephone anyone anywhere (provided there was enough small change handy to feed the pay phone); even, in Billings case, a convivial drink now and then with his guard, who went pretty heavy on the booze.

Mooney took things more seriously. He was forever busy making contacts, spreading his story, and plotting various courtroom manoeuvres that livened up the otherwise long and dreary hearing. He had the run of the jail, and was allowed to receive callers almost at will in the evenings. But the big event of the working day was lunch in a flat in the 1900 block on Polk Street, where Tom entertained famous lawyers, motion picture stars, activists of one type or another, money-raisers, money-givers, sometimes a priest or two — anyone Tom liked or felt could be helpful. Among liberals, it was considered an honor to be invited to those luncheons at The House of the Red Flower Pot — so called because the front door key was hidden under a flower pot on the doorstep. The chatelaine was a well known female radical, Myrtle Childs, known as Myrto, who, besides being as Red as a rose, was an excellent professional cook. The bedrooms of the flat were converted into workplaces for the distribution of letters and literature, complete with a forger who signed Tom's name to the flood of correspondence.

The great bulk of the testimony taken at the hearing was a rehash. Here and there, however, a sensational fact stuck out like a beacon light seen from afar.

For instance, there was the story of Draper Hand. A former

police detective who had served in the Bomb Bureau in 1916, he later made a fascinating "confession," published by Fremont Older in 1920, revealing the methods of the frame-up. He came to the witness stand at Tom's urgent request, and told how he had "wet nursed" the prosecution witnesses, entertaining them and giving them "pep talks" about their patriotic duty to testify against the accused and thus save America from anarchy. He said he had worked closely with the Edeau women, Oxman and Rigall, and MacDonald. All of them, he said, had been in a constant sweat about the reward money and how much each would get. He told of manipulating the identification of the suspects by prospective witnesses, and — a high point of his testimony — described how Oxman, on the witness stand against Mooney, had been able to pull a scrap of paper from his pocket and read off the exact license number of Weinberg's jitney.

Hand here corroborated the story as published by Older. The "honest cattleman" had been brought to the North End police station to inspect this automobile, a rather dilapidated Model T Ford. It was Oxman's "first and only sight" of that car, by then stripped of its license plate so the defense could not claim that Oxman had seen the license when making his inspection. The detective said Eddie Cunha had taken off the plate and hidden it in a drawer in the police station. Older had quoted Hand as follows:

"Cunha told me to copy the number. I did that and gave it to him [Oxman]. As far as I know, Oxman never saw the license plate itself. Cunha was nervous. He had me go back and verify the number. I did that and gave it to him; I compared my note with the plate. Only then was the number given to Oxman for his testimony."

On cross examination the former detective stood by this published account.

One of the defense witnesses in *Mooney on Habeas Corpus* was Israel Weinberg, now a prosperous middle-aged contractor, who had come from Cleveland, Ohio, at his old friend Tom's request. Like all those who had participated in the original trials, he showed the changes wrought by time. He was calm, self-assured, and although he had the same long, dark, serious face and still retained the hint of an accent, he was no longer the frightened immigrant Jew who had been held in jail for twenty months and put on trial for murder.

Weinberg told how, five days before Preparedness, a stranger had boarded his jitney at Fillmore and Sutter Streets, the uptown end of his regular run, and asked to be driven on a special trip to a roadhouse some miles south of San Francisco. The stranger, exceptionally blond and rosy-cheeked, spoke with a strong Scandinavian accent; he struck up a conversation with Weinberg and asked casually what he thought of the attempted streetcar strike that had taken place a few days earlier. Something about the man's manner put Weinberg on guard; he had suggested his passenger ask the carmen themselves. The stranger was not put off, and began to suggest that Weinberg could make a lot of money, $5000, maybe, and get out of the jitney business. When Weinberg asked the obvious question, the man identified himself: Martin Swanson, and he flashed a badge that said, "Private Detective, URR" (United Railroads). The Swede now began to put the pressure on; he knew Weinberg was a friend of the Mooneys; he knew Weinberg had attended that pre-strike meeting at the IWW Hall on June 10. He demanded: "Tell me what you know about Mooney."

Silence. Swanson: "I am a very close friend of Sergeant O'Brien and Chief White. If you don't talk to me I'll take the matter up and see that you lose your jitney license."

When this threat failed to move Weinberg, Swanson produced a printed notice offering a $5000 reward for information leading to the arrest and conviction of the men who had blown the San Bruno towers. The statement asked whoever had driven the dynamiters to the towers to contact the URR president; it promised him full protection, plus the reward money. Weinberg had received just such a notice in the mail the day before. Swanson's threats grew more ominous. He told Weinberg he had been under surveillance, just like Mooney, that he faced arrest for complicity in the dynamiting of those towers if he did not talk. More silence.

Then Swanson changed from nasty to smooth: "We don't want you. If you were in it, we can whitewash you. We're after Mooney. It'll be easy for you to claim the reward. We'll protect you fully." Finally, Swanson left the jitney with a parting shot: "If you don't give us the information you'll be very sorry. Don't answer me now; think it over."

Two days later, just three days before Preparedness, Swanson again hailed Weinberg's jitney and hastily renewed his pleas for information and his bribe offer. When Weinberg made it plain that he had nothing to tell, Swanson turned on the driver with flushed face and pointing finger: "I'll get you for this. You'll see, I'll get you!"

One week later, a few hours before the arrest of Billings and a day before the Mooneys gave themselves into police custody, two policemen halted the jitney, shooed away Weinberg's passengers, put the cuffs on him and hustled him off to the North End police station. For days he had been held incommunicado and questioned by Fickert, Brennan and Cunha of the District Attorney's office and by various police detectives — with Swanson frequently in the background, laughing as if at some joke, the rosy spots on his cheeks very bright.

There were third degree sessions; still incommunicado, Weinberg was paraded before a horde of potential prosecution witnesses, "maybe two hundred in all." Meanwhile Fickert was spreading newspaper yarns to the effect that Weinberg was about to spill his guts. A "secret report" was revealed, signed with the initials of a mystery figure who claimed to be working for a Chicago newspaper, writing an "inside" story on the case. According to this report, Fickert said, the writer believed — after several long and increasingly intimate interviews with the Jewish prisoner — that the time was ripe for officials to move in and make a deal for Weinberg's confession.

Fickert promptly ordered Weinberg brought to his office. The resulting row at the jail (as Mooney testified in the habeas corpus hearing) amounted to an attempted kidnapping. It might have been easy to strong-arm Weinberg into submission, except for one particular circumstance: by this time the bomb defendants were no longer in police holding cells at city prison. They were housed in the County Jail, under the control of a sheriff who was unfriendly to Fickert and his cronies, and who made certain that the bomb defendants received fair treatment. Sheriff's deputies stepped in and staved off Fickert's over-eager emissaries. And Mrs. Weinberg, who chanced to arrive in the middle of the uproar, telephoned Maxwell McNutt, who came posthaste. The lawyer's arrival more than equalized the situation, and Fickert's men slunk away, empty-handed.

Weinberg testified before the referee that he had never told anyone, much less a Chicago newspaperman, that he wished to see Fickert or to tell him anything. But Fickert did talk to Weinberg, after all. Since Mohammed would not come to the mountain, Fickert had gone out to the County Jail, all smiles and soft soap. His line, Weinberg related, went: "You be a good fellow and I'll be a good fellow. . . I don't think you had anything to do with making the bomb, but I think you carried them that day."

The District Attorney could think whatever he pleased; Weinberg had had nothing to say to him.

The business of fishing for confessions from Weinberg continued, a bit more subtly. One day he was visited by a *landsman* named Farber. They had been boys together in the old country, and the friendship had continued in San Francisco until recently, when they had disagreed over politics.

So Weinberg was surprised at this visit. Farber was crying; tears were running down his cheeks. Weinberg asked: "What are you crying for?"

"I will tell you, my dear, good friend. I come from a committee of three Jews; we are trying to help you. We don't like it when they make remarks against you because you are a Jew, and maybe we can do something."

They went to a corner out of earshot. Farber, his face beaded with sweat where tears had been, began to whisper:

"If you be a good fellow, we will take you out."

That phrase rang an alarm bell in Weinberg's brain; it reminded him of Fickert. Farber continued:

"They told me there was fifteen or maybe twenty thousand for you if you be a good fellow. There'll be nothing to it. We will just ship you away from here if you be a nice fellow and say what they want."

Weinberg stared at the man, saying: "Now listen, Farber, no committee of Jews sent you over to see me. Tell me the truth; who sent you?"

Farber seemed glad to shed his false front. "Fickert," he admitted. "Fickert tells me to come out here and tell you he will give you $20,000 and ship you out of the country for just something that they can hold this thing on — I mean, the conviction."

Of all this talk, four fateful words stuck in Weinberg's mind: "Say what they want." He felt terrible about them, but they refused to go away. They made him think of his family and his Jewishness. He was surrounded by prisoners and cops who told him his co-defendants cared nothing for him because he was a Jew. He had had little opportunity to talk with them and find out — and he would be embarrassed to ask such a question anyway.

His family was in dire financial straits; the strain was about to drive his wife out of her mind — he could see the trouble in her eyes when she came to visit; as he knew all too well, she was nervous and timid; he also noticed the shabbiness of her clothing, and that of their little boy. The defense seemed to have no money for a lawyer to defend him — no lawyer had come recently to comfort and advise him.

He felt alone, lost, overpowered. He put Farber off; he'd think it over.

At this, the police redoubled their hammering; they came at him daily, hours at a time, beating into his brain their theme statement: *he had driven the bombers to the fatal spot.*

Finally, Weinberg gave up. "All right!" he shouted, clutching at his mouth as though about to be sick. "Tell me what you want me to say and I will say it!"

By a happy coincidence neither Fickert nor Swanson was present to hear this bleat. Duncan Matheson was in charge, and although he wanted Weinberg's confession badly, this was not a confession. The police captain looked pityingly at the prisoner, shaking his head, and ordered a deputy sheriff to return Weinberg to his cell.

Meanwhile, Farber had doubtless reported to Fickert, who, with a typical flourish, gave reporters one of his forecasts: Weinberg was coming through, revealing the entire bombing conspiracy. This, Fickert said, would be followed by exposure of the entire network of Anarchy throughout western America. The names of all the plotters would be made known, including some still at liberty. Arrests and convictions would follow, and the streets of San Francisco would again be safe for women and children. The sanctity of The Flag would be preserved!

All this made splendid newspaper headlines. It also alarmed defense lawyers, who rushed to all five defendants, and swiftly let Weinberg know he was not alone, not defenseless, not without hope. When Farber returned for his answer, Weinberg was his own man again. He shouted "Listen, Farber, you know me! I would not do things like that. They can hang me to this post, but I will not do that!"

While these dramas of the past were being recited for the record before the referee downtown, I was uptown performing the miniscule duties of bailiff of the California Supreme Court in its austere quarters in the State Building. When court was not actually in session, the bailiff earned his keep as receptionist, taking care of the dignitaries who came to visit the justices while they were in chambers.

I could not go to the hearing on habeas corpus, but my newspaper colleagues kept me closely informed, so my concerns and curiosities were fairly well satisfied. And I was not the only one who had Mooney and his case on the mind. One day during this period, a woman came calling on Mr. Justice Preston. She was Annette Adams, who before and during World War I had been Preston's chief deputy when he was the United States District Attorney for Northern California. The mere fact that a woman had held such an office was unusual at that distant time.

Preston happened to be busy when she arrived, and while she was waiting we chatted. I asked about those times when she was in charge of the U.S. District Attorney's office, due to Preston's serious illness. The German saboteurs, the treason charges against Franz Bopp, the popular consul in San Francisco — things like that.

"You know," said Miss Adams, "there's something about that Preparedness Day bombing that has always puzzled me. We knew that a certain German saboteur was in San Francisco that very day. We knew that about ten days later the Long Tom terminal in New York Harbor, on the Jersey side, was blown up. [This was an enormous shipping pier from which munitions were being loaded for transport to the Allies.] There was a tremendous loss of life, much more than here. We knew that that German saboteur was caught and convicted. What puzzles me was that that saboteur was never asked, there never was any investigation, as to what he was doing in San Francisco on Preparedness Day."

Of all the original prosecution participants Charlie Goff had the most trouble, for he had to explain why he had changed his mind about Mooney and Billings at least three times. His explanations were rambling and depended upon rumor rather than fact, and

Finerty, the fiery defense lawyer, had uproarious moments with the police captain trying to get some sense out of him.

Then came Eddie Cunha, not so slender now, but still full of fight. He did not have Charlie Goff's trouble, for he had never changed his mind: Mooney and Billings were guilty as hell. Cunha and Finerty traded insults so heated that the referee was on the verge of calling the cops to restore order, but Mooney's prosecutor stood fast, denying every accusation the defense could throw. Finerty called Cunha "a crook." Cunha called his opposite number "dirty, cheap scum of the earth, shanty rat . . . contemptible cur, a cheap coward." The referee called a recess. After all the ranting, all the denials, Finerty coaxed Cunha with a final question: Did he still believe John MacDonald, Oxman, the Edeau women? Cunha obliged. Yes, all the key witnesses in the Mooney trial had told the truth — that he still believed!

At one point, Tom Mooney, against his own attorneys' advice, tried to conduct his case himself. In Rena's trial, there had been this incident about Fickert offering a deal through Straub, a young PG&E attorney: if Belle Hammerberg would finger Tom, she could save Rena from the gallows. All this was a bit fuzzy, and it had plagued Tom mightily, so he called various people to the witness stand, including the sisters. The problem was that the young attorney, by now chief counsel for PG&E, was a dear friend of Belle's — and, by osmosis, a dear friend of Belle's sister, Rena. The two women fought Tom's attempts to show that this man, in carrying Fickert's message, was doing the sinister work of his employer, the company which felt it had so many reasons for vengeance against Tom Mooney. The sisters and Straub left the witness stand with heads held high after Tom's questioning, in an atmosphere of mutual rancor. Tom later boasted he had obtained what he went for; I, however, would have given him a poor mark as a lawyer.

During the few hours he acted as his own attorney Tom also called "Scoop" Gleeson, the muckraking reporter to whom Mrs. Judd told her story of the "Hollywood" crew. Now middle-aged, a city editor, and highly respected in his calling, "Scoop" tried to testify regarding the Densmore Report. Yet even now, seventeen years after that report had caused screaming headlines, the referee used every device at his command to keep Gleeson's testimony out of the record, claiming the Densmore investigation was excluded because it had been conducted *after* judgment had been passed on Mooney. Tom interrupted:

"And I was still pleading for redress, as I am today, nineteen years later [after his arrest], for the correction of an outrageous wrong; and the government of the United States, the President, authorized this investigation; and this is one of the things that developed, and, to use the language of the man who was in charge of it, he says, 'This cries to Heaven for redress'."

The referee responded: "The President of the United States has no particular standing in the courts of California, and what he may have suggested or wanted to do is a matter of minor importance. . ." With this, the referee choked Gleeson off, allowing him to do little more than identify a copy of the Densmore Report.

When Fickert first learned that a man named Oxman, up in Oregon, was telling people he had seen the planting of the Preparedness Day bomb, a cop named Steve Bunner was sent up there to get the first interview with the "honest cattleman." Again, wanting to get that first interview, the defense had tried for many years to see Bunner's report. No luck. Nor were Mooney's representatives now able to question Bunner, who over the years had risen to the rank of Captain, retired, and disappeared. A few months before *Mooney on Habeas Corpus* opened, investigators probing a police scandal announced that a certain retired police captain had acquired a fortune for which he could not account. The captain was not named, but all the other retired police officers of that rank had come forward with full accountings of their personal finances.

Although Bunner was shown to have been drawing his pension for some time, Charlie Goff swore he had been unable to find a trace of Bunner despite a diligent search. All of which provoked sarcastic remarks from Messrs. Walsh and Finerty.

As the hearing dragged on, the positions of the two famous defense lawyers became more and more difficult. The fact that they were serving without fee was not the problem; they had responsibilities to clients other than Tom Mooney, matters that could be put off no longer. Walsh was the first to go. Finerty hung on a few more weeks because he hungered for a crack at the arch villain, Fickert, the last major witness to come before the refereee.

Fickert was still seen around The City now and then, often dropping into the law offices and judicial chambers of old friends, including those of Supreme Court Justices Emmet Seawell and John Preston. By 1935 it was clear his life was nearly gone. His voice was weak and halting, his eyes were dim, his mouth was relaxed and jaw drooping. As I escorted him down the quiet hall to the chambers of his old friends he was clearly having difficulty with his feet and legs, inching along with a jerk and a shuffle. Most of the court attaches laughed quietly among themselves at the thought of this oncce prominent man and his errand at the State Supreme Court. The gossip was that it once cost a judge money to get visited by Fickert; his take was said to average ten dollars per judge per visit.

When Fickert at last came to the hearing room he looked weary, with a hesitant smile flitting over his battered countenance as if begging for a little kindness. In the witness chair, he began by denying everything: no frame-up involving Oxman and Rigall, or MacDonald; never had he agreed to seek a new trial for Mooney as a result of the Oxman letters; no such thing as rigging the Mooney jury; no ôffer of a deal to Belle Hammerberg through PG&E's Straub or anyone else. Denials, denials, denials. Had Fickert met with Swanson at the Palace Hotel on the night of the bombing? Yes. At that meeting, had not Swanson named Mooney and Billings as the prime suspects? No. Was Fickert sure? Yes. Even though Swanson had testified that he and Fickert discussed those particular suspects? Fickert thought there must have been a mistake.

Finerty by this time had acquired a helper, a young, brilliant lawyer named George T. Davis, and between the two they soon had a long row of Fickert denials lined up like sitting ducks. While the famous lawyer watched approvingly, the neophyte Davis bored into the witness, showing him clippings and other documents about the 1916 strikes, the Law and Order Committee, Captain Dollar's threats. How could Fickert claim he had no memory of such things? What about scabs shooting strikers, about the employers importing gunmen? Fickert had never heard of such misdeeds.

George T. Davis and Mooney examine the twenty-volume *Mooney on Habeas Corpus.*

Davis produced recently unearthed reports from operatives of a detective agency on surveillance of Mooney and Billings on July 19, July 20, and up to and including the evening of July 21, 1916 — the eve of Preparedness Day. Why did the reports stop at that point? Was it not strange that the District Attorney had not contacted these operatives to find out whether Mooney and Billings had had the chance to make or set a bomb? Fickert neither knew or cared, even though Davis waved before him a written report, Swanson to Fickert in August, 1916, saying that the United Railroads had had this detective agency shadowing the favorite suspects up to July 22.

Satisfied that Davis could handle Fickert, Finerty took his leave. When all the ancient tale of skullduggery had been entered into the record on habaes corpus, Fickert still filled the witness chair with flesh and bone, but little more. When a man can do nothing but deny or try to explain the unexplainable, he seems to shrink in size. Not that the sneers and smirks from the courtroom audience bothered him. He was past all that.

But there was a final fillip: during the days after the bombing when the police were running around arresting suspects and searching homes without warrants, they had raided Ed Nolan's basement. There, cops had seized Mooney's motorcycle and other items, including a white crystalline substance which the prosecution had long maintained was saltpeter, for use in bombs. However, this claim had long been dropped, as the substance had proved to be epsom salts. Davis brought the matter up by mentioning certain Grand Jury testimony in which one of the raiding cops had testified the substance was saltpeter.

Fickert rose to the bait, lifting his voice and gathering himself for one last effort. He declaimed that in Nolan's basement they had found "enough high explosive to blow up this building."

Davis retorted that the witness had knowingly made a false statement.

"No!" shouted Fickert. "I know it is true."

Davis murmured inquiringly: "Epsom salts? Make an explosive out of epsom salts?"

On his mettle for probably the last time in his life, Fickert glared defiance. "Oh, yes! Epsom salts can be made into a *very* high explosive!"

13

The Crime of Consistency

After testimony which filled twenty fat volumes, covering thirteen months of shrieks and murmurs, the proceedings on petition for a writ of habeas corpus came to an end in September, 1936. Billings went back to repairing clocks and watches at Folsom; Mooney returned to San Quentin to peel potatoes and onions for the officers and guards.

Early in 1937 the referee brought in his recommendation to the State Supreme Court; to the suprise of no one, he held that Mooney's petition should be denied. The defense was eager to argue, so the court set aside five days to hear the lawyers out; Davis, now Mooney's chief counsel, estimated he would take about four days; his opposite number, a deputy Attorney General named William F. Cleary, asked for only one day.

By this time Justice Preston had resigned, and a new Associate Justice, Ira F. Thompson of Los Angeles, was on the bench. A handsome, affable man, never connected with the Mooney-Billings case, he had a reputation for mild conservatism. If he could be won over to Langtdon's viewpoint, a significant change might be wrought within the court. His secretary made no secret of the fact that Mr. Justice Thompson looked forward to the argument with an interest bordering on excitement; he was frankly curious.

George T. Davis came before the high bench like a human spring, tuned as taut as possible. He talked for 18 hours, four and a half court days, at an average rate of 250 words a minute. (I know, because I was one of two phonographic reporters, recording the words that came spurting out of Davis' mouth; the speed of his articulation made us sweat to keep up.)

It was an unusual performance in more ways than one, for Davis talked with the fervor of outrage, not in the clever, measured, and dignified terms usually heard in that courtroom. Davis listed the events of the case in all their dazzling multiplicity; he described the strange characters used as witnesses by the prosecution and the methods by which they had been exposed; he told of the evasions, misrepesentations, cover-ups and denials of Fickert & Company—and the means used to unravel all such trickery.

Furthermore, Davis described the man who sat behind him, listening intently—Tom Mooney. Although he made no bones about his client's radicalism, Davis stressed the fact that the passage of twenty-one years had brought to reality many of Tom Mooney's early dreams. For instance, all of San Francisco's streetcar men were now organized in a proper union. Organization was coming a mile a minute in the ranks of PG&E employees. FDR and his New Deal laws were giving a tremendous boost to workers who before had found it almost impossible to give themselves one voice with which to answer the voice of the employer. More than that, Tom had merely been ahead of his time when, a fifth of a century earlier, he had preached industrial unionism as preferable to the stratified organization of the innumerable, quarreling craft unions. In steel, automobile, electrical, newspaper, mining and other great industries men who never before had been successfully organized were joining the new-style "vertical" unions, picking new leaders; men like John L. Lewis and on the West Coast, Harry Bridges.

Mr. Justice Thompson was clearly fascinated by Davis. About the third day, word went around the court that Thompson was troubled—not yet convinced, but shaken. He asked no questions in open court, but in chambers he was fretting. How could any lawyer dare say such outrageous things against a former district attorney unless they happened to be true?

Knowing full well that his opponent would make most of Mooney's leftist connections, Davis touched lightly on Mooney's radical correspondence, his association with *The Blast* and Alexander Berkman, and other revolutionary activities. Davis rested at noon of the fifth day; at 2:00 PM Cleary began, uncomplaining at the shortened time. It would be ample.

The contrast between the two lawyers was striking. Cleary was huge and blond; he moved and spoke with sepulchral gravity, holding back each word until it had ripened in his throat. He had no fervor, rather the air of a man doing his job — and yet everything about his broad, placid face and weighty voice displayed confidence. He was free now from the laughs and sneers he had gotten in the hearing room, where the audience had consisted mainly of Tom Mooney's adherents. Cleary was among friends at last; no one would dare laugh at him in the solemn dignity of the California Supreme Court.

It took only a few sentences for Cleary to dispose of the issues raised by the petitioner — supression of evidence, improper identification of suspects, illegal arrests, detentions and raids, deliberate frame-up by use of testimony the prosecutors knew to be perjured. All these accusations had been denied by the State's witnesses, and Cleary expected the justices to believe them.

Tom Mooney had been a dynamiter, an associate of anarchists and Wobblies and other men of violence, a writer and speaker for revolution! These were facts that mattered most, Cleary argued. Mooney's outspoken enmity against the most sacred American institutions, his friendship with Alexander Berkman — a man who would as lief spit on the flag as not — marked Mooney as exactly the sort of man to conceive and execute as vile a plot as blowing up the parade and its marchers and spectators.

Mooney had condemned himself by his own pen, the deputy Attorney General declared, when he signed those many letters, "Yours For The Revolution." What matter an alibi here and there? Any clever Red could pre-arrange these things; they knew tricks which put them miles from the scene, with plenty of witnesses, when their handiwork wrought havoc and holocaust, taking the lives and limbs of good, God-fearing citizens.

Justice Thompson's face began to change. The worry wrinkles left his brow, his eyes resumed their natural shine, pink glowed on his cheeks, and his mouth relaxed into an incipient smile. Cleary had swept away his doubts.

Chief Justice William H. Waste had the power of assigning cases among his colleagues on the court, and he assigned *Mooney on Habeas Corpus* to himself.

The man who undertook this responsibility was of medium build and pleasant mien; a devout Methodist and something of a child when it came to money. He had an excellent salary and was by no means profligate in his ways, yet he was never more than a few dollars ahead of his bills. He admired men who had acquired wealth, found something noble about any man who had managed to earn and keep a million dollars. His few modest investment ventures never panned out. Like men in much more humble circumstances, he lived in wait for his next paycheck — which occasioned some personal problems in his home life.

The Chief Justice lived in a rented house and drove a medium-priced car. He was a joiner; his wife told me he paid dues to one hundred and four different clubs and fraternal organizations. Probably that is where his money went. His extravagance in fraternal affairs centered upon the Knights Templar, a Masonic order in which he rose to be California Grand Commander. He loved his ceremonial sword and the white ostrich plume on his cocked hat (worn, of course, only when acting in his fraternal capacity) which filled out a uniform giving him somewhat the aspect of Lord Nelson at Trafalgar.

One of his family treasures was a gilt medal, bestowed upon the Chief Justice in childhood by a Sunday school teacher, inscribed to "Willie Waste, for being a Good Boy." He lived in Berkeley, where he was credited with founding or helping to found the YMCA, the public library, various fraternal groups, and a set-up for extending financial aid to needy students at the University of California, his alma mater. Energetic and gregarious, his communal and religious activities were multifold, and eight years before he undertook to decide *Mooney on Habeas Corpus* he had been the first recipient of the Benjamin Ide Wheeler award, bestowed by the Berkeley Service Clubs' Council upon that community's most distinguished citizen. People thought and spoke of him as "Mr. Berkeley."

Within the bosom of his family the Chief Justice often confessed a hankering for beer which his principles permitted him to satisfy only during Prohibition, when near-beer was available; thus he had a very personal reason to mourn the return of alcoholic beverages. Culturally, he would not have a novel by Jack London in his home;

the writings of Zola, Norris, Sinclair, Hemingway, Lewis, Fitzgerald, Joyce, Faulkner, Rolland and Steinbeck meant nothing to him.

Since we all shared a love for Charlie Chaplin's comedies, the Chief Justice once took his daughter and me to see the comedian's latest movie, *Modern Times*. My father-in-law was shocked to the core. To him the sight of a worker thumbing his nose at the boss smacked of anarchy; the display of a red flag, even when it turned out to be an innocent misuse of a warning sign, was a hint at Revolution.

One morning a few weeks after the Mooney matter was submitted, I happened to be chatting with the Chief's legal secretary when into that office came the Chief himself, carrying a pile of documents a foot thick. There it was: Mooney, petitioner, versus State of California, respondent.

Handing his load over to the secretary with a throaty sound of relief, Waste told the young lawyer to write up the opinion. "Take your time," said the Chief paternally. "The record — for whatever it's worth — is tremendous. Taylor [Grant Taylor, clerk of the court] has the transcript and other documentation closeted away, when you need it."

"Yes, sir; and what. . . .?"

"The position will be *res adjudicata,*" interrupted the Chief, blue eyes smiling through steel-rimmed spectacles. (In plain English, the matter has been adjudged; DO NOT DISTURB.) "After all, there has to be an end to litigation sometime. Life's too short to put up with frivolous, time-wasting maneuvers."

"Yes, sir," replied the law secretary, tensing at sight of the file he was about to tackle.

The Chief nodded to the law secretary and me and returned to his chambers, light of foot and conscience. Once again Willie Waste had been a Good Boy.

For me, the California Supreme Court was insufferably dull. I was not a lawyer; I was a newspaperman, an ardent partisan of industrial unionism, known as the CIO; I was curious to explore all the new thinking, to participate in all the new action stirred up by the Great Depression. In addition, Fascism had reared its ugly head in

Spain and was challenging the democratically elected government in that country. I knew or knew about many men who were over there, fighting on the side of the angels.

There were many causes to espouse and support; all of them needed money, and fund-raising parties were a major part of my social life. Any host who gave a party only to entertain friends was a hopeless bourgeois. At parties for the budding Newspaper Guild, for Spain, for Tom Mooney, I met people who were doing things I believed in, men and women I could help and who could help me. At union meetings and social affairs I was rubbing shoulders with many different species of human, including an occasional member of the Communist Party. And every once in a while someone I had met and liked was exposed as a spy — for the FBI, Army Intelligence, Navy Intelligence, Immigration, Associated Farmers; the list grew longer every month. We were in the Pink Decade, and it was a lulu.

Among those with whom I chatted a time or two over a glass of red wine was a rather mysterious figure known to me as Arthur Scott. Neatly dressed and well spoken, he had an interesting face and manner, was a burglar by profession and had come to know Tom Mooney in "Q." Somehow or other I absorbed a story that Scott had learned the error of his ways from Tom and men like him, and upon release from prison had gone to work on the Mooney staff for a time. In fact, he was credited with arranging Tom's use of the House of the Red Flower Pot during the habeas corpus hearings. It was also said that Scott had become something of a wheel in the local Communist set-up.

Three or four days after the scene between the Chief Justice and his law clerk, Arthur Scott entered the court reception area. He stuck out his hand, called me by my first name, and glanced around to make sure we were alone. Then he said:

"I've come about the Mooney case. It's been submitted, I understand."

"Yes," I replied. It was a fact available to anyone.

"Tell me," and here I began to try to read Scott's face, "what the decision is going to be. It's very important that we know."

Quick flashes passed through my mind. I might have asked the identity of "we"; I had a suspicion. Should I show Scott the door, informing him that he had made an improper request? No, he might be merely an innocent idiot; the Left had a few of those. I might have asked Scott what good it would do the prisoner or anyone else to have pre-knowledge of the decision. It wouldn't change the outcome.

But I did none of these things; instead I fell back on one of my father's aphorisms: "The truth to him who hath the right to know it." So I told my visitor I had not the faintest idea what the decision would be.

"Could you find out?"

"Not likely," I replied. "I'm not that close to the throne. I don't even know what judge is handling the case."

Six months later the newspapers carried stories about a San Francisco ex-convict named Arthur Margolis, also known as Arthur Scott, Arthur Scott Kent, Arthur James Kent, and James Allen, who had been arrested for burglarizing a mansion in Beverly Hills. The story was played up because Margolis told reporters he was a Red who robbed the rich to help the poor. Therefore the press dubbed him "Red Robin Hood." In addition to having been a burglar and an aide to Tom Mooney, the man's basic occupation had been that of a labor spy.

My first suspicion as to the identity of "we" had been quite wrong. The Communist Party had not sent Scott.

But who had? And for what purpose?

At work in San Quentin. Most of his 22 years Mooney spent in cell #155, an 8 ft. long , 4 ft. wide and 7 ft. high unheated stone and iron cubicle.

14

Stone and Iron

Although it was pitch dark outside, morning was on the way. It was early winter and the cell was cold and damp. Tom Mooney, banging out letters all night on his typewriter, blew steam every time he exhaled. He wore all the clothes he owned, and put up a hand now and then to his lone naked light bulb to steal its warmth. San Quentin was quite a change from the comparative luxury of the San Francisco County Jail and the House of the Red Flower Pot, but after all, that hearing on habeas corpus had been merely a long vacation. Old Stone was Tom's real home, had been for nineteen years.

At six o'clock each morning, electrical impulses unlocked all the cells in San Quentin. In Old Stone the doors were opened seriatim in a rapid ripple of clicks. The cell block was of three tiers, built of stone and brick and honeycombed with cells eight feet deep and five feet wide, whitewashed inside, with arched ceilings and doors of rusty iron.

Mooney lived in the second tier. His furnishings consisted of a cot and two buckets, one for fresh water, the other for slops, a chair, a stool, and a shelf for toilet articles and books. Tom functioned in the smallest possible portion of the available space. The rest was crammed with records, transcripts, law books, newspapers and magazines, and files of correspondence.

At the click of the latch, each inmate was supposed to be standing ready to step forth, slop pail in hand, and join his fellows in a slow, single-file shuffle to a central sump in the prison yard. The wags called this the Rose Bowl; the less imaginative referred to it as the shit-pot. As the men ringed the sump and let fly, it behooved each individual to be careful. It was easy to get splashed, through negligence or intent. Plenty of cons thought it fun to decorate their fellows with dung. Also it was a splendid way to start a fight. No. 31921, however, was never splashed; his appearance, attitude, and rank as the prison's most durable celebrity rendered him immune from such indignities.

Tom's garb gave him instant distinction, for he wore a crisply starched white uniform that had some semblance of fit rather than the ordinary shapeless, dark grey. The white suit indicated that Tom served in the O & G Mess, a "bonarue" job; in free world slang, a gravy job. Another thing that set Tom apart was that all men knew why he was in "Q." One could hardly pick up a newspaper or magazine without finding some reference to him and his troubles, two days out of three. He was so obviously not a criminal that everyone from the warden to the newest "fish" knew him for a political prisoner. Such men — there were almost always a few around — were considered oddballs. During Tom's earlier years, their offense was usually "criminal syndicalism." More recently, as union organization climbed toward respectability, this law had fallen into disuse, but it remained on the books, ready for anyone who encouraged life's underlings to band together and fight. There were still some like Tom in stir, convicted of definable crimes — J.B. McNamara and Matt Schmidt for the dynamiting of the *Los Angeles Times*; three maritime unionists doing second degree murder rap for "educating" a scab too enthusiastically; direct actionists. Their motivations had not been those associated with ordinary criminality. Such convicts were usually men of great personal courage and fiery ideals. Prison guards never understand politicos; even wardens and fellow convicts have trouble figuring them out. They usually make model prisoners, and such a one was Tom Mooney. He conducted raging disputes with the various wardens who came and went, but always on the level of high policy. Tom followed prison rules as religiously as a divine is supposed to follow the Ten Commandments.

Tom was by no means the most popular man behind the walls of "Q"; it was an unusual con who could find much in common with him. For one thing, Tom was too busy; busier by far than any other con, probably busier than the warden himself. His pace would have killed a man of lesser stamina. During recreational periods, Tom ran rather than walked through the Yard. He was driven, without a minute to spare, keeping abreast of every scrap of news, every bit of gossip that might prove important, writing, planning, arguing, giving or receiving information — all concentrated upon the Mooney-Billings case, the labor movement, and political progressivism. To him all three were indivisible.

Tom's duties fluctuated, depending on his standing with the warden at any given time, but mostly he sat in a cubbyhole, surrounded by onions and potatoes and carrots, peeling, peeling, peeling, eight hours a day. The work was easy compared to the jute mill, and it absolved Tom from having to eat ordinary prison fare in the mess hall with the other cons. With his unpredictable, supersensitive guts, diet was a matter of life or death.

Had he been an ordinary convict, Tom would have been locked up at 4:30 every afternoon, with lights out at 9 and nothing to do all night but sleep. Tom, however, wangled his way into the Old Prison, and worked the O & G Mess on the night shift, from 4 in the afternoon until midnight. With this came the privilege of an electric light until dawn. Thus Tom got sixteen hours a day to devote to his own purposes — less a few hours here and there for sleep.

Always there had been frustrations. All prison mail was censored, and frequently the turnkey or the warden found a letter, incoming or outgoing, "unacceptable." Sometimes the regulations were tightened until it became almost impossible for Tom to have visitors, and those who did get through were subjected to inquisitions intended to discourage them. At other times he would be restricted to one outgoing letter per day. This put a terrible crimp in his operations, and he got around it by sending out batches of letters in a single envelope, addressed to the defense committee with instructions to forward them as indicated.

Tom's best weapon against any warden was his health. He had

saved himself the necessity of eating the regular starchy prison food by coming down with bleeding ulcers. When it became known that he might die, the uneasy stirrings of public conscience had been coaxed into a whirlwind by Tom's arts of propaganda. Sick as he was, he had managed from bed in the prison hospital a campaign that brought floods of mail to the Governor and the warden demanding that he be given the very finest medical attention and whatever diet his condition required.

The battle for health had been fought on more than one front. Tom found a hole in a corner of the prison grounds and went there on sunny days, stripping off his uniform to take sun baths. One day, however, some sharp-eyed screw spotted him from the walls and reported him to the Captain of the Yard. The Captain came running to order Tom back into his clothes. "This isn't a summer resort, you know," was the Captain's dictum.

That had been the end of the sun baths, but Tom thought of something else; he could stop eating. The first time he went on a fast the word spread that he was hunger-striking, and there was a swift rise in the temperature of the warden's office. Tom had quieted his apprehensive supporters, however, and gone on with the fast; it had done him a lot of good. Thereafter he fasted whenever he felt the need; it rested his alimentary tract. Also, on one occasion, it had given him the fringe benefit of that "after" picture used on the official Tom Mooney letterhead. It made him look like a candidate for the marble slab, and he loved it.

Tom himself could hardly have imagined beforehand the mixture of emotions that struck him when he returned from that long sojourn in San Francisco and saw the old hellhole once again. Semi-freedom had not been freedom, and this brick cell of his had become home.

Furthermore, it was good to be shut of courts and lawyers. Thirteen months of legal games had been more than plenty. For all the pleasures of the House of the Red Flower Pot, the hearings had been financially and emotionally difficult. The appeal to the United States Supreme Court was all very well, but the State Supreme Court's six-to-one repeat of all former opinions showed how deep the ruts those minds were in; Tom was haunted by the thought that the men on America's highest bench, though of greater prominence, probably had minds that ran in the same ruts. Why think otherwise, when Roosevelt was desperately pushing his court-packing scheme in an effort to circumvent the moribund opinions of the "Nine Old Men" holding those seats.*

No, the courts were not the way to justice; Tom had learned this for the umpteenth time, and he was determined not to forget the lesson again.

Lawyers! Fights between his counsel and the spokesmen for the prosecution had been part of the game, but the never-ending rows in his own camp had been wearisome; Walsh saying one thing, Finerty another, and Davis, young but not shy, barging in with a third position. As Tom wrote Roger Baldwin of the American Civil Liberties Union: "The stars in the legal fraternity demand their right to shine as well as the stars in heaven." All lawyers disagreed with each other; almost as bad as a bunch of Anarchists. Worse, sometimes they disagreed with Tom Mooney!

And the money! That problem had been acute throughout the hearing. Walsh and Finerty had served without fee, but they were accustomed to spending their clients' money in the grand manner, and although they had tried to consider the state of defense finances, habit was too strong for them. It had driven Tom crazy when Finerty took taxis all over town, or when Walsh had sent lengthy telegrams when short letters would have done just as well; or had picked up the phone and called Washington or New York on matters Tom considered inconsequential. These extravagances had been most exasperating when defense funds ran low; at one time Tom had been compelled to lay off five girls in the defense office and cut the wages of the remaining staff from $15 to $10 per week — less than half the normal wages for bank clerks and stenographers. Yet when Tom pointed out these financial anomalies to the high-powered gentlemen, they had waxed indignant!

George Davis was not so lavish with the expense account; his problem was that he needed to be paid. Tom got so he hated to see George coming, although he knew the young lawyer had no money of his own and was working full time on the case. Davis demanded more than a bare subsistence — as much more as he could get,

---

*When ageing reactionaries appointed by previous administrations to the U.S. Supreme Court did their best to frustrate President Franklin Roosevelt's liberal social programs, Roosevelt labeled them the "Nine Old Men." Congress turned down his scheme to change it's bias by appointing additional liberal judges — "packing" the court, his opponents called the scheme.

and he was persistent. Also he had a keen nose for personal publicity; this, to Tom, was *lese majeste.*

Money! If only Tom could understand the ways of the liberals who had the stuff. Here was Charlie Chaplin, who had signed a petition asking a gubernatorial pardon for Tom Mooney. But would he appear on the platform at a Mooney rally? No. For a couple of days during the habeas corpus proceedings the great comedian had been aboard a liner tied up on the San Francisco waterfront, a ten minute drive from the County Jail. Mooney had sent Chaplin letters and telegrams begging him to visit, even promising no publicity. No answer. Tom had tried to telephone Charlie aboard the liner and had been switched around from one voice to another, never reaching Chaplin. It would have been easier to get an interview with the President of the United States.

Jimmie Cagney, a tremendously popular star and a staunch liberal, was much more definitely committed to Tom. Cagney had come forward with statements and appearances, risking the displeasure of his movie bosses. Cagney made $4500 a week, even in the depths of the Great Depression; he had told Tom so. Yet it was almost impossible to reach him when there was a desperate need for money. Even a fund raiser who understood the Hollywood temperament had to work weeks to get through to Cagney and tap his checkbook for the defense. Cagney's secretaries were expert at fending off any such approach, and if the fund-raiser got past the secretaries, there was still Cagney's wife to persuade. It was often easier to get money out of some tycoon who made small claim to liberalism, having made his money the hard way.

On the other hand, there were Hollywood luminaries like Frederic March, who would do almost everything Tom asked; money, time, appearances. Whenever work permitted, March could be found at the habeas corpus hearing and at those luncheons at the House of the Red Flower Pot.

Some of Tom's financial problems stayed within his innermost circle. For example, he was unhappy when John L. Lewis, labor's great man of the Thirties, accepted a wage increase from the United Mine Workers from $12,000 to $25,000 a year. Tom was pleased to see Lewis carrying out the industrial union program that Tom had promulgated a quarter of a century earlier; it displeased him mightily that the labor leader should accept such a huge sum. Coal miners were poorly paid; not a man among them could dream of obtaining such a wage. But although Tom was shocked he made sure John L. never learned of it, nor John L.'s underlings, either. It might cut down the flow of miners' contributions to the Mooney defense.

Tom was always warning his staff people never to offend big donors, even when they deserved it. Among these was Aline Barnsdall, a Los Angeles oil heiress; easy to reach, generous beyond the ordinary, but a problem in her own right because she liked to run things and didn't know how. She had been unable to comprehend why the defense did not use a Los Angeles non-union printer, less expensive than the San Francisco competition. How could she know that the unions, a greater source of financial support to the defense than herself, would consign to the wastebasket, unread, any literature that did not bear the union symbol? When told the reason, point-blank, it had made no impression on her. Donors like Miss Barnsdall were impossible and indispensable. Tom, and Tom alone, knew how to handle them.

Whenever possible, Tom favored the new CIO unions, and for this reason sent his telegrams via Postal Telegraph, whose employees belonged to what he considered a bona fide labor organization. Western Union had a "sweetheart" arrangement with an old line craft union and consequently paid lower wages. The day came, however, when Postal refused to send one of Tom's messages. It was to a meeting of the American Students' Union, and read:

GREETINGS TO MAGNIFICENT UNITED FRONT AMERICAN STUDENTS' UNION . . . MAY YOUR DELIBERATIONS BE FRUITFUL OF GOOD RESULTS; AND I HOPE YOU WILL NOT FORGET TOM MOONEY, INNOCENT, BURIED ALIVE FOR TWENTY YEARS IN A CALIFORNIA BASTILLE ON THE RANKEST FRAME-UP CONSPIRACY EVER RECORDED IN THE WHOLE HISTORY OF AMERICAN CRIMINAL PRO-CEDURE. ACCEPT MY PROFOUND HEARTFELT PROLE-TARIAN APPRECIATION FOR YOUR SPLENDID ASSISTANCE IN THE PAST. TOM MOONEY.

Tom was forced to compromise; he offered the telegram to Western Union and that company, decreeing that business was business, sent the message.

Although he concentrated heavily on his own problems, Tom frequently revealed a deep concern for the problems of others.

While in San Francisco, Tom and Billings had talked at length with a young fellow serving a few weeks for drunkenness. Tom wrote Harry Bridges asking him to grant this man a longshore work permit; because given a chance, he might become "a good, class conscious, militant union member." On another occasion, Tom sought to involve a famous judge, Ben Lindsay, in an effort to secure justice for a young man serving time in "Q" for a crime arising out of a difficult domestic problem. Tom had become convinced this prisoner was innocent.

Many ironic incidents kept Tom's sense of humor bubbling; for instance, a letter from the American Research Corporation addressed to a list of the nation's most prominent persons, asking: "What is your favorite hobby, and why?" Tom replied: "My greatest hobby and the chief aim of my life and the object of my greatest interest is the freedom from exploitation of the class of which I am a part . . . I have been the victim of the large corporations and bankers in California because of my militant loyalty and devotion to the working class in their fight for freedom. This . . . is my hobby and the reason why."

Always there was a plethora of difficulties, some brought about by mischance. David Dubinsky, president of the International Ladies' Garment Workers' Union, had been one of Mooney's staunchest supporters and good friends. Yet Dubinsky, seeking to block the Italian Fascist Red Cross from extracting donations from Italian workers in New York, suddenly prohibited fund-raising for any purpose in the garment factories. This was a blow to Mooney's cause, and Tom wrote Dubinsky: "Surely there can be no comparison between the Tom Mooney case for freedom with that of the Italian Fascist Red Cross activities."

And then there were the cranks trying to gain cash or notoriety out of Mooney-Billings. The chairman of the Mooney Molders Defense Committee in Buffalo, New York, got a scare from a woman claiming to have a letter written by Tom in 1917, asking her to do some dynamiting for him. After a wry chuckle, Tom soothed his Buffalo supporters by reminding them that in 1917 he had been in jail under sentence of death, and every letter he had written, then and ever since, had had to pass censorship.

More than one union passed resolutions of financial and moral support and then fell down on the financial end. In such cases Tom's letters of thanks carried a bite, such as one to the Maritime

Federation of the Pacific acknowledging receipt of a check for $46, representing proceeds from a sale to members of "Free Tom Mooney" buttons at ten cents each. While Tom gave thanks, he also commented that, as the organization had 35,000 members salesmanship must have been less than vigorous.

There was no sarcasm, however, in letters of appreciation from Tom to many helpers, like the San Francisco florist who regularly sent flowers to Mother's grave, or the barber who gave Mooneyites haircut tickets to be sold for the benefit of the defense.

Although his chances of freedom had often seemed brighter, Tom's situation became vastly improved shortly after the habeas corpus proceedings ended. At long last he found the ideal defense secretary, a young man just out of law school named Herbert Resner.

Resner and several more or less leftist classmates came out of Boalt Hall Law School at Berkeley in 1936, looking for jobs. Resner happened to meet George Davis, who invited him to the habeas corpus sessions. Thus Resner met Mooney, and a father-son affection sprang up instantly between them.

Resner had an excellent personality and a penchant for getting to know lots of people — people who counted. He was soon on a first-name basis with every labor and civil liberties lawyer in the Bay Region. He knew labor leaders in the Web Pressmen, the Teamsters, the various groupings of the Railroad Brotherhoods, the Machinists, and hosts of others, plus officials of the local Communist Party. More than that, Resner was full of ideas, bursting with energy, able to make a good speech, write a fine pamphlet, organize a successful rally and spur others into action. He was an organizer; above all, he was young enough and eager enough to do exactly as Mooney told him.

Resner had no thought of supplanting George Davis. Davis was taking care of the legal end; Resner was to handle everything else, postponing his own professional career to perform the exciting tasks Tom was asking him to take over, with Tom's confidence the only reward.

Beyond his personal qualifications, Resner had the luck of good timing. The American working class was making a great surge forward, and the Mooney-Billings case became part of that surge. The sit-down strikes in the automobile industry, and a thousand other strikes; the organization of millions of new union members; the formation of Labor's Non-Partisan League to encourage working stiffs into practical political action, all helped Resner achieve the goals set by Tom Mooney.

The Tom Mooney Molders' Defense Committee began to flourish anew; headquarters were established in downtown San Francisco where people would not hesitate to come for night meetings. There Resner and three other full-time employees, a stenographer, a book-keeper, and a boy who did everything, made use of a host of volunteers. They set up an addressograph system that included an updated version of the old Sacco-Vanzetti list and many other "cause" lists; it became the country's finest compilation of persons and organizations known to be interested in civil liberties and trade union activities.

Resner had different hats. One hour he was the secretary of the Bay Region AFL Committee to Free Tom Mooney; the next hour he would be secretary of the Railroad Brotherhoods Committee for Mooney and Billings; the hour after that, secretary of yet another Mooney committee. Each had its distinct letterhead, its list of distinguished sponsors, its special operational sphere. One hat Resner wore on top of all others was that of Tom's personal factotum.

One of Resner's tasks was to work with those Hollywood actors who became very concerned over the imprisonment of innocent men but did nothing more than emote. He started with a nucleus of Frederic March and his wife, Florence Eldridge, Dorothy Parker and her husband, Alan Campbell, a writer named Humphrey Cobb, and Tanya Tuttle, wife of a leading movie director. In a matter of weeks, with their help, Resner created the Hollywood Committee for Mooney and Billings, with many luminaries listed on its official stationery and with himself as executive secretary. Hollywood protocol required that this committee be launched with some sort of a super-colossal affair, and so there was a pay party, proceeds to the Mooney defense, at the home of Ira Gershwin. Everybody was there, from script girls to top-flight directors, plus most of the more popular actors and song writers. It was fun to go Left in Hollywood in the Pink Decade.

As always, Tom was demanding, even dictatorial, persistantly piling on too much work, and then nagging. None of this bothered Herb Resner. He loved Tom Mooney. The man might very well be the most supreme egotist he would ever meet — but he loved Tom just the same. Herb got so he could make a speech like Tom would have had he been free. Herb copied Tom's writing style, omitting some of the bombastic verbosities and cleaning up the grammar. When No. 31921 could not find time to handle his voluminous correspondence, Resner filled the gap.

Resner roamed California, appearing at union meetings, fighting for the chance to speak at all labor conventions. In San Bernardino County, a region historically hostile to unions, Herb would find his way to dingy little upstairs meeting halls where twenty or thirty men would come sneaking, as if outside the law, to hear him speak for Tom Mooney and Warren Billings. Sometimes the results seemed hardly worth the effort, and occasionally confusions or transportation difficulties meant he lined up more meetings than could be covered in one night. In his nightly report to Tom, Resner apologized for these small failures. Tom serenely replied:

"I don't mind your making mistakes; the fact that you make mistakes shows you're trying to do something."

Very few of those who had served as Mooney's defense secretary — especially his wife and her sister, Belle — would ever believe he could be so complacent over errors.

One hangover of the summer of 1916, with the defeat of the longshoremen and the tragedy of Preparedness Day, was a series of anti-picketing ordinances passed in virtually every San Francisco Bay community. These ordinances made it impossible to conduct a successful strike unless the authorities chose to look the other way (when they did, there was usually well-founded suspicion of hugger-mugger between labor officials and city hall). It was a situation that encouraged an odd form of union bossism: unions which did not conform to the wishes of The Man at the Labor Temple could count on serious trouble with the cops if they went out on strike, no matter how peacefully.

In 1936, my union, the Newspaper Guild, had no recognition from any publisher and no contracts, but it had a one-room office and about a dozen devout members, including me, doing our best to make a strong, healthy union. We were young but not shy, and our voices were heard in many a union hall. Since I lived in Berkeley, I was the Guild delegate to the Alameda County Central Labor Council.

One evening, the Guild's executive board considered (among many other matters) a request for adoption of a resolution demanding that the Berkeley City Council rescind that city's anti-picketing ordinance. We adopted it, pro forma, and left it for our volunteer office person to mail out next day — hoping there was enough money for stamps in the office kitty.

By some fluke this resolution wound up not in Berkeley, but before the San Francisco Board of Supervisors. We first learned of this when we received a formal notice from that body that our request would be considered before a committee at 2:00 PM two days hence. We pricked up our ears: what The City did, the smaller communities usually followed. With the help of a friendly legal secretary at the court, I was able to do some quick research and prepare a powerful presentation. And since court chambers were only a short way from City Hall, and nobody minded if I took an extra hour now and then to tend to my own affairs, I could make the presentation. So it happened that I made a speech before a room crowded with representatives of every important union group in the city — and the Supervisor's committee voted unanimously to recommend that a measure repealing the anti-picketing ordinance be put on the ballot at the upcoming election. Pretty good for a pip-squeak union like the Guild! We were proud that night.

Then came the morning after. Hearst's *Examiner*, in reporting the action, identified me not as representing the Newspaper Guild, but as *bailiff of the California Supreme Court*. It was a neat piece of newspaper nastiness: at the hearing I had never mentioned any personal connection except with the Guild.

Every conservative lawyer in town hit the telephone to the court, demanding to know what the hell went on up there. Did not the Justices know what their staff was doing? Did not staff members know that the court took no sides in anything, lest it be prejudiced when matters came before it for decision?

My former father-in-law was the first to call me on the carpet. I apologized for the embarrassment I had caused, and explained my innocence. Apparently the Justices took the matter up in conference, for Justice Langdon, the lone Mooney supporter, was chosen to give me a paternal lecture on the mystique of the court and the necessity to keep its skirts clean. He made it clear that if I wanted to work for the court I could not go around representing the Guild in public places. I was seething; nobody blamed the *Examiner.*

It was no news to me that some of the Justices referred to me, in private, as "that pinko"; now I knew for certain that the sooner I quit, the happier they all would be. And I ardently wished them to be happy.

On the positive side, my performance before the Supervisors had put me, and therefore the Guild, on the trade union map, so to speak. The newer unions, operating under the banner of the CIO, were being expelled by the old-line AFL set-up and were establishing labor councils of their own. Not long after my speech to the Supervisors, I ran for office in Alameda County, and the morning came when the press reported that I had just been elected executive secretary of the Industrial Union Council in the East Bay.

The Chief Justice was away on one of his Knights Templar trips, and the Acting Chief was Seawell — who had presided at the trials of Rena Mooney and Israel Weinberg. It was my duty to inform him that in two weeks there would be a vacancy in the office of bailiff. His obvious pleasure at my news was marred by a suspicion that I might go around criticising the California Supreme Court. He did not mince words: "I hope that, whatever you may do in the future, you will always have good thoughts and kind words for the court. Remember, we have been good to you."

"Of course," I responded. And I could say that honestly; I had plenty of problems ahead; no need to add a hopeless fight against that court.

In a very real sense, the day I left that court was a day of newfound freedom.

Daylight came, raw and foggy, to San Quentin, and the light in Tom's cell went out. To continue working he would have to open his cell door and let in the light of day; the peep-slit allowed only a faint gleam. Keeping that door open was fine in summer, but in winter the wind whistled down the corridors, condensation sweated the brick and stone, and flinging the door wide was to invite frostbite. Perhaps a nap. . . .

By mid-morning on the average day No. 31921 would be awakened by a trusty tapping on his door. Visitors awaited him in the reception room. Tom would wash the sleep out of his eyes, comb what was left of his hair, put on a clean white shirt and a freshly starched pair of pants, and check his shoeshine. He was ready to go out and receive the first of the day's faithful.

I was sometimes one of the visitors, often as leader of some union delegation; occasionally by myself. From Tom, and later from Frank Spector, I learned many things about prison life; and from both men, hundreds of tips as to how to stir people and get things done. On occasion at San Quentin I found myself in the company of men of whom I stood in awe; like the day Theodore Dreiser arrived at the same moment I did, and Tom introduced us to each other.

Tom also helped me gloat over Labor's victory at the polls in 1937: the voters, taking the lead of the Guild, the Longshoremen and Warehousemen, and other progressive unions, repealed San Francisco's anti-picketing ordinance. We took it as a good omen.

15

Eqinox

Assuming that the Nine Old Men would run true to form, the Mooney habeas corpus petition would be denied, proving beyond all doubt that the American courts were solid against No. 31921. A trial had been held on a remaining murder indictment arising from the bombing, and it had brought nothing but a farcical, meaningless acquittal. Jimmy Walker of New York and other prominent people had pleaded for Mooney at special hearings; *coram nobis* and *audita querela*, used as legalistic cannon to bombard judges with words and theories, had changed not a single mind. For Mooney and Billings there remained only one hope — politics.

If the political climate of California could be changed so timid governors could be assured that the majority of the citizenry wanted freedom for these famous men, then — and then only — would prison gates open for them.

There were now a number of able and prominent individuals who could help create such a climate. Defeat of Upton Sinclair in 1934 had been a stepping stone, not a disaster, for the Left. Sinclair's EPIC (End Poverty In California) program had been rejected, but all sorts of progressive movements had sprung up in its place. The voices of the senior citizen were heard in the land, speaking through the Townsend Plan, Ham 'n Eggs, and cooperative groupings. More and more organizers were willing to brave the criminal syndicalism laws and the night riders of the Associated Farmers to unionize the agricultural workers and all kinds of militant and political action broke forth in the huge, corporation-owned valley farms described in a book by Carey McWilliams as "Factories In The Field." Democrats were threatening Republican control of California for the first time in the twentieth century. New unions proliferated everywhere. Old-line labor leaders and employers rushed into each others' arms, preferring "sweetheart" union contracts to those demanded by the CIO, that rascally bunch of radicals headed by John L. Lewis.

Although Upton Sinclair had left politics, many of his former associates were edging toward the seats of power. Sheridan Downey, who had run for Lieutenant Governor on Sinclair's ticket in 1934, was building rapidly toward the election which would send him to the U. S. Senate. A significant number of Assembly seats were held by men who had campaigned on the EPIC program. And Culbert Olson, a handsome lawyer with Democratic affiliations and a Socialist background, had already become State Senator from Los Angeles County.

Olson had only one vote in the 40-man California Senate, but he spoke for more than a third of the state's voters; such was the population of Los Angeles County. He had come out of Idaho and Utah, earning his legal spurs fighting for the rights of union men from headquarters in Salt Lake City. Long before coming to California, Olson had made speeches demanding freedom for Mooney and Billings. He knew the radical history of the old Western Federation of Miners, and had been acquainted with Big Bill Haywood, one of Tom Mooney's heroes. Olson thought Clarence Darrow's fight to smash the murder frame-up of Haywood, Moyer and Pettibone had been the most exciting story the Wild West ever produced; the pulse of courage beat in every word of it. Now, at long last, Olson was moving into a position where he might do Tom Mooney some good.

Poll-takers and wind-sniffers were aware that something was up. In 1935 a resolution asking the governor to pardon Mooney unconditionally had failed in the Assembly, 35 for to 47 against. Shortly thereafter, Assemblyman James F. Brennan — the same Brennan who prosecuted Billings in 1916 — introduced a resolution calling upon the Governor to commute Mooney's sentence to time served. This resolution (which the prisoner opposed) passed 51-28. Two years later, 25 of the 35 pro-Mooney legislators were re-elected, whereas only 28 of the 47 opposed made it back to their Assembly seats. It no longer hurt a man politically — except in certain areas — to be for Mooney, and so the Assembly passed a resolution calling for a direct legislative pardon. Such a move had never been made before, and there was serious doubt as to whether the State Constitution gave the Legislature such powers. Doubts or no, the majority was a handsome 45 to 28.

The measure went to the Senate, where the picture was utterly different. This chamber was dominated by the "cow counties"; Senators were elected by acreage, not population, and the Senate was often the graveyard of progressive legislation. As one liberal Assemblymen quipped: "A California Senator will vote money to combat horse syphilis, but not a cent to fight human syphilis; horses are important."

Olson spearheaded the fight in the Senate; the opposition was led by the Senator from Alameda County, William F. Knowland (son of the man who fired and blacklisted me from newspaper work). Knowland relied on the technical question — whether the Legislature could grant pardons; he had the easy oar and the resolution was defeated, 34 to 5. A second try, this time avoiding the constitutional problem by merely requesting the Governor to grant the pardon, whizzed past the Assembly but did only slightly better in the Senate, 8 for and 30 against.

(At Tom's suggestion, Resner tallied the number of voters represented by the eight Senators who had supported the resolution, as compared with the number represented by the 30 who had been opposed. By these calculations, the voters of California favored pardons for Mooney and Billings by a majority of 557,891.)

The issues of the day were many and clamorous; organizations like the Workers' Alliance, composed of people unemployed or working on New Deal projects at pittance wages, had little money but lots of people; and there were causes — Free Tom Mooney, Loyalist Spain, the Simon J. Lubin (agricultural) Society, Labor's Non-Partisan

League; and the fight to organize social workers, public workers, Federal workers, office workers, agricultural workers; support of a strike or defeat of a lockout; money-raising for some Leftist or labor publication.

Mass rallies, often for Tom Mooney, were an important part of the process of public fermentation. A Free Tom Mooney rally in San Francisco drew twelve thousand persons.

The new labor movement did more than go to pay parties, sing "Solidarity Forever," and hand out leaflets. We learned how to organize precincts, register potential voters, and get out the vote. The left was growing stronger, and the right more alarmed. Haywood Broun, president of the Newspaper Guild and a famous columnist and long-time supporter of the Mooney-Billings cause, went on a rampage against Red-baiting.

He kept his column hot, commenting that a few communists in the Republican and Democratic parties might help politicians keep up with the times, and taking shots at various investigating groups, such as the House Un-American Activities Committee, then run by Congressman Martin Dies. Broun wrote:

> Once a man begins to see Red in everything it is worse than useless to try to cool him down with facts. You will merely tantalize him into stretching the word 'communistic' so far that it becomes loose as ashes. Tell him that men like Fremont Older and Frank Walsh were mighty fighters for Mooney and he will merely add the names of those two departed veterans to his list . . . . If the radicals of America asserted they were in support of a campaign to wipe out infantile paralysis the super-patriot would be compelled to defend disease rather than share a single wish with [Communist Party Chief Earl] Browder.

The spies proliferated; there must have been at least one in every meeting of five or more persons, those days. We had to learn quickly, often the hard way. A young lady friend, a teller at the Bank of America, became enthused over the possibility of organizing her fellow workers, and helped arrange a meeting attended by three thousand of them. They signed membership cards in droves. There was strong reason: at that time, bank clerks were making $65 to $75 per month, $20 to $30 below the average for office workers. However, a few swift, strategic dismissals, including that of my friend, brought the bank clerks back to meekness and non-unionism, where most of them remain to this day.

Interestingly enough, Arthur Scott had been on hand with advice and suggestions for the bank clerks right up to the time of their debacle. Later, when this mysterious man emerged as the "Red Robin Hood" of Beverly Hills, a few knowledgeable people were not surprised. Arthur Scott had not been seen in San Francisco for quite a while, and there had been good reason for his absence.

When "Scott" had been Tom Mooney's close friend and top defense worker, he had had a stunning Titian-haired assistant and personal companion named Norma Perry. Tom had called her "Noni." Gradually the relationship between Scott and Mooney loosened; others took over the bulk of the defense work, while Scott became known as the contact man between the prisoner and the Communist Party. The rumor was that Scott's ambition was to achieve fame and power as a Communist leader; certainly he moved among the higher-ups in local Communist affairs, and also had the confidence of several labor leaders. Norma, however, drifted away from Scott and the Mooney case, going to work as office secretary for Harry Bridges.

There had been a dramatic purge among Communists in Northern California, resulting from the discovery that the party had been infiltrated from top to bottom by people secretly on the payrolls of various government and private intelligence services. This put the real Reds on guard. One such was a man known as "Pop" Hanoff. A person whose garb came close to foppishness, Hanoff was blond and bald and as Russian in appearance as a samovar. A bit of knowledge he had brought from the old country was that a man who had been converted to the left while in prison bears watching — particularly if, on release, he makes it his business to ingratiate himself with leftist leaders. Perhaps he wishes to know too much.

Hanoff was nervous about Scott's involvement with the House of the Red Flower Pot, which gave him access to a lot of people. "Pop" kept a discreet eye on Scott, particularly after learning some of the aliases that man used, and discovered a thing or two. For example, when Harry Bridges went to Portland, Oregon, for a longshoremens' union convention, Arthur Scott also went to Portland. A microphone was discovered in Bridges' hotel room; the finger of suspicion pointed to Larry Doyle, a known operative for the Associated

Farmers and the shipowners. Hanoff, however, felt positive that Doyle had not worked alone — so he asked Arthur Scott why he had been in Portland at that critical time. Scott's answer did not check out.

Quietly, without fuss, the word went out. Gradually, Arthur Margolis Scott found that doors normally open to him had been shut tight, and he disappeared from Northern California. Soon his "Communist" days were over.

It happened during that same period that Harry Bridges and a shipowner did each other a favor. As sometimes occurs between opposite numbers, they liked each other: Bridges felt this shipowner was a good guy who happened to be on the wrong side of the fence. They met every few weeks as the labor leader and his committee went from pier to pier, settling grievances in the toilsome manner necessary before arbitration machinery was established. The shipowner, according to office worker organizers, had quite a reputation as a skirt-chaser. One day, after a grievance session, Bridges tapped his friendly enemy on the shoulder.

"Just a word to the wise," whispered Bridges. "You might want to be careful for a while; your wife is having you tailed."

The shipowner took affront: "You keep your big nose out of this . . . "

Bridges spread his hands like a baseball umpire calling a runner safe at first. "All right, take it easy," he murmured. "No harm meant."

A month later the men met at another session; this time it was the owner who tapped the labor leader on the shoulder.

"One good turn deserves another, Harry," he whispered. "You might like to know your secretary is working for us!"

Bridges laid a trap, caught Norma red-handed, and faced her with the proof as she sat at her desk in the union office.

"You bitch!"

"You bastard!"

Bridges had caught men out like this, but never a woman. He took an excited swing at her; she ducked, he slipped, and instead of walloping her he cracked his chin on the edge of her desk.

Next day Norma Perry went to work for Harry Lundeberg, the right-wing maritime labor leader who was Bridges' most dangerous opponent. The story became commonly known in and near the port, and thereafter longshoremen referred to this quick-change office worker as "the iron cunt of the waterfront."

The great red bridge across the Golden Gate had been in operation only a few months when Herb Resner drove over it with four visitors, a woman and three men. This was an official delegation from the Republican Government of Spain, come to the United States to beg money for guns and planes with which to fight off the modern machines of war provided to Spanish Fascists by Hitler and Mussolini. The delegation had been given short shrift by American officialdom, and had been forced to hunt out individuals willing to donate tens to hundreds of dollars, when they needed millions. As a matter of honor and duty, they wished to pay Tom Mooney a call.

The hills of Marin County made the visitors feel at home; they told Resner the panorama reminded them of the beautiful hills that rim Barcelona.

They came to the high yellow walls of "Q" and through the gate to the office of the Captain of the Yard, where Tom was now permitted to receive most of his visitors. A new warden had tried to be strict with Tom, but soon learned the realities of life with No. 31921, as letters of protest poured in from all over California, all over the nation, all over the world.

Now Resner could come as often as he liked and bring anyone he wished; even a stenographer so Tom could dictate letters by the hour. Still, he could not answer half his mail. In fact, the prison postoffice had come to be known as "the house that Mooney built," for during his imprisonment the mail service had grown from nothing into a regular setup, with its own building and an official San Quentin cancellation stamp. At first, Tom had sent only personally signed letters from this office. Later, as it became necessary to use a green-inked signature stamp for the less personal correspondence, mail was prepared in San Francisco and brought by the sackload to the prison postoffice so each envelope might bear the San Quentin cachet. Tom took good care to see that the postmark was printed with indelible clarity, so that all who noticed would get a thought-wave from No. 31921.

So here were Resner and the Spanish Loyalists, and Mooney embraced them. The visitors' English was not perfect, but it was adequate. Mooney was eager to know how the civil war was going, and to hear tales of Indalecio Prieto and Alvarez del Vayo and La

Pasionaria and Hemingway and Andre Marty of France — and also of the young American fighters who formed the Abraham Lincoln Brigade. Speaking in the third person, as he did with all visitors except relatives and intimates, Tom offered suggestions as to whom to approach for money and advice regarding political figures who might be helpful. Most of all, Tom sought to give these Loyalists courage; perhaps Republican Spain might yet be saved.

It was 1938, the year of another gubernatorial election, and much of the pre-campaign maneuvering took place in the Legislature. In March, the Assembly voted, 36 to 30, to subpoena Mooney so he could tell his own story before the Legislature. A bloc of 22 Assemblymen attacked this move, arguing that the body had no right to pardon or subpoena witnesses. (The opposition also held that if the Legislature heard Mooney, it would have to hear the 147 witnesses who had testified at his original trial, an argument easily laughed off, since most of those witnesses, including the most important, were now dead). All protests were overridden, the subpoena was issued, and the warden appeared with his prisoner.

Assembly leftists tried, unsuccessfully, to have the Mooney proceedings broadcast by radio; the Assembly invited the Senators and Governor Merriam to attend. The Governor ignored the invitation, but more than half the members of the upper house came to watch California's most famous convict smash all precedents. By the time Mooney entered the Assembly chamber, the place was packed.

The opening formalities were as brief as possible; No. 31921 was given the speakers rostrum and told to go ahead. Mooney talked for several hours, asserting for the thousandth time that he was convicted because he was an "active, aggressive, militant trade unionist," and for no other reason. Outside the chamber, the Sacramento newspapers carried flaming headlines, and there were some excited discussions on streets and in bars — but nothing more. When Tom finished, the warden returned him to prison and the Assemblymen began debating a new concurrent resolution granting a pardon. The vote came at midnight, 39 yes and 35 no — the resolution failed for lack of a majority of the 80-member body. The next day a couple of missing Assemblymen were rounded up, one so ill he had to be flown to Sacramento by ambulance plane. Then, with two extra votes in sight, Mooney's friends moved for reconsideration.

A hitch developed. Police Captain Charles Goff demanded equal time to answer Mooney. After some confusion the demand was granted; Goff, like the man for whom he had once requested clemency, took the dais and spoke for several hours. Goff denied all accusations against the prosecution, and for the fourth time changed his mind as to who did that bombing — this time he said it must have been Tom Mooney.

The police officer wasted his time — worse: as soon as he finished the Assembly adopted the resolution on reconsideration, 41 to 29. Goff had lost his side six votes. However, the Senate again turned all this into an exercise in futility; the resolution was tabled in committee.

Pollsters differ; no sooner had the Mooney defense publicized its claims that if put to the voters they would have given Tom a half-million majority, than a Gallup poll brought more conservative results, 52 percent declaring Mooney guilty and 48 percent holding him innocent. Analyzing this poll by political affiliation, Gallup found that 64 percent of Republicans said guilty, while only 42 percent of the Democrats felt that way. Analyzed by occupation, the poll showed 65 percent of the farmers, 60 percent of the business men, and 53 percent of the professionals were against Mooney, while 65 percent of unskilled labor, 55 percent of skilled labor, and 57 percent of white collar workers thought he was innocent. The younger generation was much stronger for Mooney than its elders; city dwellers were 57 percent sympathetic, rural people only 47 percent.

In April 1938, State Senator Culbert Olson became a formal candidate for Governor (he had actually started campaigning the summer before). Every Californian who had ever heard of Olson knew the candidate was deeply committed to freedom for Mooney and Billings, so there was no deception when he suddenly fell silent on that issue. Olson felt this caution was needed to quiet some barking dogs. The McClatchy papers, for instance, were powerful influences in the Sacramento and San Joaquin valleys, the great farmlands of the state, and their fervor for Olson was exceeded only by their venom against Mooney. The same could be said for many oil executives who were placing their political bets on the handsome Senator from Los Angeles — and oil support could not be sneezed at, for to elect a Governor in California costs far more money than organized labor could hope to raise. The election was of interest nationwide: John L. Lewis tossed in a $25,000 donation from Labor's Non-Partisan League. It was gratefully accepted, but at campaign peak it met expenses for slightly less than a single day.

Olson and Governor Frank Merriam, arch enemy of Mooney and the unions, emerged from the primaries as the featured fighters in the main event; for the first time since some year way back in California's political infancy, the Republican Party was not a cinch to win.

At this juncture the Right made a whopping big mistake. By initiative, it put on the ballot a constitutional amendment proposing to bind California unions in a legal straitjacket. The proposed law would have virtually extinguished the right to strike and picket, made the unions more vulnerable to employer attacks, and promoted industrial strife on levels as terrible as those of the old, lawless days. The possibilities stirred all the unions to the depths. Even those which would not have lifted a finger for Tom Mooney now laid aside other problems and got down to political fundamentals.

The new unions set up political action committees, and their educational and organizational work sparked over to many of the older, more sedate unions through Labor's Non-Partisan League. Surveys showed that a large percentage of working people failed to register, much less go to the polls. Registration machinery was set up on a grand scale; local politicians were pressed to appoint vigorous and qualified union members as deputy registrars. In the union halls and at shopgates workers were signed up and instructed in their rights and duties as citizens; wives and families were approached in door-to-door canvassing, at shopping centers, wherever people gathered.

The Workers' Alliance gave access to the many thousands working at meagre wages and make-work projects provided by the Federal government. There the Alliance took on the challenge of poverty, ignorance, and indifference, educating and registering voters right and left.

Tom and Resner produced a pamphlet entitled "Tom Mooney's

Message — On The 1938 Elections." The defense committee, however, had no money. Feeling that it was now or never, Resner borrowed $5000; the pamphlet was published by the tens of thousands and was distributed up and down the state. Tom Mooney's Message was — elect Culbert Olson Governor!

As the campaign neared its peak, Olson asked Resner to take him to see Tom. At the prison gates, the man on guard paid little attention as Resner signed in, but showed a polite curiosity about Olson. This seemed to embarrass the candidate, and Resner watched as Olson pulled the brim of his hat over his eyes and turned up his coat collar.

Once past the guard, Resner and Olson walked past the floral array known to convicts as "The Garden Beautiful" and into the Yard Captain's office where Tom was waiting. He and Olson had never met before; first they shook hands, then they embraced. Olson took the lead, telling of his early life in the mining country, his admiration for Big Bill Haywood and the Western Federation of Miners. He said the Mooney-Billings case was one of the most shocking of modern times, truly "an American Dreyfus case." Then he spoke the words No. 31921 had been waiting to hear: "Tom, my first official act as Governor will be to pardon you."

Some professed friends proved more fickle: in his salad days as a backer of John L. Lewis, William Green, president of the American Federation of Labor, had been one of Mooney's supporters. That position had long since changed; in recent years Green had done all he could to discourage AFL unions from donating to the Mooney defense. Now, from his seat of power in Washington, D.C., Green endorsed Merriam. Mooney retorted with an open letter: "You have betrayed Tom Mooney and Warren K. Billings and the entire labor movement of California by this malicious endorsement of labor's Number One Enemy in California." Green's act was repudiated by all but a handful of the most reactionary unions.

Scharrenberg and his group made a gesture at the 1938 convention of the State Federation of Labor by adopting, with loud hosannas, a declaration withholding endorsement from any candidate with a bad record on Mooney and Billings. Then, in the closing session of the convention, delegates quietly endorsed eight such candidates.

Yet Mooney's pamphlet was having an impact. The San Francisco *News* editorialized: "We have here just one more demonstration that Mooney in prison is an agitator of higher potency than all the soap boxers in the country and that he will remain so until the issue that he personifies is settled and is settled right."

Once more the San Francisco Civic Auditorium was the scene of a great protest rally for the defense, with valiant predictions that it would be the last of its kind. "Freedom within six months!" was the rallying cry. Eighty-five thousand unionists marched in The City's Labor Day parade. Every unit carried signs and banners for Mooney and Billings, and there was a striking and impressive Mooney float.

The struggle grew more sinister when Congressman Dies announced that his Red-hunting committee had made a startling discovery — all the leading nominees of the Democratic Party in California were either card-carrying Communists or had associated with Communists. Some of this nonsense was put forth by Dies in the form of an affidavit from Arthur Scott, under the name of "Arthur Kent." Harper Knowles, a man who wore two hats — secretary of the Associated Farmers and chairman of the Americanization Committee of the California American Legion — assured the public that Culbert Olson "fraternizes with and accepts the program of the Communist Party." The Los Angeles *Times* lashed out at Olson, pin-pointing the Mooney issue. Liberals and labor leaders sucked in deep breaths: such tactics had defeated Upton Sinclair in 1934. Would that trick work again?

A month before the election, the United States Supreme Court delivered its anti-climax, rejecting Mooney's petition for a writ of *certiorari* on the ground of lack of jurisdiction. But Tom, who had again been measured for a "going-away suit," did not cancel the order this time. The court's decision was not the crusher it might have been a year or so earlier. Tom took the opportunity to stick a thumbtack in Governor Merriam's chair by filing a new petition for pardon with the demand that it be acted upon before election day. A delegation of labor and Mooney defense leaders waited upon the Governor with a well-publicized demand for his answer. The Governor, whose shiny bald head, porcine jowl and glacial expression had won him the nickname of "Marbletop," replied that he had not been officially informed of the Supreme Court's action; all he knew was what he had read in the press. Until he received official assurance that Tom Mooney had no possible further recourse to the courts, he would not consider the pardon application. In the next breath Merriam took the offensive, claiming that the pardon ploy was nothing but a concoction by Culbert Olson, Tom Mooney, the CIO, Harry Bridges and the Communist Party.

Olson, however, had an invaluable shield against all the Red-baiting — the political blessing of Franklin Delano Roosevelt — something Sinclair had tried desperately to obtain in 1934 without success. FDR was at the zenith of his popularity, and what he gave or withheld could make a great difference.

Election day came. My lady and I, and everybody else we knew, did little else that day but take assigned posts: watching polls, pounding precinct pavements, providing transportation, prodding forgetful voters, all the chores needed to get every single vote possible into the ballot box and properly counted. We worked from mid-morning until the polls closed. With aching feet, throbbing heads, and weary to the marrow, we struggled up Telegraph Hill to join a small group in a quiet but nerve-wracking wait for the election returns. The first scraps of news were teasers — Merriam ahead by six votes in a mountain town, Olson leading by four in a precinct inhabited by oil workers. By ten o'clock however, an Olson trend was discernible; by ten-thirty the trend had firmed up.

After midnight Olson's lead became comfortable; his election was assured. The anti-labor proposition was whipped decisively. Sheridan Downey would be the new United States Senator from California. The only dark spot for us was that Earl Warren, the tough, anti-labor district attorney of Alameda County, would be the next State Attorney General.

Too tired to do much in the way of celebration, my lady and I took off, driving down Montgomery Street into the dark, empty canyons of San Francisco's financial district. In the turtle-back of my car was an armload of left-over Mooney pamphlets and other campaign material, now waste paper. Suddenly a thought came. In the middle of a block I stopped the automobile, opened the trunk, piled the literature in Montgomery Street right in front of the Bank of America, and touched a match to the pile. It wasn't much of a fire, but I took Angela by the hand and led her around and around the blaze in a victory dance.

A police prowl car drove up with two uniformed men in the front seat. One of them got out, inquiring: "What's going on here, folks?"

"Just having a little election celebration, officer," I responded. "We won."

"I see," said the officer. He shined a flashlight into our faces, decided everything was all right and gave his benediction: "Well, you've got something to celebrate, all right. Have fun — and drive carefully."

The fire soon died down. I stamped out the embers and resumed driving — carefully.

One of the juicier moments of the evening came to mind, and I asked Angela: "Do you remember what that UCLA political science professor said on the air tonight?"

"I'll never forget it."

The professor had summed up the election's meaning in a paraphrase of Horace Greeley's famous quotation: "Go Left, young man; go Left!"

16

The Moment of Doubt

Winning a hard-fought election is a wonderful thing — for two or three days. Then the glow fades and a new set of problems pops up for those who live by politics. Such was the case with Mooney.

Culbert Olson could not take office until January 2, 1939, almost eight weeks after election day; many anxieties could build during that time. It was good that, within 24 hours after the polls closed, the Governor-elect had issued a public proclamation of his proposed program, including the pardon of Tom Mooney. No longer did No. 31921 need to sit all night at the typewriter, pleading, cajoling, educating and inciting people into helping him win freedom. But — he was not yet free.

Tom fretted. He felt Olson should consult him on program, on the choice of personnel needed to flesh out the skeleton of power which would be the new Governor's. But Olson had asked nothing from No. 31921; in fact, since the election he had not communicated with Tom at all.

Tom continued working his regular eight-hour shift, and the flow of visitors increased, but now Tom had spare time. This, to him, was like living in a vacuum. Seeking mental exercise, Tom took to assuming that the pardon had already been given. As a free man, how should he go about unifying the labor movement?

Tom thought of two women he admired, Minnie and Jennie. They had much in common: both belonged to the same local union, both were of Old Country Jewish origin and were short, sturdy brunettes, incandescent speakers, mentally quick and powerful in argument. Both were faithful supporters of Tom Mooney. But — and it was a tremendous "but" — one was a Communist, the other a Trotskyite. They hated each other. They fought over anything and everything, from the right candidate in union elections to how to free Mooney. Visitors had told Tom it was worth a month's union dues to watch and listen when those two went into battle.

How to bridge the gap between these two personalities and the forces behind them? No answer came to Tom, except it might be better to work from the top down than from the bottom up. So — what about Labor's top men?

Several antagonists came to mind: Sidney Hillman *versus* David Dubinsky; Jay Lovestone against Earl Browder; John L. Lewis as opposed to William Green. Oh, not Green! Tom would have fired Green the moment labor unity was achieved.

All right, take Hillman and Dubinsky, both of Russian Jewish background; Dubinsky was closer to Tom Mooney, but Hillman was a powerful CIO leader and as such, Tom thought, a force for betterment in the American labor movement. Dubinsky, on the other hand, preferred to remain in the AFL, home for the more backward-looking unions. Hillman and Dubinsky were either Socialists or just next door, and both staunchly anti-communist. Yet both men lived knowingly with Communists. Hillman sometimes went out of his way to hire a Communist, provided the person had talent as an organizer. Tom had heard of Hillman's philosophy about such hirings: "Who gets the bird, the hunter or the dog?" Clever way of calling a man a son-of-a-bitch!

One of Tom's dearest recollections was the temporary unity around his case that had been established by two normally antagonistic Jewish organizations in New York City. Of course, that had happened twenty years before, and the groups had not been large or particularly decisive. However, Tom reasoned that what had once been done in a small way might be done again in a much larger way. His vision might be fanciful, but it was a lovely fancy: Tom Mooney, blending all the opinions, wiping out the hatreds, winning common men and women into one great mass where truth and honor and dignity and justice should prevail! It would be worth any sacrifice to do that one great job and do it well.

On the more practical side, Tom worried when a member of his staff joined the Communist Party. He did not want his helpers to get all tied up in ideological cocoons; they might hamper the fulfillment of his dreams. It was best to be a friend to the entire Left; witness his own example.

But Tom had employee morale to consider. He did not have the right to impose his own ideas upon any other man simply because that person took his pay check. At most, if Tom had not wanted a Communist in his employ, he should have laid down that condition beforehand. Tom let the person know of his feelings, but made no demands. All he did was hope for the best.

The continued silence from the Olson camp became alarming. Less than a week before inauguration, Tom still had no word as to how or when the pardon was to be issued — not even a word of thanks for the campaign pamphlet. Without Tom Mooney, Culbert Olson might well have been defeated; his margin had been only 220,000 votes, comfortable but not overwhelming. Tom, by his mere say-so, could swing twice that number of votes in California; probably more. So thinking, No. 31921 fumed until his apprehensions drove him to send inquirers; what did Olson have in mind?

Word came promptly from Sacramento. Olson himself would not be pinned down, but he was clearly under pressure to postpone any action on Mooney until after the Legislature adjourned, a delay of five or six months. The Senate was the bogeyman.

Nobody knew better than Culbert Olson the temper of those cow county Senators; he had fought them in the Upper House for four long years. The election just completed had made a State Senator out of Jack Shelley, a San Francisco labor official who had come up out of the Bakery Wagon Drivers under the tutelage of George Kidwell, and there would be a handful of others of similar persuasion. However, the Senate was still solidly conservative, and the majority was angered at all the liberalism about to be thrown in its face. It had the power of veto; it could kill Olson's bills, withhold approval of most of his key appointees. It could wreck the Olson regime administratively and legislatively, and about thirty of the forty Senators were eager to do so.

If Olson was to achieve any part of his liberal program, he must find ways and means of bargaining with those thirty men; and several of his closest advisers were talking of throwing the Mooney pardon up for grabs. Immediate clemency, they argued, would be a slap in the face to the Senate conservatives. Let Mooney peel onions and potatoes a while longer. After 22½ years, what matter another half year?

The news made Tom sick at heart. There had been so many promises, so many betrayals. Delay was no good. Appeasement was suicide. If the California Senate could keep Tom in prison another month, it could keep him there until death settled the problem. He called a council of war, and the discussion vividly recalled to Resner that moment at the prison gate when Olson had acted as though he wished he'd never thought of visiting Tom Mooney. Talking the right thing was all very well, but actually doing it might be expensive. Would the cost be too high for Culbert Olson?

Tom decided to break through Olson's palace guard with a showing too powerful to be ignored. The inauguration was to occur on Monday, January 2, and here it was, late afternoon of Friday, December 30. Resner put in a call to Olson's private apartment in Sacramento, making an appointment, through a secretary, for a delegation of union leaders at 7:00 PM Sunday, New Year's Day. At that moment, there was no such delegation. To repair that lack, Resner made telephone calls all over the State that night, all of Saturday, and on and off during a New Year's Eve dance (for a cause) at Dreamland Rink.

About twenty labor leaders, myself included, responded to the call. Some came from San Diego and Eureka, at either end of the State; we represented virtually all the California labor groups that had supported Olson.

Everyone arrived on time; there were no stragglers. We were ushered into a living room sufficiently large for such a gathering; the Governor-elect, it developed, had gone for a short after-dinner ride after a long day of conferences, and would be back shortly. Before the wait got long enough to breed impatience, the door opened and there stood Olson, tall and strongly built, with white, wavy hair, a well-shaped head and face, and smiling blue eyes.

He threw up his hands, crying: "The Reds are here!" Then he circulated around the room, shaking hands with each visitor. The amenities completed, he sank into an easy chair and asked what the purpose of the delegation might be.

Resner took the lead, exchanging sweet political smiles with Olson. (Davis was not present; it was not his type of show). "We have a letter here from Tom Mooney. You know, he's been waiting a long time and he'd kind of like to get out." Resner unfolded the letter and read it aloud. It congratulated Olson and put in writing his request for an immediate pardon. It was a most carefully written letter; no animosity, no anxiety, no bombast; just a straight-forward request, couched as diplomatically as possible.

Here tricks of memory come into play; Louis Goldblatt, who attended as secretary of the State CIO Council, recalls that Olson erupted briefly, angry that there should be any doubt about his promise, but mastered himself very shortly. I remember Olson's face flushed a trifle, but when Resner handed him Tom's letter he glanced at it and responded: "Of course! I can imagine how he feels."

"Starting tomorrow morning, it's going to be a busy time in Sacramento," Olson said. "Have you any suggestions as to a date, Mr. Resner?"

"Well, I think Tom would hope — within a week, say?"

Olson looked up at the ceiling, then down at his fingertips, counting. "The first three or four days will be impossible," he declared. "How would next Saturday do?"

"Fine!" said Resner. "Fine," echoed the members of the delegation.

"Saturday will be good because the Legislature will be out of session and we can have the Assembly chamber," Olson continued. "Say 10 o'clock next Saturday morning. To avoid confusion, admission had better be by ticket." He turned to an aide, asking him to help Resner with details. Then Olson had another question: "Don't you suppose I ought to be presented with a formal petition for pardon? Every Governor has, since 1916."

"Of course," replied Resner. "When should we do that, Governor?"

Olson stroked his chin, beginning to enjoy the prospect. "I promised Tom my first act would be to pardon him. I can't exactly do that, but I can receive his pardon petition and announce the time and place of the pardon as my first act."

"You mean . . . ?"

"As soon as I am sworn in, I will go to the Governor's office and there receive the pardon petition. It will indeed be my first act as Governor."

Thus the question was resolved. We left soon, intent upon the morrow and the Saturday to follow. No one had said "boo" about the Senate.

On our way out of Sacramento that night, we noticed the lights burning late in the well-known "corner office" on the ground floor of the Capitol. There the outgoing Governor was busy appointing judges and performing various other "deathbed" acts. Among these was a pardon for one Arthur Margolis, alias Scott, alias Kent, et cetera, burglar, because of "services to the government."

The ceremony the next morning was held in the Governor's office, all right, but the room was so bare it looked as if it had been vacant for years instead of for hours. Part of the previous night's delegation was present, including Resner, Kidwell and Harry Bridges, and myself plus George Davis, who formally presented the pardon petition. The new Governor announced the time and place for the pardon hearing; pictures were taken; the news went out to the world by telephone, telegraph, and radio.

With Germain Bulcke of the Longshoremen as his chauffeur, Resner rushed to San Quentin where the warden, apprised by telephone that they were coming, had Tom in his office, waiting.

"Tom, you're leaving here next Saturday," announced Resner.

"And you're never coming back!" added Bulcke.

Tom stood speechless, a tear coursing slowly down either cheek. Finally he found voice: "What about Billings?"

On Saturday morning there were more uniformed police than usual around the Capitol. Plainclothesmen mingled with the people coming along the avenues and through the park toward the assembly chamber. These men, however, were not there to harass the Left; their duty that day was to guard against the Right.

Ever since Preparedness there had been men who had sworn that if Tom Mooney ever got out of prison they would kill him with their own hands. The most openly vengeful was Ben Lamborn, a prominent citizen of the suburban town of Alameda; his brother, Lea, had been among those killed in the bomb blast.*

Other sorts of disturbances were also possible. The occasion, technically, was a pardon hearing; all parties must be given the opportunity to be heard. Olson was willing to hear such protests for the record, but not in a way that would taint the atmosphere. Still, if some group of determined men sought to turn the hearing into a riot, could the Governor control them? He thought so; he had had that problem in mind when suggesting that admission should be by ticket only.

Angela and I got to the Assembly chamber early enough to find good seats down front at some legislator's desk — and then to turn around and watch the faithful filtering in. The leaders of the Los Angeles "reform" movement were there. Hollywood was well represented. Myrto, the ribald cook from the House of the Red Flower Pot, came with friends, all dressed up and dignified. Lots of politicians, quite a few unionists. Suppressed gasps greeted William Schneiderman, head of the California-Nevada Communist Party, as he entered at the head of a group that some identified as members of the CP State Committee.

But quite aside from the prominent or near-prominent was the influx of the little people, the workers and their wives and uncles and aunts and cousins who had given time and shoe leather and a hard-earned coin now and then, week after week, month after month, year after year for so many years, so this great day should come to pass. Among them was Lou Goldblatt's mother — who had been attending Mooney defense meetings since Lou was in second grade in New York City. Goldblatt had arranged to fly his mother up from her Los Angeles home so she could see for herself that all her toil for justice, not only for Tom Mooney but for all the little people of the world, had not been in vain.

It was great to watch them coming through the doors of the chamber with those faces shining with pride, with anticipation of a happiness that comes but rarely in human affairs. It was almost

---

*I watched and heard Ben Lamborn, at a social gathering where Chief Justice Waste was present, shake his fist in the air and proclaim his murderous intent. Waste was not affronted. His private comment later was: "An eye for an eye and a tooth for a tooth."

ten o'clock; the chamber was jammed full. My thoughts turned to that small cortege that must be nearly at the climax of the trip from "Q."

At the stroke of ten technicians quit fussing with wires and microphones set for radio broadcasts that were to be relayed around the world. Then everything happened at once. Governor Olson appeared on the platform and advanced to the speaker's dais; a bustle of people entered from a cloakroom off right. Tom and the warden came slowly down the right-hand aisle; no handcuffs now. Behind them were Davis, Resner, Bridges, Goldblatt, Kidwell, and a couple of the more helpful legislators.

Craning my neck, I caught sight of Rena, halfway up the right-hand aisle. It seemed an age as husband walked those last slow steps toward wife. Somehow they managed a gesture that satisfied the necessities. He put out a hand, she put out a hand; they touched, then embraced. They were like an old and weary couple meeting in a railroad station. No kiss; just a light touching.

They drew slightly apart and looked into each other's eyes. I saw her lips move; she seemed to be asking for something; I swear I saw his lips form a gentle but decisive "No." Tom passed on, mounting the steps to the platform with Resner and others, leaving Rena to one side. Perhaps by prearrangement, George Davis chivalrously helped Rena up the stairs and found her a chair in the back row. She was on the platform, to be sure, but as a mere onlooker.

Governor Olson announced the purpose of the meeting and stated he had received two letters protesting the proposed pardon. He proceeded to read them. The first was from Ben Lamborn, declaring that justice for his dead brother required the continued incarceration of Tom Mooney, without mercy, until death. No threats, however — not in writing. The audience sighed with relief. If that was the sum of the protest by relatives of bomb victims, well and good. The second letter was from California's newly elected Attorney General, Earl Warren. Announcement of his name drew a murmur of distaste from the audience, but his letter proved mild. It did little more than express the hope that Governor Olson would conduct the matter of a pardon for Thomas J. Mooney so that no discredit would fall upon the prosecuting authorities and the courts.

With these letters read and filed, Olson looked out over the crowd and asked the required question: Was anyone present who wished to oppose the pardon? There was a pregnant hush; everyone turned this way and that, searching for the raised hand, the rising figure.

The Governor did not hold the moment overlong, for there was no need. He called upon George Davis, who briefly summarized the defense position; the attorney declared that the "most sinister aspect" of the Mooney case had been the refusal of the California Supreme Court to act in accordance with justice, adding: "The issue . . . was not Mooney . . . it was the integrity of the judicial process."

Then Olson spoke for himself, earnestly but without flourish. He said he had thoroughly familiarized himself with the case, and that "there is no doubt that Mooney was convicted on false and perjured testimony." He expressed deep regret that he could not, under the law, grant a pardon to Warren K. Billings, uttering the hope that the State Supreme Court, in the near future, would open the doors for Mooney's fellow convict.

The Governor proclaimed his faith in Tom Mooney and sympathy for the cause of "industrial and social justice" which had been Mooney's "life obsession." Olson expressed confidence that the man he was about to set free would use his new opportunities wisely and peacefully, in accordance with the finest democratic traditions. Thus Olson led up to his climax; saying he had prepared and signed an Act of Clemency granting Thomas J. Mooney a pardon; the Governor unrolled a scroll, looking like the parchment diplomas handed to scholars, and read aloud the fateful words inscribed thereon.

The Assembly chamber was a great cup of emotion, full to the brim, as the Governor turned and beckoned Tom to join him on the dais. Ears strained to hear every word and intonation as the tall, handsome Governor said to the rotund man who had just quit being Prisoner No. 31921:

"I now hand to you, Tom Mooney, this full and unconditional pardon." The two shook hands, and there was a split second of silence. Then the Governor gestured toward the waiting microphones, saying: "And now, Tom, you are free. We are waiting to hear whatever you may have to say."

Mooney's first words came haltingly. But he quickly gathered confidence. Microphones were new to him; freedom was new; the

world was new! He gave due thanks to the Governor. Taking note
of the discretion inherent in Olson's remarks, Tom avoided dwelling
on the infamies of the past. But when he tried to express his
gratitude to the helpers and supporters in the hall and all over the
globe, his feelings nearly overcame him; we could recognize the
telltale quaver in his voice. He mastered himself, but his listeners
could bear no more; sobs, some muffled in handkerchiefs, burst
forth everywhere. Men and women sat staring at Tom Mooney
while tears slid down their cheeks.

Gone was the prisoner, the man of bitterness and suspicions
and fiery demands. In his place stood a gentle soul, speaking of the
most urgent task confronting him — freedom for Warren Billings.
Then, enlarging slightly upon the Governor's remarks about social
justice, Mooney set forth his belief that "the force of economic
organization of workers" would be the best guarantee the world
could have "against the onward march of the terrific and dark and
sinister Fascist reaction." And further: "Our economic system is in
a state of decay, here and throughout the world. Out of it I hope
will grow another and better social order. And to that end, Governor
Olson, I shall dedicate my life . . . "

He stopped, left the dais, and stumbled into Resner's outstretched
arms. The pardon hearing was history.

Nothing had been left to chance. Mooney and his party were led
through back labyrinths of the Capitol to a spot where a fleet of
automobiles furnished by the state Highway Patrol waited to make
the dash to Folsom Prison.

Prisoner Billings and Ex-Prisoner Mooney met in the official
reception room. Tom was blooming, his orotund self again, swearing
he would not rest until Billings walked out free. Billings' smile was
wan; he said congratulatory, optimistic words, but his look and
tone spoke of underlying resentment. It would not be easy to see
Tom leave that room, going anywhere he pleased, while Billings
could only march back to his cell.

When all the right words had been said, Tom and his party left,
shaking off the chill of the prison and the look on Billings' face.
Back in Sacramento, the Mooney group found newspapers with

Governor Culbert Olson granting Mooney his pardon. Mooney's acceptance speech would not be out of place today: "Our economic system is in a state of decay, here and throughout the world. Out of it I hope will grow another and better world."

big, black headlines — but they were not about the pardon; that story had become secondary. The new sensation concerned Governor Olson, who had collapsed three hours after freeing Mooney and was now under emergency treatment in a hospital, in danger of his life.

That night doctors debated whether Olson had suffered a heart attack or whether he was suffering extreme exhaustion from the strain of the campaign, the inaugural, and the pardon hearing. Quite a few Californians attributed the Governor's misfortune to divine retribution. To them, a man who would free Tom Mooney deserved the worst.

Before retiring that night, Tom sent a message of solicitude to the man who had so magnificently befriended him. However, there was another matter high on Tom's personal agenda just then. For the first time in twenty-two and a half years, he was about to go to bed with a woman — and she was not Rena.

17

Up Market Street

The Sunday after the pardoning was blessed with weather fit for rejoicing; the sun was bright and the air smelled like early Spring.

Angela and I rejoiced, not only for Tom Mooney but for ourselves, for we were newlyweds. We had taken the rest of Saturday off: Sacramento was halfway to Nevada, where couples could get married without the three-day wait imposed by California law between marriage license and ceremony; then we had driven back that night to see what Sunday might bring.

In the morning the Mooney party came across California into Marin County and to the grave of Mother Mooney on Mount Tamalpais. Tom had never seen it. Someone with forethought provided a bunch of roses for Tom to place at the headstone as he knelt, paying his respects to the memory of the one he had held most dear. His chubby face was solemn and his eyes were bright, but there were no tears. He had had four and a half years to become used to the fact of Mother's death.

Ever since Olson's announcement of the pardon hearing, plans had been in progress for a public observance of Tom's return to San Francisco; something to make amends to the man whom The City had once condemned to death. There were to be no silk hats or brass bands and flags or police honor guards and pink-faced bureaucrats out for a little unearned publicity! The Mayor now was Angelo Rossi, (whom I had witnessed giving the Fascist salute, Mussolini style, at a right-wing rally.) None of us wanted such a man to officiate at Tom's home-coming. Nor did the planners want the mounted police, or the Chief of Police, or any police at all. Memories of 1916 and the great waterfront strike of 1934 were still green.

These same painful memories led to some concern over the possibility of violence. The parade was to proceed up Market Street from the Embarcadero to the Civic Center, but on Sunday, with stores and office buildings closed which simplified the task of protection. Men were assigned to scan the rooftops and windows along the route for snipers or bombers. One hundred of the huskiest longshoremen, armed with their hooks, were designated an honor guard to march with Tom and form a hollow square around him at any sign of menace. Unions were requested to show their banners in the line of march, with that of Mooney's own Local 164, International Molders' Union, in the vanguard. A small speakers' platform was set up on the steps of City Hall.

The publicity announcing the parade was explicit — no glitter, no frills, no spectacle. The time had come to see what plain, ordinary Mr. and Mrs. San Francisco thought of Tom Mooney and his pardon.

The Mooney automobile rolled into its reserved parking space at the foot of Market Street exactly at the appointed hour. The longshoremen set up a cheer and closed around Tom. Labor leaders who had supported Mooney and helped elect Olson formed a line on the Embarcadero facing the broad canyon that leads uptown through the heart of San Francisco. That line spoke eloquently of the division in labor's ranks over Mooney; neither Ed Vandeleur, secretary of the State Federation of Labor; nor John O'Connell, secretary of the San Francisco Labor Council; not Mike Casey, reactionary leader of Teamsters' Local 85; nor Harry Lundeberg, head of the Sailors' Union of the Pacific and foe of Harry Bridges; no Paul Scharrenberg of the maritime unions and the State AFL. They and their kind would have been unwelcome.

For a few steps it looked like a medium-sized affair at best. Tom, bareheaded and wearing his going-away suit, dark grey with

Victory parade in San Francisco. In the front line are Harry Bridges, Belle Hammerberg, Rena Mooney, George Davis, Anna Mooney, John Mooney and John (later Mayor) Shelly.

a faint pin stripe, was in the lead, followed by his local union banner, the Longshore honor guard, and the line of progressive labor leaders. One short block brought them to the corner of Steuart and Market. Passage of time had changed the tragic spot beyond recognition, but many gave it a passing glance.

Except for the spearhead, any semblance of parade quickly vanished. Those who had notions about keeping the lines straight and marching eight abreast had to give up. There were no ropes, no police to hold back the onlookers — so the onlookers joined the parade. Marchers who started four or five ranks behind Mooney were half a mile behind by the time Tom reached the Civic Center. He was a human magnet, pulling people off the curbs to follow joyously in his wake. The longer that wake became, the more the participants reveled in the sensations of strength and brotherhood that rewarded their exertions. As a parade it was a mess; as a demonstration it was a miracle.

One of those who watched from the curb was a man in mufti who had just returned from a two year-year tour of duty in the Orient as a Marine Corps officer — plus a private mission for Franklin D. Roosevelt. He was Captain Evans Carlson (soon afterward to become Colonel Carlson, leader of the famous "Carlson's Raiders" in World War II). He was spending a few days in San Francisco for a reunion with wife and family before going on to Washington to give the President his personal evaluation of the Sino-Japanese situation. San Francisco had always been one of Carlson's favorite cities, and it was good to be walking its streets after many months abroad. Son of a preacher and deeply religious, more concerned with the political and social aspects of events than most of his military colleagues, Carlson, out of curiosity, made it a point to be standing on the curb when Tom Mooney passed by.

When he caught sight of the plump, middle-aged man with the bushy black eyebrows and that smiling Irish face, the professional soldier felt the impact of an emotion he had not counted upon, although he had known something similar during his adventures with the Eighth Route Army in China. It was a sensation of strength and joy, attainable only when surrounded by human beings who are gripped with the certainty that something good has been achieved. Carlson himself was the physical opposite of Tom, tall and gaunt and with a face like sunshine on a crag of New England granite.

Carlson stepped off the curb at a point about a block above the spot where Oxman had sworn he stood and watched Mooney and Billings place the infernal machine. Without making any conscious decision, Captain Carlson let his body move out into the stream of marchers; his pulse quickened, his spirits lifted. He walked with working stiffs and university professors and bank clerks and girls from high school and old men who could tell stories of San Francisco as it had been before the bombing. It made Carlson feel — as he had sometimes felt in China — that perhaps the day would come when he could put his finger on the common denominator of all mankind and be able to say to himself: "This is the reason for our existence."

The parade advanced steadily up Market Street; as they passed the Hearst Building at Third Street, Tom turned and raised his hand in the Bronx salute, thumb to nose. It was a throwback to the years when Hearst's *Examiner* had been the principal outlet for Fickert's inflammatory blasts. Tom felt that the *Examiner* had contributed more to his convictions than the perjured testimony of Oxman and MacDonald.

Actually, over the years, Hearst's own relationship to the Mooney case had not been so simple. In New York, where the pro-Mooney movement was popular, the Hearst papers had become friendly soon after the Oxman disclosures and the Petrograd incident. But Hearst's San Francisco editors never got the word: the difference could not have been more marked if one paper had been printed with red ink and the other with green. Under Older, of course, the Hearst-controlled *Call* (which soon absorbed the faltering *Bulletin*) had become the great spokesman for Mooney and Billings — but this made little difference to the four other Hearst papers in California.

For years Tom had tried to win the powerful publisher to his side, importuning famous persons such as George Bernard Shaw, Charlie Chaplin, Mary Pickford and Douglas Fairbanks to use their influence for the defense with Hearst. He had even sought to gain the support of Marion Davies, the movie star, in hopes she might be willing and able to influence her immensely rich and powerful friend. Somewhere along the line something had worked, for in the early part of the Pink Decade all five of Hearst's California papers suddenly came out for Mooney. The change had been of great importance, but Tom always thought the San Francisco editors made it grudgingly and only because William Randolph Hearst had ordered them to straighten up and fly right. At any rate, the underlying antipathy remained.

Those close enough to see Tom's gesture knew the background and shared his feelings. They were well aware that, because of Labor's outrage at the paper's editorial slant, *Examiner* editors had lived in terror during certain strikes, installing steel shutters at all ground floor entrances to the Hearst Building and keeping armed guards on duty day and night. No actual attack had occurred, but the hate was there; that was why Tom's placement of thumb to nose drew such a roar of approval.

There was not a uniformed cop in sight; unpleasant incidents were few and trifling. When the rearguard of the paraders reached the Civic Center the entire area, two square blocks, was packed with humanity. Police estimated the attendance at twenty thousand; Labor spokesmen and the *Call-Bulletin* said it was "nearly 100,000."

There were no seats; it was a standing-room-only affair. The speeches began, and some men talked too long, but nobody left. The City wanted to hear Tom Mooney, even if those hundred thousand pairs of feet wore holes in the pavement.

When Tom finally took the microphone he expanded a bit on his remarks of the day before. He was specific about his lifelong belief in the principles of socialism, and blasted the divisive, old-fashioned labor hierarchy typified by the leaders who were not there to hear him. He recounted with pride his early struggles to bring about industrial or "vertical" unionism, and how his dreams were now being realized via the CIO. He preached labor unity, but he preached not too long or too demandingly. Within twenty-four hours Tom had become an easier, softer man.

When he finished the loudspeakers fell silent, the speakers' platform emptied. The crowd stirred, separating slowly as though people were loath to break the bond that had held them all so close that day. Exultation had been replaced by a feeling of satisfaction; a great hunger had been appeased.

Tom Mooney set up his personal headquarters in a modest suite of rooms in a modest hotel, two minutes' walk from his defense office. Both places buzzed with activity, for Tom was plunging into all sorts of plans. There was a pressing problem — money. In the final push for victory it had seemed advisable to spend without worry for the future; now the Tom Mooney Molders' Defense Committee was $15,000 in debt.

This might not have been too serious a matter if Tom had followed the advice of almost all his friends and helpers, including the local and national Communist leaders. New York wanted him; Chicago begged for him; Washington, D.C. and Boston were sending telegrams and calling. But Tom held back. He was committed first to see that Billings was also free; he felt that barnstorming around the country would not be consistent with that pledge.

It was not an easy decision. In Chicago a Newspaper Guild strike against a Hearst paper had been dragging along for months and the strikers badly needed a boost, something they felt Tom could provide. While discussing the invitation over long distance with a Chicago Guild officer, he and Tom both noticed interference on the telephone line, as if some bungler was trying to listen in.

Tom finally hit upon a compromise. The state's parting gift to all discharged prisoners was a $10 bill. Tom still had that bill. And here was the San Francisco-Oakland Newspaper Guild, an actual union at last, recognized by most local publishers, with contracts and all the paraphenalia of labor-management relations, eager to help the Chicago strikers in any way possible. Tom went to the Guild office and presented half of the State's farewell gift to the Chicago Guildsmen — a bit of the symbolism so dear to him. A recording machine was in readiness, into which Mooney spoke his best wishes to the strikers in Chicago and assured them that if they kept their picket lines firm and worked in unison with the older unions in the newspaper industry they would unquestionably achieve their goals.

How best to use the other five dollars? The biggest strike in San Francisco at the moment was that of a new AFL union, the Retail Clerks, against a leading chain store. Tom therefore proceeded from the Guild office to the Clerks' office, where he spent the other half of the State's beneficence. In both instances there was a little ceremony, some speech-making, and much shaking of hands for the benefit of photographers.

Longshoremen thought it might have been triggered by the nose-thumbing; Guildsmen were sure the cause had been the five dollar gift to the Chicago strikers. Certainly the Hearst organization was quick to take offense and brooked no opposition in fields where it had power — and there were many such fields. Whatever the cause, the San Francisco *Examiner* suddenly went for Tom Mooney's jugular.

Any newspaperman covering the Mooney story, unless he was dead drunk, must have noticed something very odd about Tom Mooney's domestic affairs. Now that his every move was a public matter, it was plain to see there was no wife at his side. Rena was not a party to the goings and comings at the hotel suite or the defense offices; Tom did not go to the house where she and Belle lived.

There were encounters, for Rena was certain to show up whenever a victory meeting was staged for Tom. I witnessed one such scene when, as secretary of the Alameda County CIO Council it fell to me to arrange a mass meeting celebrating Mooney's freedom at the Oakland Civic Auditorium. This was a huge affair, with ten thousand in attendance.

As Tom and I emerged from a car in front of the Auditorium, Rena appeared. A muted drama ensued — like that of the aging actress hanging around the stage door, begging for a chance to make a triumphal entrance with the leading man; it was painful to see. She looked Tom in the eyes, extended a hand as if to pet him, and asked in a low tone, "Please, Tom, let me walk down the aisle with you. Let me sit beside you on the stage." Tom's face hardened: "No, Rena, you know that is impossible." Resner was prepared for such meetings. He had arranged for some kind man to take her by the elbow and steer her to a seat where her presence could be noted, leaving Tom unencumbered.

Gradually Tom and Resner became aware of an *Examiner* reporter who seemed to be always under foot; Ernie Lenn, a tall, dark-haired young fellow with pouty lips, thick-lensed spectacles and a perpetual frown. At 5 o'clock one morning there came a rap on the door of the Mooney hotel suite. It continued until Tom got out of bed and opened up — and there was Lenn, trying to shoulder his way in and see who was sleeping with whom. Resner happened to be spending the night there; he was awakened by the noise of the struggle and joined in the fray. He and Tom shoved Lenn away and locked the door.

One of the points at issue at that doorway was the reputation of the young woman who had become Tom's lover. I met her once or twice; a small, mousy person, affectionate but not pretty. In the years immediately preceding the pardon, defense activities had brought her to the attention of the prisoner, and they clicked. She had offered herself without strings — nothing but a desire to love, help, and cherish Tom, and he had found her wonderful.

Tom was furious at the intrusion; Resner was worried. Men like Lenn did not act that way out of idle curiosity. But after a few days of more or less open surveillance, Lenn faded away, knowing little more than the obvious — Tom and Rena were not living together. His next move was clear — Rena might be easier to deal with than her doughty husband.

Double headlines screamed the story across Page One of the *Examiner* on the morning of February 3, 1939, less than four weeks after Tom's release:

MOONEY WANTS DIVORCE, SAYS WIFE; SHE'LL FIGHT

Rena, Stunned by Outlook, Describes Many Sacrifices

Fears Cheers of Crowds Have Alienated Mate

by ERNEST LENN

Tom Mooney wants a divorce.

"But I won't let him have it," Rena Mooney told The Examiner yesterday.

The young bride who grew old and grey waiting for her man to be released from San Quentin, whose wedding anniversaries were merely forlorn milestones on a lonely road, was emphatic.

"Tom has talked to me about a divorce. I can't understand why, after what we have been through. Maybe it's because he wants all the applause—the crowds, the cheers, the bands.

"What is there left for me? This . . ."

She was seated at her copyists desk at the local Federal Music Project. She was wearing a neat pink smock. It was faded, like her tired eyes.

Under it was a plain yellow dress, formless as a sack. It was all in contrast to the well-groomed, well-to-do business man appearance of Mooney today.

All day, she said, she sat at her desk, peering through tortise shell glasses, transcribing orchestra scores. Thundering symphonies. Gay, light pieces.

But to her they are merely black dots and hieroglyphic musical terms, all to be spaced by bars—bars almost as grim as those that once held Tom Mooney. These bars hold her prisoner. For Rena Mooney is on relief.

Through those endless nights during Tom Mooney's San Quentin years she had but one thought. And that was how they would start life anew some day, together.

She was at his side when he was released from San Quentin, at the pardon hearing in Sacramento, and on his return to San Francisco. She thought they would continue on through life like that.

Which is why Rena Mooney is so stunned at this talk of divorce.

"Tom is the hero," she said. "He takes trips on planes, makes personal appearances, wears nice suits. I earn only $45 a month here. They won't let me see the books on Tom's income.

"They figure I'm an anchor to Tom.

"We've been through too much to think of divorce. We've been married 27 years. I'm 61 now. We're old. I want to spend the remaining years with Tom Mooney—the old Tom Mooney.

"I fought to save him from the gallows. I fought for his freedom. I never had much money, only what I could eke out from my little music studio. I'm a music teacher.

"What money I earned went for Tom. I remember making out-of-town trips, to speak in his behalf, and having to borrow the train or bus fare.

"During the 1933 depression things were blackest. I was honestly considering digging worms in my back yard, and selling them for bait, to the fishermen at Municipal Pier.

"I'd like to go with Tom and be present at his personal appearances. But they won't let me. Well, I won't let them part us. Not even San Quentin could do that."

People who knew of Rena's fondness for liquor surmised that Lenn had unlocked her mouth by getting her drunk. However, it developed that much greater pressure had been required before Rena would say a public word that might harm Tom. When she had a chance to tell her side of the story, Rena declared that "somebody threatened to take me off relief now that Tom was out of prison and could support me." Tom told everybody who would listen that Lenn had gone to Rena's project and represented himself as a Federal agent, threatening to have her fired unless she gave him something he could build up into a scandal.

The story was hung on the frailest of pegs. Lenn had asked Rena, if Tom should file suit for divorce, what would she do? She had replied that she would fight such a move; she was Tom's wife and wished to remain so; she wanted nothing more than to be with him and help him, as she had always done to the limit of her capabilities.

Nowhere did Lenn say in his story that Tom had sued for divorce, which would have been untrue, or was known to be contemplating such action. The quote had been extracted from Rena in such a way that Lenn reported nothing libelous, yet smeared Tom as a heartless, ungrateful wretch.

The America of 1939 demanded that its villains be villainous and its heroes pure. Once a man had achieved heroism in the public mind, President or prisoner, he dared not put aside the wife of his bosom. However one wronged the other, any couple that wanted America's love must love each other — at least in public. (Except, of course, for movie stars; they were exempt from all the rules.)

Tom had perpetrated a fraud upon his public — harmless, but a fraud nonetheless. It need not have been so, for if Rena had yielded to his urgings and divorced him when they first split all would have long since been over and forgotten. But she had been stubborn, and now Tom stood in the ruins of a shattered illusion. Love had *not* conquered all; stone walls *do* a prison make; the wife who waited after her own fashion could not share in the vindication of the man who had served the hard time. The wire services picked up the story and raced it around the nation. It was clear Tom had been severely damaged, but it took time to realize he had suffered a disaster.

On the night Lenn's story was published I attended the regular monthly meeting of the Eastbay Mooney Defense Committee. Most of the members had spent years helping Tom. Now they found their idol splattered with mud, and they were aghast. Was it true, this divorce story?

I tried to defend Tom, telling the group that it was impossible for a marriage to survive the strain of such a long separation. I told my grieving audience that Tom believed Rena had taken up with George Sayles, and after Sayles with other men.

An Irishwoman spoke up, a grandmother, a worker herself and the widow of a worker, militant all her life:

"And what did he expect the poor woman to do? Keep it on ice for twenty-two and a half years?"

She flounced out of the meeting; the men looked down their noses, shamed that she should have said such a thing. Very shortly the meeting adjourned, without setting the time and place for the next meeting. There wasn't going to be any.

Women of the intelligentsia were also put out with Tom, although they were not so blunt as the old Irishwoman. Among the most knowledgeable of Tom's critics was Miriam Allen de Ford, widow of a prominent Socialist, writer and correspondent for the Federated Press, member of the Newspaper Guild, and a practicing feminist with a labor and socialist background. She had written for Mooney and in support of his cause, but their relationship had not been easy. It had been difficult for her to accept his contention that because he was "the man who is doing the time" he knew better than a professional writer how to tell the world about the Mooney-Billings case. The Mooney family also got under Miriam's skin; she felt that Mother and Anna and John had done altogether too much to stir Tom up against Rena.

"It's that damned Irish morality," was her verdict. "Putting Rena in with the Mooneys was like throwing a kitten into a cage of wildcats!"

Tom's first venture outside of Northern California, a mass meeting in Los Angeles, turned out poorly. There the AFL unions absolutely refused to cooperate with the CIO.

And there was another reaction that the more intelligent among the anti-Mooney people had foreseen many years earlier. Mooney, free, was rapidly losing his value as a symbol and becoming nothing but a pleasant, aging man with grandiose ideas.

The pay parties changed in character; no more for Mooney, because he had won; no more for the Spanish Loyalists, for they had lost. No one, after the fourth glass of red wine, broke into Spanish and sang *Los Cuatros Generales* or *No Pasaran!* — in fact, any such effort would have brought the whole group to tears. The major cause of the moment was an effort to halt shipment of American scrap iron to Japan. Already the wind-sniffers sensed that this metal might be coming back at us, and soon.

On top of everything else, Tom was again having trouble with Warren Billings. Everyone had agreed for more than twenty years that the two cases were inextricable, that what was fair for one man must be fair for the other. Therefore, Billings' imprisonment had become more inexcusable than ever. Only the State Supreme Court, however, had the power to recommend pardon for "two-time losers," and the majority of the justices could not see why they should reverse themselves simply because a damned fool Governor had given freedom to a dangerous man.

Olson recovered from his long illness, but found himself facing many frustrations beside his inability to pardon Billings. His legislative and administrative programs were in shreds. Until some change in the court, by death or resignation, made it possible for Olson to appoint liberal justices, there was nothing he could do.

Even though Mooney visited him often, Billings felt neglected and forgotten. As he had done years before, the Folsom prisoner began to turn away from Tom and the radicals, thinking he could make better progress toward liberty through the more "respectable" elements of California unionism. Billings decided to woo Paul Scharrenberg.

One day, facing Tom in the Folsom reception room, Billings became nasty; he accused Mooney of deserting him. This brought on indignant denials, but Billings refused to be mollified and the visitor departed in a huff. Years later, Billings claimed he had deliberately planned this scene to win Scharrenberg's support. The prison reception room was known to be "bugged"; he hoped his bit of acting would be taken as a genuine break with Mooney. He further hoped that the record of that meeting would be reported to Scharrenberg, and presto! bring the whole AFL hierarchy to Billings' side.

Whether Billings' version came from forethought or afterthought, Tom took Billings' "play-acting" for the real thing. Tom could understand the impatience and suspicion of a man under lock and key — for he himself had been that way — but he was certain that Billings was mistaking enemies for friends. It was too much for Tom to take; he and Billings never saw each other again.

By summer Tom felt free to undertake the national tour that had promised so much in January. Easterners had always been more supportive of Tom Mooney than the citizens of his home state. But the long delay had been a great mistake; Tom and Resner made the trip, only to discover the full extent of the damage done by the passage of time and by the *Examiner* revelations.

Most of Tom's working class supporters in the industrial centers of the East were Catholics — Irish and Polish and Italian and German. When they learned that Tom Mooney had disowned his wife, they kicked his pedestal out from under him. Liberals came to see and hear him — but not the workers! There were nice little meetings in places like Washington, D.C.; rooms full of people who did not mind if a couple agreed to disagree. But the meetings in Chicago and Buffalo and Cleveland and Cincinnati were disastrous flops. Even Detroit was a near-flop.

Still hoping to recoup, Tom planned a smashing rally in New York's Madison Square Garden and sent Resner and another aide ahead to do a month's spade work. As the meeting date approached, Tom came to New York and went from office to office, asking advice from old friends. He talked to David Dubinsky and Sidney Hillman of the garment trades and to CIO people like John Brophy, whom Tom had always admired; to his first defense secretary, Bob Minor; to Earl Browder, head of the American Communist Party, and to Browder's worst enemy, Jay Lovestone.

As gently as possible, Browder told Tom: "When you were in prison you were everywhere in the world. Now that you are out, you are only wherever you happen to be. Your rallying cry is gone."

By dint of extraordinary effort on the part of his advance men

Herbert Resner and Mooney at New York's Grand Central Station. New York Governor Jimmy Walker and Mayor "Little Flower" La Guardia showed up for well-publicized welcomes, as did Communist Congressman Vito Marcantonio and dozens of national labor leaders.

and New York friends, Tom drew a full house at Madison Square Garden, but the speech he had hoped to make into a rallying cry turned out to be his swan song. The goals he tried to set before his audience were too tenuous, too far off in a suppositious future. The response was listless, and Tom knew that he had failed.

Hitler invaded Poland, and as his troops moved up from the south the Red Army came down from the north. France and England declared war on Germany. World War II had begun.

Nine months after the pardoning of Mooney, a way out suddenly opened for the little man left behind in Folsom Prison. The State Supreme Court would recommend commutation of sentence to time served. This would leave Billings carrying the onus of guilt and the question of citizenship rights unresolved. But The Kid was now 46, and eager to get free and marry a woman who had been visiting and writing him for the past several years. When George Davis told him what the prospects were, it did not take Billings long to decide — indeterminate imprisonment, with life and love passing by outside, was more unthinkable than acceptance of the compromise. Once Olson was informed that Billings would accept commutation, things moved so quickly there was no time for the prison tailor shop to make him a going-away suit; available clothing was hastily altered instead. On his last night in Folsom, Billings stayed up until almost dawn, repairing as many clocks and watches as he could. This was the trade he had learned in prison, and he hoped it would provide his livelihood in free society.

It was October 17, 1939. At a press conference in the warden's office Billings discussed his plans for marrying Miss Josephine Rudolph as soon as possible. While many aspects of his future remained uncertain, he was sure of one thing; he would dance with his lady at the Warren K. Billings Victory Ball, to be held on the tenth of November in Moose Hall, San Francisco. He had the tickets right in his hand.

Rena Mooney was there but no one paid her any attention; Billings and George Davis barely nodded to her. Tom probably would have been on hand, but he was lying desperately ill in a hospital in Pittsburgh, Pennsylvania. He did manage a telegram of congratulations, couched in terms of good cheer.

The Billings party went by motorcade to the Governor's office in Sacramento, where Olson presented the clemency papers, along with an apology that the law prevented the Governor from giving the unjustly imprisoned man his obvious due, a pardon.

Rena was again present, standing in a corner, again ignored by all. One could hardly imagine what compulsion forced her to put herself into such a humiliating position. All the newspapers commented on the contrast between Billings' quiet exit from custody and the hoopla of the Mooney pardon. Next day, in San Francisco, Billings told newsmen of telephoning his former ally at the Pittsburgh hospital. It was a "get well" call in return for the congratulatory telegram. Mooney had asked about Josie, and had offered some advice: "Keep after that pardon, Warren. If Olson said you'll get it, you will. He's a great Governor."

The doctors patched Tom up enough for him to travel back to San Francisco, where he was taken directly to St. Luke's Hospital. His freedom had only lasted nine months; he was to be a prisoner again, for the rest of his days, confined by ailments brought on by those early years of deadly prison diet.

Great changes were again taking place in America. As Europe fanned its smouldering war into world holocaust, the factories of the United States began humming day and night, turning out weaponry. New Deal agencies established under President Roosevelt to absorb the unemployed became obsolete; organizations of the jobless fell apart for lack of membership. The workers now had real jobs bringing real paychecks and new problems. The Great Depression was over, the Pink Decade was at an end.

With another old friend, I visited Tom one day while it was still hoped he might again defeat his balky guts. We tried to be optimistic, but Tom grimaced and shook his head. One of us offered a joke:

"The only trouble, Tom, is you worked yourself out of your job."

The man on the bed made the beginnings of a smile, but a twinge of pain caught that smile aborning and banished it.

Tom never left that hospital room alive. Although he had the best doctors and the finest treatment, he who had clawed his way out of San Quentin Prison could not find the strength to fight much longer. When he read of Pearl Harbor and other terrible events of the war, Tom's pains became mental as well as physical; he was in double anguish.

I was not there at the finish; work had called me to Los Angeles. Only a few of the faithful came during those last days; John and Anna, of course, and notably Herb Resner and the quiet, faithful woman who could be found at his bedside every night, eager to give him what happiness she could.

On the night of March 6, 1942, she telephoned Resner:

"Herb," she said, "Tom is gone."

Epilogue

Once again the great hall of San Francisco's Civic Auditorium echoed with sounds of adulation and grief over the fate of Tom Mooney.

This time his body was there, encased in a fine casket and surrounded by an honor guard of labor leaders, but his spirit was there only in the words of the memorial service speakers and in the minds and hearts of the five thousand men and women in the throng that came to say goodbye.

During all those years of imprisonment for Mooney and Billings there had been meetings in that same hall as big or bigger than this one for the dead martyr, but the motif that formerly had been militance mixed with hope was now changed to militance bolstered by remembrance.

America was nearly a year into World War Two; the memorial service had been organized by union officials from the American Federation of labor, the Congress of Industrial Organizations, and the Railroad Brotherhoods under the name of Labor's Unity for

Victory Committee. Speaker after speaker repeated American Labor's pledge to do all possible to win the war against Hitler, Mussolini and Hirohito, and to support and improve upon President Franklin D. Roosevelt's programs for the rights of working people.

Alexander Watchman, president of the California Building Trades Council, speaking for the AFL, put it this way: "We pledge that labor will continue Tom's fight to defeat world fascism in the factories and on the battlefield."

Herbert C. Carrasco, a State Labor Commissioner, spoke for the Railroad Brotherhoods, begging that "Mooney's spirit forgive the State of California for his unjust imprisonment."

Speaking for the CIO, Harry Bridges said of Tom: "He died in bed but he died with his boots on. To the very end he did all he could and in every way he could. I know that when any group of workers anywhere, regardless of affiliation, were involved in a struggle with employers, Tom would send them a telegram. A group of Negroes in the South, workers in other lands — they all received aid from him."

Reverend Robert Whitaker, an old friend of Tom's, said: "He spoke so effectively that the whole world heard him."

Warren K. Billings, "The Kid" who had spent nine months more time in prison for the Preparedness Day bombing than Tom, spoke of the fight to save labor militants and radicals from framed-up charges, turned to the coffin and said: "Tom, I will continue that fight."

George T. Davis, the last of a long string of Mooney-Billings defense attorneys, declared that "Tom's was the fight of the common man."

Robert Minor, who abandoned growing fame as a cartoonist to become a prominent radical and secretary of Mooney's first defense committee, gave his remarks a touch of poesy: "In the membership card of each member of organized labor is a little bit of Tom Mooney."

Herb Resner was chairman of the day, and he closed the memorial service by calling to the platform a choral group which sang the famous song about Joe Hill, the Wobbly organizer who was executed for a crime most working people believed he did not commit:

"Joe Hill ain't dead," says he to me;
"Joe Hill ain't never died.
"Where working men are out on strike
"Joe Hill is at their side."

Comparative quiet reigned the following day at graveside services in Cypress Lawn Memorial Park as John and Anna Mooney and a few close friends watched the casket being lowered into the earth.

The last words were spoken by Reverend Herrick Lane of Olivet Presbyterian Church: "Tom Mooney's life was part of the battle to see that 'government of the people, by the people, for the people shall not perish from the earth'."

The gentle dynamiter.

Reference Notes

In 1982 a handful of people may still believe that Tom Mooney was a devil and should have been hanged by the neck until dead. But those who write, read or think about the Mooney case usually agree on only two things — that he did not commit the Preparedness Day bombings and that Governor Olson was right in pardoning him.

Conflict and confusion persist on almost all the other issues and attitudes regarding Tom Mooney, most of them nit-picking, some quite important.

I respect those writers on this case who show thorough and diligent research to back up their statements — although I frequently disagree with them on matters of attitude as well as fact. These are honest disagreements, for the material available to the researcher is so vast and voluminous, so various, that the inquirer can find authority for almost any statement he chooses to make. A writer's ingrained opinions and ideas have great bearing on what he finds in his search through the haystack of facts.

If this seems to say that all writers are biased, I admit it. I also admit that my personal bias differs considerably from that of other writers on the Mooney case. Take for example differing assessments of Mooney's character: Prisoner No. 31921 was, without question, a difficult and demanding man, hard to work with and harsh on those who thought they knew better than he how to get him out of San Quentin. There are those who harped on that. But within hours after he *was* out he became a sweet, kindly middle-aged socialist whose thoughts dwelled on how to help Billings and other underdogs, how to defeat fascism and prevent war. I saw that change myself.

So be it.

Bibliography

Tom Mooney willed his only property, a vast accumulation of trial transcripts, affidavits, petitions, briefs, pamphlets, letters, accountings, and other written and printed material documenting the Mooney-Billings case, to the Bancroft Library of the University of California at Berkeley. This bequest, catalogued as the "Mooney Papers," is undoubtedly the most comprehensive source of information regarding the famous case. In addition, The Bancroft has several separately catalogued books and documents pertaining to Mooney and Billings. These include:

Tom Mooney's Monthly, a *quondam* defense publication.

Frost, Richard H., *The Mooney Case and California Politics*, an unpublished dissertation for a Master's degree, 1954.

Burke, Robert E., *Olson's New Deal for California*, (Berkeley, CA., University of California Press, 1953)

Frost, Richard H., *The Mooney Case*, (Stanford, CA., Stanford University Press, 1968)

DeFord, Miriam Allen, *California's Disgrace*, an unpublished manuscript.

Hopkins, Ernest Jerome, *What Happened in the Mooney Case*, (Brewer, Warren & Putnam, 1932)

Wells, Evelyn, *Fremont Older*, (New York, Appleton-Century Co., 1936)

Hunt, H.T., *Case of T.J. Mooney and W.K. Billings*, (C.G. Burgoyne, 1929)

Densmore, John T., *Report to the U.S. House of Representatives*, submitted to Congress by the Secretary of Labor, W.B. Wilson, on July 22, 1919.

Wickersham, George T., *Report on Law Observance and Enforcement*, made by the Wickersham Commission to President Hoover in 1931, partially suppressed, but published in full, by Gotham House, 1932

Federal Mediation Commission Report to President Wilson, 1918

Marcet, Anna, *The Amazing Frame-up of Mooney and Billings*, (Chicago, Haldeman-Julius Publications, 1931).

The original version of *The Gentle Dynamiter*, by Estolv E. Ward gives greater detail on the Mooney-Billings case than in the present book.

Newspapers of the San Francisco Bay Region, 1916-39, provide much valuable information on the case. For a general background for the "direct action" of trade unionists prior to the enactment of laws protecting labor's right to organize and bargain collectively, *Dynamite* by Louis Adamic, Viking Press, 1931, New York, should be helpful.

Unless otherwise noted, newspaper citations will refer only to the San Francisco press, and all other citations will refer to the Mooney Papers and other documentation in the Bancroft Library.

The Mooney Papers have been assembled in six parts, of which Part I (Mooney's letters from prison) and Part IV (legal records and trial transcripts) are most frequently referred to. The most important material in Part IV will be found in twenty bound volumes of transcript of *Mooney on Habeas Corpus*, abbreviated herein to MHC.

The detailed reference Notes follow:

Chapter 1 Notes

Detailed accounts of labor strife on West Coast, S.F. Chamber of Commerce million dollar union breaking fund, Law and Order Committee, shootings, arrests of strikers (including Rena Mooney): reported in the *Examiner, News, Chronicle* and *Bulletin* between July 1 and 22, 1916.

General Pershing and U.S. troops entered Mexico on March 8 and 9, 1916 and returned to U.S. soil on Feb. 5, 1917: U.S. Reference Library, Presidio, San Francisco.

Oakland R.R. bombing: *Examiner* and *Chronicle*, July 1, 1916.

Theodore Roosevelt calls for war with Mexico, *Examiner,* July 5, 1916.

Wm. Randolph Hearst denies his Mexican property a problem: *Examiner,* July 8, 1916.

President Wilson pledges "I'll Stand To The Last Against War": *Examiner* and *Chronicle,* July 1.

Wilson pledges to respect sovereignty of Mexico: *News,* July 10, 1916; *Chronicle,* July 11, 1916.

German diplomats, including Consul-General in San Francisco and his agents, were accused (and some convicted) of sabotaging munition trade to Allies: *Examiner,* July 1, *Chronicle,* July 2, 1916.

Court trials for violation of neutrality laws against Consul-General Frans Bopp, E. H. Von Shaack, Wilhelm Von Brinken, C.C. Crowley and others: *Examiner,* July 11, 1916 (This was the same Crowley who was a pal and employee of Fickert, who reportedly planned to use Crowley as a prosecution witness in the bombing trials): MHC Vol. VIII, pp. 4887-91.

For details on German sabotage see all San Francisco daily papers, April 22, 24, 25, 1918, *News,* April 25 and 26 and May 28, 1918. *Examiner,* May 28 and 29, 1918.

The Anarchists — Emma Goldman speaks tonight at Averiil Hall on "Education and Sexual Mutilation of the Child": *News,* July 20, 1916; Emma Goldman speaks tonight on "Preparedness, the Road to Universal Slaughter," ad, *News* July 22, 1916. Emma Goldman's speeches and the atmosphere in which they were made are described in a pamphlet, *Law and Order in San Francisco — A Beginning:* exhibit, MHC Vol. XX, p. 12,951 and letter from George P. West to Alexander Berkman: *Examiner,* Jan. 7, 1917. Mayor Rolph speaks out against anarchy and revolution at a Chamber of Commerce mass meeting: *Chronicle* and *Examiner,* July 27, 1916. See also defense pamphlets, Mooney Papers, carton 43 and 44.

Preparedness Day Parade buildup: *Chronicle,* July 12-22, 1916; *Examiner, Call,* July 19-22, with both *Examiner* and *Chronicle* giving full-page plugs on July 22. Opposition to militarist and labor opposition to parade: *News* July 8, 14; the *Bulletin* reported on protest meeting at Idora Park, Oakland, July 17, big plugs for Dreamland protest rally on July 18 and full accounts of that rally on July 20 and 21.

Threatening postcards and letters: Frost, Richard H., *The Mooney Case,* pp. 82-3.

Swanson fingers Mooney and Billings to Fickert: Frost, *The Mooney Case,* p. 99-100; see also MHC Vol. IX, pp. 5706-7, Vol. XIV, p. 9244 and Vol. XV, p. 9518.

Chapter 2 Notes

Ed McKenzie told the story of the courtroom death signal, plus a wealth of other details regarding defense dealings with Cunha, Fickert and the foreman of Mooney's trial jury in testimony he gave during Mooney on Habeas Corpus in 1935-36: MHC Vol. IX, pp. 5256-73a and pp. 5308-27.

Cunha crows at courtroom door: MHC Vol. IX, p. 5288.

Fresno woman: MHC Vol. XX, p. 12,924.

Rigall to Ellis in office: MHC Vol. V, pp. 2627-44.

Newspaper hints at witness to corroborate Oxman: *News* Jan. 26, 1917; *Examiner, Call*, Jan 27, 1917; *Chronicle*, Jan 29, 1917.

Oxman's testimony *vs.* Mooney: MHC Vol. V, pp. 2561-2617.

Ellis: "It's a hell of a thing. . . ": MHC Vol. V, p. 2645.

Rigall's telegram to Cunha: MHC Vol. V, p. 2643.

Cunha's reply to Rigall: MHC Vol. V, p. 2827-9.

Matheson distrusts Rigall: MHC Vol. XIII, pp. 7943-5.

Cunha hides Oxman: MHC Vol. XII, pp. 7797-8.

Cunha's argument before Judge Griffin: *Examiner*, Feb. 21, 1917.

Chapter 3 Notes

Description of the issues and moods of America upon entering World War I and of the world situation in the later part of 1917: *Sunset Magazine*, August, 1917, MP, Part V, Scrap Book 6, pp. 16 and 500; *Oakland Tribune*, Oct. 1, 1917; letter from Mooney to "Noni and Sidney," Jan. 14, 1932.

Problems of the Kerensky government and the Bolsheviks: Browder, Robert P. and Alexander F. Kerensky, editors, *The Russian Provisional Government (Documents)*, Hoover Institution of War, Revolution and Peace, Stanford, CA, and the *Bulletin*, April 19, 1917.

The account of the Petrograd demonstration is an interweaving of information from various sources, minor conflicts have been rationalized by the author. See news stories carried by most American dailies on April 25, 1917; *Bulletin*, same date; Ambassador Francis's first cabled report and reply by Secretary of State Robert Lansing on April 30 (National Archives, Washington, D.C., Record Group 59 — Dept. of State); interview with Charles R. Crane, a member of the Root Commission to Russia; *N.Y. Times*, Jan. 22, 1918; Stevens, Walter B., *David R. Francis Ambassador Extraordinary and Plenipotentiary*, privately printed, 1919 (Local History Section, Library of Congress); Ambassador Francis, *Russia From the American Embassy*, (Scribners, N.Y., 1921).

Official reaction in Washington: Lansing's memorandum, National Archives, Section 59, under "Official Papers to and from the President, 1917-18"; also under "Mooney" in the same card catalog; *Bulletin*, August 31, 1917.

Investigators come to Greyville: MHC Vol. V, p. 2645-6.

Mullholland gets to Ellis: MHC Vol. V, p. 2646.

Ellis' office ransacked: *Bulletin*, April 23, 1917.

McKenzie gets involved: MHC Vol. III, pp. 1731-2 and Vol. IX, p. 5380.

McKenzie comes to grips with Rigall and Ellis: MHC Vol. III, pp. 5290-2 and
5330-9; also Mooney Papers, Part IV, Vol. 29, pp. 262-3.

Rigall agrees: MHC Vol. V, pp. 2645-6.

Judge Dunne calls Oxman's letters unimportant: Statement by Fremont Older,
appendix to McNutt's brief to Governor Stephens; Mooney Papers, Part IV,
Vol. 17, p. 159; MHC Vol. XX, p. 13, 191.

Chapter 4 Notes

Mooney's background and early life: Letters from Mooney to Waldo Cook, Nov. 3,
1927; to M.A. Thompson, Nov. 13, 1932; to Joe Doyle, Sept. 19, 1933; MHC
Vol. XX, pp. 12, 836 *et seq.*

Mooney's adventures as adult: Marcet, Anna, *The Amazing Frame-up of Mooney
and Billings* (Haldeman-Julius Publications, Chicago, 1931), p. 58; and personal
talks with Mooney.

Hidden transcript of third-degree on Mooney: MHC Vol. II, pp. 661-731.

Billings spies in shoe factory strike: MHC Vol. IV, pp. 1875-86.

Billings hired to transport dynamite: MHC Vol. IV, pp. 1891-1913.

Billings refuses to implicate Mooney: MHC Vol. IV, pp. 1909-10.

Mooney promises ILWO will pay Billings' fine: MHC Vol. XIII, pp. 8062-3.

Swanson talks to Billings: MHC Vol. III, pp. 1422-35; MHC Vol. XX, pp. 13,115-7.

Billings returns Mooney's camera: DeFord, Miriam Allen, *California's Disgrace*,
p. 56.

Mooney's philosophy on non-violence: MHC Vol. XX, p. 12,804.

Details of conference in which Fremont Older showed Police Captain Matheson ir-
reconcilable conflicts in the prosecution's case and the exposure of Estelle Smith as
a fabricator of testimony: Photostats of two pages of the *Bulletin*, April 20, 1917
in MHC Vol. IX, p. 5443; *Bulletin*, April 17, 1917.

Nolan's release from jail: MHC Vol. III, p. 1408 and 1411.

Fickert's "society women": *Examiner*, Aug. 22, 1916.

Edeaus apply for work: MHC Vol. VII, pp. 3855-63, 3887-95, 3900-29, 3933-41.

Mrs. Edeau and Chief Peterson: MHC Vol. VI, pp. 3795-3820.

Mrs. Edeau talks to Inspector Smith: MHC Vol. VI, pp. 3821-30.

Mrs. Edeau's "confession" to her clergyman: MHC Vol. X, p. 5953, *Call* Jan. 29,
1917, *Chronicle*, Jan. 30, 1917.

Mrs. Edeau's testimony implicating the Mooneys, Billings and Weinberg: *Call*,
Nov. 12, 1920 and MHC Vol. XI, p. 6888.

Fickert's discussion with Inspector Smith, the visit to Mrs. Edeau's home and resulting gunplay and the "astral body" business: *Examiner* and *Bulletin*, April 13,
1917 and MHC Vol. VI, p. 3830.

MacDonald claims he saw bombing: MP part IV Vol. 9, pp. 383-94, 429.

MacDonald tells cops: MP Part IV, Vol. 55, pp. 110-11 and 113-4.

Frank Drew helps MacDonald: MP Part IV, Vol. 55, pp. 13 and 47-48.

Discrepancies in MacDonald's stories: MP Part IV, Vol. 9, pp. 381-3.

MacDonald's story to Grand Jury: MP Part IV, Vol. 55, pp. 161-4

MacDonald's different story in Mooney trial: MP Vol. 55, p. 26.

Rena nicknamed "Lady Macbeth": *Examiner*, June 16, 1917.

The "conspiracy" witnesses: MP Part IV, Vol. 21, pp. 1060-1105; 1257 *et seq.*, 1270 *et seq.*

Letter from Mooney to Mother Jones, Oct. 28, 1914: MCH Vol. XVI, p. 10373 *et seq.*

Towers blown up: MP Part IV, Vol. 21, p. 1207 *et seq*; Vol. 22, p. 1802 *et seq.*

Fickert plays with dynamite: *Examiner*, June 30, 1917; MP Part IV, Vol. 21, p. 1589.

Preparations for trouble at Rena's trial: *Examiner, Bulletin*, July 24, 1917.

Rena is acquitted: *Examiner, Bulletin*, July 26, 1917.

Summation of Weinberg's trial: *Bulletin*, Nov. 29, 1917 and Dec. 5, 1917; MHC Vol. II, pp. 943-96.

Chapter 5 Notes

Judge Dunne's explosive denial of bail for Rena Mooney and Israel Weinberg: *Bulletin*, April 30 and Dec. 10, 1917; *Chronicle*, Jan 27, 1918.

State Supreme Court orders bail for Weinberg: All S.F. newspapers March 21 or March 22, 1918.

State Supreme Court denies Mooney's appeal: All S.F. dailies March 1, 1918.

German use of Mooney case for propaganda: *Call* Aug. 27 and Oakland *Tri-City Labor Review*, Sept. 6, 1918.

Mooney's opposition to nation-wide strike: Oakland *Tri-City Labor Review*, Mar. 22, 1918.

First public revelation that President Wilson wrote to Governor Stephens on Mooney's behalf: *Bulletin*, March 29, 1918.

Rena Mooney's release on bail: *Bulletin* and *Call*, March 30, 1918.

Big Mooney mass meeting in S.F.: *News*, April 17, 1918; Oakland *Tri-City Labor Review*, April 19 and Oakland *The World*, April 26, 1918.

The El Centro kidnapping: *Call* and *Chronicle*, April 20, 1918.

U.S. Senate discussions on Mooney case: All S.F. dailies, April 22, 24 and 25, 1918; *Examiner*, May 28 and 29; *News* May 28, 1918.

Anti-Allies activities of Consul-General Franz Bopp: *News*, April 25, 26, 1918; letter from Mooney to U.S. Senator Thomas Schall, Nov. 14, 1929.

Mooney's telegrams to pro-strike unions and President Wilson: All S.F. dailies, April 29, 1918.

First Mooney juror to doubt validity of the conviction says Mooney deserves a new trial: *Examiner*, June 16, 1918; *Bulletin*, June 21, 1918.

Attitudes of California newspapers: *Los Angeles Times*, Jan. 31, 1918; *Sacramento Bee*, Jan 28, 1918; *Wasp*, March 23, 1918; *Examiner*, March 28, 1918.

Labor strife for and against Mooney: *Bulletin*, Nov. 3 and Dec. 1, 1917; *Chronicle*, March 13, 1918; *Bulletin*, March 23, 1918.

New York State Legislature: N.Y. *Mail*, March 16, 1918, MP Part V, scrapbook 8.

Detroit mass meeting: Detroit *Labor News*; March 22; *Detroit News*, March 25, 1918.

Tom Mooney Day: *Bulletin*, July 24, 1918; *Bulletin* and *News*, July 26 and 29; *Examiner*, July 30; S.F. *Labor Clarion*, August 2, 1918.

Chapter 6 Notes

The remark that set Densmore ajangle: *Call*, Nov. 22, 1918.

The strange story of Fickert's promise to the defense and then double-cross: *Bulletin*, April 19, 1917; MHC Vol. IX, pp. 5275-85.

Accusations made by Densmore: *Densmore Report*, pp. 4-76.

Documentation of the exposure of Justice Henshaw: *Call*, Nov. 23, 1918.

Older's "scoop" on Densmore report: *Call*, Nov. 22, 1918; Document No. 157, 66th Congress, House of Representatives; MHC Vol. X, pp. 6272-86.

Duncan Matheson's blast at Fickert: *Examiner*, Nov. 24, 1918.

Fickert's violence against Older: Evelyn Wells, *Fremont Older*, p. 329; Miriam Allen DeFord, *California's Disgrace*, p. 120; *Examiner*, Nov. 25, 1918.

Furman's statement about Judge Oppenheim: *Call*, Nov. 25, 1918.

Archetect Diggs' story about saboteur Crowley: *Bulletin*, Nov. 25, 1918.

S.F. Grand Jury's demand on Densmore, his reply and report on Oil Workers official: *Call* and *Bulletin*, Nov. 26, 1918.

Commutation of sentence and Mooney's reaction: All S.F. dailies, Nov. 29, 1918.

Chapter 7 Notes

Difficulties among the left; particularly with Robert Minor: letters from Mooney to Clara Leiser, March 12, 1935 and Roger Baldwin, Aug. 31, 1928.

The Rena-Sayles problems are described through interviews I had with Billings, Herbert Resner and Miriam Allen DeFord in 1965 and 1966. These interviews conflict in that Billings said Sayles had comforted Rena with drink but had told him (Billings) that he had tried to seduce Rena without success. Resner and DeFord, however, indicated conclusively that Sayles must have told Billings a gentlemanly lie. Certainly Mooney felt he had been cuckolded: see his letters to Mary Gallagher, Dec. 23, 1928, May 14 and Oct. 11, 1929 and Jan. 6, 1930; Aline Bransdall, May 14, 1929; sister Anna, Sept. 30 and Nov. 28, 1929.

Mooney's early request for a divorce: *News*, Feb. 3, 1939.

Rena's blunders in defense work described in letters from Mooney to Rena, Aug. 20 and Nov. 17, 1929; Anna C. Wellbreck, Jan. 26, 1929; Mary Gallagher, Feb. 18, March 11, Aug. 29, 1929 and Jan. 6, June 9, 1930; Fremont Older, Aug. 28, 1929; Defense Committee, June 24, 1931; sister Anna, Nov. 28, 1929.

A sampling of letters from Mooney to his jurors tells the story of that phase of his pardon campaign: John Forsythe, Thomas Kennedy and William V. McNevin (the jury foreman who gave prosecutor Cunha the death signal), Jan. 28, 1926; John Miller, Jan. 29, May 17, May 20, May 22, 23, 24, 25 and 26, 1926. McNevin again, May 28, 1926. Reverse polling of the Mooney jury: MHC Vol. XIII, pp. 7858-60. More pressure on Miller in letters on June 26, 1923; Sept. 14 and 17, 1925; May 25, July 5 and Oct. 6, 1926 and April 10, 1927; Belle Hammerberg, July 12, 1926; Miller's cave-in described in letter to Mary Gallagher, Dec. 5, 1929.

Initial contacts with Oxman: MHC Vol. XIV, pp. 8850 and 9316; Vol. XV, pp. 9573-5.

Oxman's Kansas City statement: MHC Vol. XIII, pp. 8518-19; Vol. XIX, pp. 12,768-9.

Billings told me the story of his early life in an interview in his home in December, 1964. Details of his imbroglio in the shoe factory and his capture while carrying dynamite: MHC Vol IV, pp. 1875-86 and pp. 1891-1913.

Change in Scharrenberg's support: letters from Mooney to Martin Egan, July 30, 1928; Walsh, Oct. 4 and 16, 1927; Kate Crane Gartz, Oct. 19, 1927; Ed Nockels, Sept. 15, 1928; Anna Mooney, Sept. 30, 1929; Mary Gallagher, Sept. 13, 1929; Roger Baldwin, Nov. 18, 1930.

Tom fights parole proposal: letters to Older, Oct. 6, 1927 and Jan. 31, 1928; to Dan Regan, July 7, 1927; to Keough, Oct. 1, 1927; to Walsh, Oct. 4 and 20, 1927.

Billings suspects Madeline Weiland: letters from Mooney to Mary Gallagher, Sept. 17, 1929; sister Anna, Nov. 21, 1930; Madeline Weiland, Nov. 29, 1930.

Scoldings from Tom: letters to Liggett, Feb. 13 and May 23, 1930; Frank Brown and Mary Gallagher, April 7, 1930; to "Trade Union Supporters," May 31, 1930.

Governor Young makes a proposition: letters from Mooney to Older, Sept. 23, 1929 and Bruce Bliven, March 14, 1931.

Liberals favor Billings: letter from Mooney to Mary Gallagher, Oct. 17, 1929.

Story about Justices: letter from Older to Mooney, Dec. 16, 1929.

Supreme Court votes against Billings: all S.F. afternoon papers, July 4, 1930.

Mooney's pardon application denied: all San Francisco papers, July 8, 1930.

Chapter 8 Notes

Rena's sorrow at court decision: *News*, July 5, 1930.

Mooney's blast at Governor and Supreme Court: *News*, July 8, 1930.

Fremont Older's editorial reaction: *Call-Bulletin*, July 8, 1930.

MacDonald's 1921 affidavit and its result; *Call*, Feb. 8, 1921; MHC Vol. VIII, pp. 4887-91.

Billings' rejection of the court's hint: *Call-Bulletin*, July 12, 1930.

Big hunt for MacDonald: *News*, July 9, 1930; all S.F. papers, July 12, 1930.

Governor Young delays hearing: *News*, July 14, 1930.

Cockran lays down to die: letter from Mooney to Pollock, April 20, 1928.

New York City rally: MP Part IV Vol. 55, pp. 102-7, 118-22, p. 235 and pp. 358-9; MHC Vol. X, pp. 5861-3.

Mother Mooney gets in: *Examiner* and *News*, July 29 and 30, 1930.

Goff's search for lost document: *Examiner*, July 28, 1930.

MacDonald's testimony that he was paid by Drew: MP Part IV, Vol. 55, pp. 195-7; his letter to Matheson, p. 47 and in MHC Vol. VIII, p. 4885 and Vol. X, pp. 5904-5.

McKenzie's use of the alibi picture: *Call-Bulletin*, July 30, 1930; MP Part IV, Vol. 55, pp. 158-65.

Detective's discovery of discrepancy between photo and actual scene in 1930: MHC Vol. XVII, pp. 11,475-96.

McKenzie's effort to get MacDonald to exculpate Fickert and company: MP Part IV, Vol. 55, pp. 141-2 and 165-6.

Goff's waffling over his change of mind: *Examiner* and *News*, July 31, 1930; MP Part IV, Vol. 55, pp. 358-61.

Goff's aid in the Densmore Report and remarks about MacDonald: MP Part IV, Vol. 55, pp. 356-8.
Clash between Fickert and MacDonald: *Examiner*, July 31, 1930; MP Part IV, Vol. 55, pp. 263-4 and 269.
MacDonald's letter to Older: MHC Vol. VIII, pp. 4887-91.
Preston's final question to MacDonald: MP Part IV, Vol. 55, pp. 282-9.

Chapter 9 Notes

Description of Fremont Older and his office: Evelyn Wells, *Fremont Older*, pp. 98-9.
Estelle Smith's sordid background: MP Part IV, Vol. 23, pp. 2043-54 and pp. 2226-34; letters from Mooney to John Miller, July 25 and 26, 1926.
Peculiar clemency granted to Estelle Smith's uncle for the murder rap: document on file under "Executive Clemencies," a commutation signed by Gov. Stephens April 10, 1917, State archives, Sacramento.
Estelle's performance at the judicial hearing plus ensuing results: MP Part IV, Vol, 3, pp. 885-979 and MHC Vol. V, pp. 2561-97.
Duncan Matheson's denial of cigarette paper story: MP Part IV, Vol. 4, pp. 1522-3, 1535-40, 1563-5 and 1567-8.
Night interview with Billings at Folsom: MP Part IV, Vol. 4, pp. 1471-6.
Justices' session with Billings at Folsom: MHC Vol. II, pp. 1069-70; and MP Part IV, Vol. 4, pp. 1515-21 and 1608-17.
McKenzie's belief in a "gentleman's agreement": MHC Vol. III, pp. 1729-31.
California Supreme Court's denial of Billings pardon application: 210 California Reports, p. 717, California law libraries; Justice Langdon's dissent: p. 783.
The division between the prisoners deepens and other results of Billings' pardon application: undated statement entitled "Warren K. Billings" filed between two letters dated June 16, 1932, MP Part I, Carton 1; letters from Mooney to sister Anna, Dec. 11, 1930 and J.P. Farrell, Jan. 2, 1931.

Chapter 10 Notes

Tom's dissertations on publicity ploys, use of pictorial gimmicks, handcuffs, etc.: letters from Mooney to sister Anna, Jan. 13, 1931; Leonard Craig, Jan. 24, 1931. Stuart Scott, April 23, 1931; William Busic, Aug. 1, 1931; Aline Barnsdall, Aug. 11, 1931 and Byrd Kelso, Jan. 14, 1932; handcuff story: *News*, Sept. 17, 1935.
Mooney uses 1932 Olympics: letters from Mooney to Si Gerson, May 26, 1932; to "Counter-Olympic State Elimination Meet," Fresno, Calif., July 1, 1932.
Description of Olympic games demonstration: *Western Worker*, Sept. 1, 1932.
Defense lawyer loses job: *Western Worker*, Sept. 1, 1932.
Defense delegations to the local press: letters from Mooney to Arthur Scott, Aug. 21, 1932; the Defense Committee, Aug. 23, 1932; sister Anna, Aug. 24, 1932.
Tom Mooney's "hearse": letter from Mooney to Defense Committee, Aug. 3, 1931; *Open Forum*, April 16, 1932.
The story of the Wickersham report and what happened to it: letters from Mooney to Todd, Stern and Jackson, Aug. 16, 1931; to various members of the Wickersham

Commission, Aug. 3 and 4, 1931; *The Suppressed Mooney Billings Report* (Gotham House, N.Y., 1932).

Chapter 11 Notes

Tom's troubles with his siblings: letters to Waldo Cook, Nov. 3, 1927; M.A. Thompson, Nov. 13, 1932; Joe Doyle, Sept. 19, 1933; MHC Vol. XX, pp. 12,836 *et seq*.

Mother Mooney's interviewer was Sherman Montrose, July 7, 1930: *see* MP Scrapbook 26.

The Mooney difficulties with bad diet and oversensitive stomach: letters from Tom to brother John, Aug. 11, 1926; John-and-Mother and John, Jan. 21, 1928; Fickert, Aug. 25, 1926; Belle Hammerberg, Sept. 22, 1926; Life Extension Institute, May 10, 1927; Miss Bauer, Dec. 10, 1927; Educational Press, Jan. 6, 1928; Dr. Haynes, Mar. 3, 1928; MacFadden Publications, Mar. 8, 1928.

Mother's actions at Labor Council meetings described to me in 1967 interview with Miriam Allen DeFord.

Mooney family imbroglio about how best to help Tom: Tom's letters to Mary Gallagher, Feb. 2 and June 6, 1929; brother John, Jan. 21, 1928; and Mary Gallagher, Mar. 17, 1929.

Tom's complaints about John's singing and other follies: letter to Mary Gallagher, Sept. 13, 1929.

Anna got her lumps: telegrams to Anna, Nov. 19, 1930 and Dec. 11, 1933; letters to Anna, Nov. 20 and Dec. 4, 1930; Dec. 13, 1933, July 16, 1934; Mar. 1, 1935.

Money troubles: see Tom's letters to Mary Gallagher, Mar. 13 and 19, May 5, June 26, July 12 and 31, Aug. 6 and 24, Dec. 14, all 1929; to Robert W. Dunne, American Fund for Public Service, June 8, 1929.

Mooney tells why he made peace with the International Labor Defense: letter to sister Anna, Jan. 31, 1931.

A description of Mother Mooney's physical condition: *Irish World*, Dec. 26, 1931, Scrapbook 26.

Tom's travel instructions: letter to "Dear Members of the Committee," Aug. 28, 1932, to Bob Minor, Sept. 14, 1931, Dorothy Murphy, Aug. 5, 1931.

The Socialist-Communist row over Mother Mooney's presence at their respective meetings: N.Y. *New Leader*, Feb. 20, 1932, N.Y. *American* and *World-Telegram*, Feb. 25, 1932; Scrapbook 26.

Hoover-Harlow incident: Pittsburgh, PA, *Amalgamated Journal*, March 17, 1932; *Cincinnati Chronicle*, April 23, 1932, Scrapbook 26.

Mother's Youngstown, Ohio appearance: Youngstown *Telegram*, July 18, 1932.

Mother's attack of blindness in Chicago: London *Daily Herald*, June 15, 1932.

Criticism from Labor's ranks of Mother's efforts: Rochester, N.Y., *Labor Herald and Citizen*, Oct. 3, 1932, Scrapbook 26.

Tom's letter to Stalin: N.Y. *Herald-Tribune*, Nov. 23, 1932, Scrapbook 26.

Dorothy Parker's account of transAtlantic voyage: Holyoke, MA, *Transcript*, Nov. 11, 1932, Scrapbook 26.

Foolhardiness of British Home Secretary: Paris edition of *Chicago Tribune*, Dec. 8, 1932; London *Sunday Sun*, Dec. 11, 1932; London *Daily Worker*, Dec. 13, 1932; MP Scrapbook 26.

Mother's return to New York: N.Y. *Evening Post*, Dec. 23, 1932, Scrapbook 26.

Mother's visit to F.D.R.: Chicago *American*, Dec. 30, 1932, Scrapbook 26.

Other pro-Mooney efforts described in Russell, Bertrand, *Autobiography of Bertrand Russell* (Little, Brown & Co., N.Y., 1938) pp. 313-14.

Unfavorable Memphis reaction: Memphis, TN *Commercial Appeal*, Dec. 22, 1932 Scrapbook 26.

Mother's last problems: *Call-Bulletin*, Sept. 3, 1934; *Examiner*, Sept. 4, 1934; letter from Tom to Aline Barnsdall, Sept. 25, 1934.

Row about funeral and funeral itself: N.Y. *Daily Worker*, Sept. 4, 1934; *Call-Bulletin*, Sept 7, 1934; *Chronicle*, Sept. 9, 1934; *Western Worker*, Sept. 10, 1934, Scrapbook 28.

Tom's farewell letter and John's graveside remarks: Minneapolis *Labor Review*, Sept. 21, 1934, Scrapbook 28.

Chapter 12 Notes

I checked out the location of the House of the Red Flower Pot personally with the help of friends who had been there. From them I got descriptions of Tom Mooney's luncheons, his aides, his cook, and his visitors and guests. Frederic March was a frequent visitor from Hollywood. I knew Myrto personally, her Rabelasian songs were a pleasure to listen to and her cooking was delicious.

Draper Hand's story: MHC Vol. XI, p. 6762 *et seq.* and p. 6888; *Call*, Nov. 12, 1920.

"Secret report" about Weinberg: MP Part IV, Vol. 4, pp. 1489-90; MHC Vol. XVIII pp. 11,974-82.

Farber carries the message to Weinberg: MHC Vol. III, pp. 1272-3 and 1346-8; *Bulletin*, April 5, 1918.

Goff admits writing pro-defense letter to Mooney: MHC Vol. XII, p. 7414.

Goff renegs: MHC Vol. XII, p. 7507 *et seq.*

Cunha denies almost everything: MHC Vol. XII, p. 7736 *et seq.* and 7925 *et seq.*

Cunha gets affidavit from Oxman: MHC Vol. XIII, pp. 7844-5 and 7925-6.

Tom acts as his own attorney: MHC Vol. X, pp. 6192-6263 and 6305-32; see also *Bulletin*, June 26 and 29, 1917; *Chronicle*, June 27, 1917.

"Scoop" Gleeson's attempt to tell about Densmore Report: MHC Vol. X, pp. 6272-86.

Inability of police to find Captain Bunner: MHC Vol. XVIII, pp. 11,705-27.

Fickert's peculiar walk: MHC Vol. XIV, p. 9229-30, *et seq.*

Fickert "forgets": MHC Vol. XV, pp. 9498-9519; pp. 9601-24; pp. 9636-99.

Chapter 13 Notes

For a more impersonal account of the oral arguments on *Mooney on Habeas Corpus: Examiner*, April 13, 14, 15, 16 and 17, 1937.

Chapter 14 Notes

The description of Mooney's life in prison derives from my conversations with Tom in "Q" in 1938 and in the hospital in 1941 and letters from Mooney to: Mary Gallagher, Feb. 10, 1924, Jan. 11, 13, 18 and 20 and Feb. 8, 1930; Warden Holohan, Jan. 23, 1930.

Mail censorship: letters from Mooney to Older, Dec. 7, 1928; Mary Gallagher, Aug. 19, 1929; open letter to Baldwin, Hunt, Older, Gallagher, etc., Jan. 12, 1931; and Louis B. Scott, Sept. 23, 1933.

Political campaign accounts in: CIO *Labor Herald*, Oct. 20 and 27, Nov. 3, 1938; *Labor Clarion*, Oct. 21, 1938; Art Eggleston's column, *Chronicle*, Oct. 13, 1938.

Tom Mooney's campaign pamphlet: MP Part V carton 43.

Olson's visit to San Quentin was described to author by Resner in 1966.

William Green's efforts against Mooney: letter from Mooney to John Antonson, Sept. 20, 1934; see also in Frost's dissertation, which also describe Green's and Scharrenberg's hostile acts, pp. 220-7.

Mooney's best weapon, his health: letters to Ed Nockels, May 6, 1924; Older, May 3, 1928; Mary Gallagher, April 11, July 10, and Oct. 21, 1929; Walsh and Finerty, Sept. 17, 1937; Dan Regan, Mar. 28, 1926; also author's interviews with Resner.

Difference between semi-freedom and freedom: conversation between author and Mooney in San Quentin, 1938.

Mooney's problems with lawyers: author's interview with Resner, 1965; letters from Mooney to: Walsh, Nov. 16, 1932 and Dec. 14, 1935; Aline Barnsdall, Sept. 25, 1934 and Feb. 18, 1936; Baldwin, Jan 24, Feb. 12 and April 7, 1936; Lena Morrow Lewis, Feb. 7, 1936; Walsh, Feb. 22, 1936; Finerty, Feb. 23, 1936; telegram to Finerty Feb. 26, 1936.

Some lawyers wanted to be paid: author's interview with Resner; letters from Mooney to Baldwin, Nov. 12 and 18, 1937; John W. Jenkins, Nov. 13, 1937; George Davis, Nov. 15 and 19, 1937; and Walsh, Nov. 19, 1937.

Troubles with donors: letters from Mooney to Charles Chaplin and Aline Barnsdall, Feb. 20, 1937.

Mooney criticizes John L. Lewis' pay raise: letters from Mooney to John L. Lewis, Jan. 23, 1936 and Gardner Jackson, Feb. 7, 1936.

Mooney warns staff about big donors: letters from Mooney to: Mary Gallagher, April 9, June 9, 13, 21 and 22 and July 3, 1930; Aline Barnsdall, Dec. 6, 1930 and Mar. 15, 1931.

Tiff with Postal Telegraph: letter from Mooney to company, Jan. 22, 1936.

Incidents of helpfulness to others: letters to Ethelwyn Mills, Jan. 21, 1936 and Harry Bridges, Feb. 18, 1936.

Crank letters and more money problems: letters from Mooney to David Dubinsky, Feb. 24, 1936; James Campbell, Feb. 19, 1936; F.M. Kelly, Jan. 24, 1936; Robert Minor, Feb. 10, 1936.

Mooney expressed gratitude for favors large and small: letter to Admiral Florist Shop, Jan. 31, 1936 and E.J. Barrett, Feb. 8, 1936.

Chapter 15 Notes

Background of Culbert Olson and the struggles over Mooney in the California Legislature were related to me by Herbert Resner in 1965; also described in unpublished dissertation for Master's degree by Richard H. Frost, 1954 pp. 184-214 *passim.* Heywood Broun's opinion: *News* Nov. 8, 1934, Dec. 30, 1936 and June 13, 1939.

Troubles in trying to organize bank clerks were described to me by one who labored in that vineyard, my wife.

Labor spy activities of Arthur Margolis (Scott) and Norma Perry, first heard of as waterfront gossip, was confirmed by me in an interview with William Schneiderman in 1967, and in conversations with Harry Bridges in 1967 and 1968.

Herbert Resner told me about the Spanish Loyalist's visit to Tom.

Mooney's appearance before the Assembly, polls about voters' attitudes toward Mooney and Olson's sudden silence: Frost's dissertation mentioned above, to p. 227.

Chapter 16 Notes

The scene where Resner and Bulcke dashed to San Quentin to give Tom the good news was described to me by both men in 1966 and 1968. At that time Bulcke was president of Local 10, ILWU, (San Francisco longshoremen).

There are conflicting recollections as to whether Rena met Tom at the prison gates on the morning of the pardon. Resner and others are positive she did not ride to Sacramento with him.

For other accounts of the pardon hearing: *News*, Jan. 7, 1939; *Chronicle* and *Examiner*, Jan. 8, 1939.

What Mooney and friends did during the afternoon and evening of Pardon Day was related to me by Resner and Al Richmond, who was then editor of *Peoples World*, a leftist newspaper.

Chapter 17 Notes

Gravside scene: itinerary in the *News*, Jan. 7, 1939; Resner's recollections.

Parade precautions were common knowledge among the longshoremen and CIO officials.

I learned about Colonel Carlson's participation in the parade in an interview with him, Dec. 5 or 6, 1945, and his biography, Blankfort, Michael, *The Big Yankee* (Little Brown & Co., N.Y., 1947) p. 354.

Thousands saw the Bronx salute; the background for Tom's act will be found in letters from him to Jim Tully, March 13, 1927 and William Randolph Hearst, July 17, 1927.

Attendance figures for the Civic Center rally: January 9, 1939, *Examiner*, 20,000; *Chronicle* and *News*, 50,000; *Call-Bulletin*, nearly 100,000; Jan. 12, 1939, CIO *Labor-Herald*, 100,000.

The defense debt: letter from Tom to Matt Meehan, Nov. 15, 1940, ILWU Library, San Francisco.

What Tom did with his $10 bill: *News*, Jan. 9, 1939.

Tom-Rena imbroglio and activities of reporter Linn: my own recollections and interviews with Resner.

I spent considerable time and effort to locate the young woman who comforted Tom in his final years. However, she disappeared completely from my ken and I could not learn if she was willing to be identified as the woman who played the wifely role in the freedom years; therefore her name remains my secret.

Miriam Allen DeFord told me what she thought of the Mooneys in conversations in 1965-67.

The story of the Los Angeles fizzle comes from Phillip M. Connelly and other CIO officials of that city in 1939.

Resner described to me the Eastern trip in the summer of 1939.

Billings told me what he did immediately after leaving Folsom prison in the 1965 interview; *News*, Oct. 17, 1939.

Exchange between Mooney and Billings: *News*, Oct. 18, 1939.

Epilogue

Memorial service for Mooney was reported by all the San Francisco dailies on Monday, March 9, 1942. The memorial and graveside services are described at length in the *CIO labor Herald,* March 13, 1942.

Page 153.

Index

ABOUT THE AUTHOR

Estolv Ethan Ward was educated on glowing accounts of ancestral involvement in the American Revolution, occasional bouts with public educational institutions, five years of Latin, tutorial coaching in history, mathematics, socialist literature, and at age 18, an unusual amount of travel.

Ward was in Manila when the U.S. entered World War I, and was in Harbin, China, about to board the Trans-Siberian for Petrograd, when all inbound traffic was closed. Thus he missed "Ten Days that Shook the World" by 48 hours.

After a year at Virginia Military Institute, plus an early marriage and early fatherhood, Ward became a reporter for the *Oakland Tribune*. Ten years in that vineyard found him with the Great Depression at hand, salary reduced from $55 a week to $40.50, and talk of an editorial union in the air. He joined the American Newspaper Guild, promptly was elected chairman of the *Tribune* unit, and just as promptly fired and blacklisted from the newspaper industry. Meanwhile he had covered the 1934 San Francisco general strike, seen Harry Bridges in action, and learned more in three days than many learn in a lifetime.

A nepotistic fluke landed him a job on the California Supreme Court as a bailiff and later as a court reporter. From this haven he continued his efforts on behalf of the burgeoning unions sweeping the country, met Tom Mooney and eventually resigned to become a CIO official at one-third his court salary.

Union positions were: Executive Secretary of the Alameda County Industrial Union Council; first vice-president, California Industrial Union Council; CIO-PAC representative, California Legislature, 1939-40; Exec. Secretary, Harry Bridges Defense Committee, 1939-40; Exec. Vice-President, Labor's Non-Partisan League, 1940-41; script writer for CIO radio programs in Los Angeles, Las Vegas and San Francisco during WW II years; Mine-Mill and Smelter organizer in Los Angeles and Nevada; CIO-PAC representative for the CIO San Francisco Council; participant in 22 strikes and approximately 150 labor-management negotiations.

Ward is the author of *Harry Bridges on Trial*, (Modern Age, 1940) and *The Piecard* (published in translation as *Renegat* in Poland in 1953); plus three other unpublished manuscripts. Since 1964 his major effort, aside from travel and gardening, has been this book on Tom Mooney. The job of collating and condensing the overwhelming accumulation of documentary material amassed during the 22½ years Mooney and Billings spent in prison required four completely different re-writes to reach the present work.

Ward now lives in Berkeley, California with his second wife, herself an active trade union organizer in the flaming Thirties and Forties. He is *pater familias* to three children, eight grandchildren and four great-grandchildren.